Bertolt Brecht
Plays : Two

Fear and Misery of the Third Reich
Mother Courage and her Children
The Good Person of Szechwan

The second volume in this selection of Brecht's best-known work for the theatre contains three great plays written in exile in the late thirties and early forties. *Fear and Misery* offers 24 episodes showing different aspects of life under the Nazis: it is the nearest to contemporary realism that Brecht ever got. By contrast, *Mother Courage* is set during the Thirty Years War, where the apparently indomitable Courage, one of Brecht's greatest creations, strives to live off the war while, one by one, the war devours her children. And in the parable of *The Good Person*, set in China, the good-hearted good-time girl, Shen Teh, has to invent a tough masculine counterpart to resolve the contradictions of trying to be good in a persistently evil world.

Each volume is introduced, with a chronology of Brecht's life and work, by Hugh Rorrison.

BERTOLT BRECHT was born in Augsburg on 10 February 1898 and died in Berlin on 14 August 1956. He grew to maturity as a playwright in the frenetic years of the twenties and early thirties, with such plays as *Man Equals Man*, *The Threepenny Opera* and *The Mother*. He left Germany when Hitler came to power in 1933, eventually reaching the United States in 1941, where he remained until 1947. It was during this period of exile that such masterpieces as *Life of Galileo*, *Mother Courage* and *The Caucasian Chalk Circle* were written. Shortly after his return to Europe in 1947 he founded the Berliner Ensemble, and from then until his death was mainly occupied in producing his own plays.

The front cover shows a detail from 'Dulle Griet' by Pieter Bruegel reproduced by courtesy of Museum Mayer van den Bergh.

BERTOLT BRECHT
Plays : Two

Fear and Misery of the Third Reich
Mother Courage and her Children
The Good Person of Szechwan

Translations by John Willett

Introduction by Hugh Rorrison

Methuen Drama

METHUEN WORLD CLASSICS
This collection first published in Great Britain as a paperback original
in 1987 by Methuen London Ltd
by arrangement with Suhrkamp Verlag, Frankfurt am Main.
Reprinted 1991 by Methuen Drama
an imprint of Reed Consumer Books Ltd
Michelin House, 81 Fulham Road, London SW3 6RB
and Auckland, Melbourne, Singapore and Toronto

Reprinted 1993
Reissued with a new cover design 1994

Printed in Great Britain by
Cox & Wyman Ltd, Reading, Berkshire

British Library Cataloguing in Publication Data

Brecht, Bertolt
Plays : 2 — (A Methuen paperback) —
(Methuen's world dramatists series)
I. Title II. Brecht, Bertolt. [Furcht und Elend des Dritten Reiches.
English]. Fear and Misery of the Third Reich
III. Brecht, Bertolt. [Mutter Courage und ihre Kinder. *English*].
Mother Courage and her Children
IV. Brecht, Bertolt. [Der gute Mensch von Sezuan. *English*].
The Good Person of Szechwan
832'.912   PT2603.R397
ISBN 0-413-15150-6

Contents

Bertolt Brecht
Chronology of life and work

Brecht's life falls into three distinct phases demarcated by his forced exile from his native Germany during the Hitler years. From 1898-1933 he is in Germany; from 1933-1947 he is in exile in various parts of the world; in 1947 he returns to Europe, first to Switzerland then to Berlin.

Germany

1898 Eugen Berthold Friedrich Brecht born on 10 February at Augsburg where his father was an employee and later director of the Haindl paper mill.

1908 Brecht goes to Augsburg Grammar School (Realgymnasium) where he is an indifferent pupil and a rebel in his quiet way, numbering among his friends Caspar Neher, later his designer. Brecht was almost expelled for taking a dismissive, anti-patriotic line when set an essay with the title 'It is a sweet and honourable thing to die for one's country'.

1917 Brecht enrols as a medical student at Munich University, where he also attends Arthur Kutscher's theatre seminar. He samples the bohemian literary life of the city.

1918 Brecht is conscripted and serves as a medical orderly, though he still lives at home. He writes *Baal*, a rumbustious, even outrageous dramatic tribute to natural drives and anarchic sexuality, and writes articles for the local newspaper, *Augsburger Neueste Nachrichten*.

1919 Brecht writes *Drums in the Night*. His Augsburg girlfriend, Paula Banholzer, bears him a son, Frank.

He meets the comedian Karl Valentin, the theatre
director Erich Engel, and actresses Elisabeth Bergner,
Blandine Ebinger, Carola Neher and the opera singer,
Marianne Zoff. He writes theatre reviews for *Volkswillen*,
a local Independent Socialist daily.

1920   Brecht visits Berlin.

1921   Brecht's registration at Munich University is cancelled.
An attempt to make himself known in literary circles
in Berlin ends with him in hospital suffering from
malnutrition. His new friendship with Arnolt Bronnen,
the playwright, leads him to change the spelling of his
name to Bertolt, or Bert.

1922   Brecht marries Marianne Zoff. He writes *In the Jungle
of Cities*.

1923   Brecht's daughter Hanne is born. The activities of
Hitler's National Socialists are hotly discussed in
Brecht's Munich circle. The first productions of *In the
Jungle of Cities* and *Baal* take place in Munich and
Leipzig respectively.

1924   Brecht directs Christopher Marlowe's *Edward II* which
he and Lion Feuchtwanger had adapted. He was
already using certain devices (plot summaries before
scenes, white face make-up to indicate fear) to induce
critical detachment in actors and audience. He finally
settles in Berlin and is taken on as dramaturg (literary
adviser) at Max Reinhardt's Deutsches Theater.
Elisabeth Hauptmann becomes his secretary/assistant.
The actress Helene Weigel bears him a son, Stefan.

1925   Klabund's *The Chalk Circle*, premiered at Frankfurt
and Hanover in January, is directed in Berlin in
October by Max Reinhardt with Elisabeth Bergner in
the female lead.

1926   *Man Equals Man* premiered at Darmstadt and Düssel-
dorf. Brecht's work on a play (which he never finished)
called *Joe Fleischhacker*, which was to deal with the
Chicago Grain Exchange, leads him to the study of

Marx as the only adequate method of analysing the workings of capitalism.

1927 Brecht divorces Marianne Zoff. He works with Erwin Piscator, the pioneer of communist political theatre in Germany, on a dramatisation of Hasek's novel *The Good Soldier Schweik*. He publishes a volume of poems, the *Hauspostille* (Domestic Breviary).

1928 *The Threepenny Opera*, music by Kurt Weill, words by Brecht (based on a translation of John Gay's *Beggar's Opera* by Brecht's friend and collaborator Elisabeth Hauptmann) opens at the Theater am Schiffbauerdamm and becomes the hit of the season. Brecht had provocatively transferred bourgeois manners to a Soho criminal setting.

1929 Brecht works with Elisabeth Hauptmann and Weill on *Happy End*. He marries Helene Weigel. Elisabeth Hauptmann attempts suicide. *The Baden-Baden Cantata* is staged at the Baden-Baden Music Festival, music by Hindemith.

1930 Brecht's daughter Barbara born. His Lehrstück or didactic play, *The Measures Taken*, is given its first performance in Berlin. The communist didactic plays for amateur performance were intended to clarify the ideas of the performers as much as the audience. The first performance of *The Rise and Fall of the City of Mahagonny*, an opera with words by Brecht and music by Kurt Weill, causes a riot as the Nazis voice their criticism at Leipzig. In his notes on the opera Brecht tabulates the difference between the traditional *dramatic* (or Aristotelian) and the new *epic* (or non-Aristotelian) theatre at which he is aiming. Brecht objects to the *Threepenny Film*, sues Nero Films and loses, but accepts an ex gratia payment to refrain from an appeal.

1931 Brecht completes *St Joan of the Stockyards* (first performed in 1959).

1932 Brecht's only film, *Kuhle Wampe*, is held up by the censor. He visits Moscow when it opens there in May. His dramatisation of Maxim Gorky's novel *The Mother* is performed by a left-wing collective in Berlin, music by Hanns Eisler. It demonstrates the development of a worker's mother towards proletarian class-consciousness. Beginning of Brecht's relationship with Margarete Steffin. Brecht studies Marxism under the dissident communist Karl Korsch.

Exile

1933 The Nazis come to power. The night after the German parliament building (the Reichstag) is burnt down, Brecht flees with his family to Prague. He moves to Vienna, then Zurich, finally settling on the island of Fyn in Denmark. His relationship with Ruth Berlau begins. He visits Paris for the opening of *The Seven Deadly Sins*.

1934 Brecht visits London. The themes of flight and exile enter his poetry.

1935 Brecht is stripped of his German citizenship. He visits Moscow where he talks to the Soviet dramatist Sergei Tretiakov about the 'alienation effect'. He attends the International Writers' Conference in Paris. He visits New York to look in on a production of *The Mother*, which does not meet with his approval.

1936 Brecht attends the International Writers' Conference in London. He writes anti-fascist poetry.

1937 Brecht attends the International Writers' Conference in Paris with Ruth Berlau. *Senora Carrar's Rifles* is premiered in Paris.

1938 Franco's right-wing Falangists emerge as the likely victors in the Spanish Civil War and Chamberlain signs away the Sudetenland in the Munich Treaty in an effort to appease Hitler. *Fear and Misery of the Third Reich* is given its first performance in Paris. Brecht writes *The*

Earth Moves in three weeks ending on 23 November. He revises it with the assistance of Margarete Steffin, adds a fourteenth scene and retitles it *Life of Galileo*.

1939   In a radio interview with scientists of the Niels Bohr Institute he hears of the discovery of a great new source of energy, nuclear fission. His first response is positive. In April he moves to Stockholm with his family. He finishes writing *Mother Courage and her Children*.

1940   German forces march into Denmark. In Lidingo Brecht completes *The Augsburg Chalk Circle*, a short story set in the Thirty Years War. Brecht's household moves to Helsinki in Finland where his friendship with the writer Hella Wuolijoki begins.

1941   Brecht completes *Mr Puntila and his Man Matti*, *The Good Person of Szechwan* and *The Resistible Rise of Arturo Ui*. He writes war poetry and 'Finnish Epigrams'. Leaving Finland Brecht travels through the Soviet Union via Leningrad and Moscow (where Margarete Steffin dies) to Vladivostock and sails to the U.S.A. He arrives in Los Angeles in July and settles with his family in Santa Monica. He makes contact with other exiles (Heinrich Mann, Lion Feuchtwanger and Fritz Lang, the film director) and with the natives (Orson Welles). First performance of *Mother Courage and her Children* in neutral Switzerland.

1942   Brecht prepares his *Poems in Exile* for publication. He works on the screenplay for Fritz Lang's film, *Hangmen also Die*. He participates in the anti-war, anti-fascist activities of exile groups. He meets Charles Laughton.

1943   The first performances of *The Good Person of Szechwan* and of *Life of Galileo* take place in Zurich.

1944   Brecht becomes a member of the newly formed Council for a Democratic Germany. In April Jed Harris, an American producer and director, enquires about *Galileo*, and Brecht looks afresh at its 'moral'. He writes the first version of *The Caucasian Chalk Circle*, and almost immediately starts reworking it. He studies Arthur Waley's translations of Chinese poetry. In September he begins to revise *Galileo* with Charles Laughton. Ruth Berlau bears him a son who does not survive.

1945   *Fear and Misery of the Third Reich* is performed in New York under the title *The Private Life of the Master Race*. Brecht and Laughton complete the English version of *Galileo* but the dropping of the atomic bombs on Hiroshima and Nagasaki in August gives rise to another revision which stresses the social responsibility of the scientist.

1946   The first performance of Brecht's adaptation of Webster's *The Duchess of Malfi* takes place in Boston.

1947   Charles Laughton appears in the title role of *Life of Galileo* in Beverly Hills and New York. Brecht appears before the *House Committee on Unamerican Activities* and proves himself a master of ambiguity when cross-examined about his communist activities.

Return

Brecht and Helene Weigel go to Zurich, leaving their son Stefan, who is an American citizen, in the U.S.A. Brecht meets Max Frisch, his old friend and designer Caspar Neher, and the playwright Carl Zuckmayer.

1948   Brecht's adaptation of *Antigone of Sophocles* is performed in Chur, Switzerland, and *Mr Puntila and his Man Matti* is given its first performance in Zurich. He publishes the *Little Organum for the Theatre*. Brecht travels to Berlin and starts rehearsals of *Mother Courage* at the Deutsches Theater in the Soviet sector of the city. *The Caucasian Chalk Circle* is first performed in Eric and Maja Bentley's English translation by students at Northfield, Minnesota.

1949   *Mother Courage* opens at the Deutsches Theater with Helene Weigel in the title role. Brecht visits Zurich again before settling in Berlin. The Berliner Ensemble, Brecht and Helene Weigel's own state-subsidised company, is formed and opens with *Puntila*. Brecht adapts J.M.R. Lenz's *The Tutor*. At Gottfried von Einem's suggestion Brecht applies for an Austrian passport (H. Weigel is Austrian) as Caspar Neher had already done. He works with Neher on a play for the Salzburg Festival, which is to be an international showcase for his work.

1951 *The Mother* is performed by the Berliner Ensemble. Brecht finishes the first version of his adaptation of Shakespeare's *Coriolanus*. His opera with music by Paul Dessau, *The Trial of Lucullus*, is tried out and meets with official disfavour.

1953 Brecht writes *Turandot*, and the *Buckow Elegies*. Ethel and Julius Rosenberg are executed in the U.S.A. for betraying atomic secrets to the Russians. Brecht is elected President of the German section of the PEN Club, the international writers' association. On 17 June there are strikes and demonstrations protesting about working conditions in the German Democratic Republic. Brecht writes a letter to the Secretary of the Socialist Unity Party which is released to the press in a doctored form.

1954 The trial of atomic physicist Robert J. Oppenheimer begins in the U.S.A., and Albert Einstein writes an article inveighing against this modern 'inquisition', but the idea that science is subordinate to state security gains currency. Brecht is awarded the Stalin Peace Prize. The Berliner Ensemble moves into its own home, the Theater am Schiffbauerdamm (where he had triumphed with *The Threepenny Opera* in 1928), and performs *The Caucasian Chalk Circle*. The prologue, *The Struggle for the Valley*, is now designated as Act I. Brecht makes public his objections to the Paris Treaty (which incorporated the Federal Republic of Germany

into NATO) and to re-armament in general. The
Berliner Ensemble's productions of *Mother Courage* and
Kleist's *The Broken Pitcher* are enthusiastically received
as the highlights of the Paris Théâtre des Nations
festival. *Mother Courage* is awarded the prizes for best
play and best production.

1955   Brecht adapts Farquhar's *The Recruiting Officer* as *Drums
and Trumpets*. He goes to Moscow to receive the Lenin
Peace Prize. In December Brecht begins rehearsals of
Life of Galileo using the third version of the play, a
modified retranslation into German of Laughton's
English version. Ernst Busch takes the title role. Harry
Buckwitz, directing the West German premiere of *The
Caucasian Chalk Circle* at Frankfurt, omits *The Struggle for
the Valley* as politically inopportune.

1956   Brecht's health prevents him from carrying on with
Galileo and he hands over the direction to Erich Engel.
He visits Milan for Giorgio Strehler's production of
The Threepenny Opera at the Piccolo Teatro. Brecht is
preparing the Berliner Ensemble, which by this time
has become generally recognised as the foremost
progressive theatre in Europe, for a visit to London
when he dies of a heart attack on 14 August. The visit
goes ahead and *Mother Courage*, *The Caucasian Circle*, and
Trumpets and Drums are presented at the Palace Theatre
at the end of August for a short season – a landmark in
Brecht's reception in the United Kingdom.

Introduction

Bertolt Brecht: 1898–1956

Brecht is an elusive figure, part Baal, part Schweyk, part Galileo – the list could go on. He could use people and yet command absolute loyalty, not least from the many women in his life. He was a dedicated survivor who learnt to co-exist with many masters. A Communist from the late twenties, he never joined the Party. Aware of the excesses of Stalinism (which devoured some of his friends), he never took a public stand against the Soviet Union, yet in 1941 he ended up in California rather than Moscow. Arraigned by McCarthy's House Committee on Unamerican Activities, he convinced his interrogators that he was not a Communist without prejudicing his long-held convictions. When he returned to Europe he chose to have an East German theatre, a West German publisher and an Austrian passport, all for the best of reasons.

His work can be as ambiguous as his behaviour. Try as he might to make plays like *Mother Courage and her Children* and *Life of Galileo* say one thing, they always ended up saying something else behind his back, and they are the better for it. The pragmatic British on first acquaintance took an overdose of Brecht's theories and made him seem dull. Brecht himself was too pragmatic to take his own theorising seriously when he had a stage in front of him; since the days in Berlin when, unathletic as he was, he consorted with boxers and racing cyclists and pointed to their fans as the kind of connoisseurs and enthusiasts he would like to see watching his plays, his aim had always been to entertain as well as inform.

Brecht was born in 1898 in the sleepy Bavarian provincial town of Augsburg, where his father managed a paper mill. He grew up in comfortable circumstances with an avenue of

chestnut trees outside the door and a moat full of swans not
far away. His mother was Protestant and his father Catholic
but this seems to have caused no tension; indeed, being
brought up in his mother's church produced the bonus of
early familiarity with Luther's German Bible, which remained
a fertile source of vocabulary and incident all his writing life.
His schooling was also free from pressure, and he later
claimed that if he had learned anything, it was in spite of his
teachers. He certainly pitted his wits against the system: one
anecdote tells how the young Brecht watched one of his
friends erase some red pencil and claim, unsuccessfully, that
his homework was undermarked. Brecht then added a few
underlinings and asked for an explanation of the 'errors',
forcing his embarrassed French teacher to raise his mark.
Brecht was not very good at French.

Out of school he pursued his own cultural interests,
admiring, at one time or another, Napoleon, Nietzsche and
Hauptmann, and developing a taste for literary outsiders.
The bohemian lives of the French poets Villon, Rimbaud and
Verlaine fascinated him, and in German he was drawn to the
anti-classical tradition of Büchner and Wedekind and often
sang the latter's saucy little songs to his friends, accompany-
ing himself on the guitar.

Brecht was already gregarious and his circle included
Caspar Neher, who would later be his designer, Georg Pfanzelt
(nickname: Orge), Otto Müller (nickname: Müllereisert).
Their adolescent discussions on life and art in Brecht's attic
den or on the river bank were the germ of his later production
teams. According to Brecht he had his first experience of sex at
seventeen, and from then on he seems to have been something
of a stud – an Americanism that would have appealed to him.

In 1917 Brecht enrolled as a medical student at Munich
University, possibly to stave off conscription to the Great
War, since he certainly was never committed to medicine.
One course which interested him was Artur Kutscher's drama
seminar. Professor Kutscher was a friend of Wedekind and

his biographer, and he enjoyed a reputation as a theatrical pundit. But Brecht was unimpressed and did not hesitate to criticise one of Kutscher's favourites, the minor expressionist Hanns Johst, who later became a prominent Nazi. Johst's *The Lonely One*, a stage biography of the nineteenth-century dramatist, boor and misfit, C.D. Grabbe, was deemed by Brecht to be sentimental and nauseating, and he volunteered to write a better play on the subject himself. *Baal* was the result, and it was the professor's turn to be nauseated. They parted in mutual contempt.

Brecht sampled what Schwabing, Munich's artistic quarter, had to offer. He saw Wedekind play *The Marquis of Keith* and was impressed with the way, as the immoralist hero of his own play, he controlled his audience, despite his shortcomings as an actor. He met the eccentric popular comedian Karl Valentin, and his one-acter *Respectable Wedding* is his homage to Valentin's zany Bavarian sketches.

In 1919 Brecht wrote his second play, *Drums in the Night*, a cynical response to the post-war months. Its hero, Kragler returns late from the war to find his fiancée Anna pregnant and engaged to an 'upwardly mobile' war-profiteer of whom her family approves. Snubbed by her, Kragler repairs to a pub and mobilises support for a Communist rising in the newspaper quarter. It is 1919 and the 'German Revolution' is in progress. Then Anna comes after him and he cops out with the line, 'I am a swine, and swine go home'. Kragler's abandonment of the revolutionaries in favour of 'a big, broad, white bed' later embarrassed Brecht, and he tried to argue that Kragler was a negative, comic figure. His next play too, *In the Jungle of Cities*, is cynical: it is set in Chicago and shows an unmotivated rivalry between Schlink, a Malayan timber merchant, and Garga, an assistant librarian. Brecht wanted the audience to forget about meaning and sit back and admire the technique of the combatants. He was already trying to sharpen audience responses: for *Drums in the Night* he had festooned the auditorium with banners which instructed the audience to take an unromantic view of the proceedings.

The first of Brecht's plays to be performed was *Drums in the Night*, with which Otto Falckenberg opened the 1922/23 season at the Munich Kammerspiele. It received a rave notice from Herbert Ihering, one of the top two Berlin critics, who praised the imagery and power of the writing and claimed that Brecht had altered the literary landscape at a stroke. Ihering then gave Brecht's career a further boost by awarding him the Kleist Prize, Germany's premier dramatic award. 1923 saw productions of *The Jungle of Cities* at Munich and *Baal* at Leipzig, and in 1924 Brecht, whom Falckenberg had taken on as dramaturg, or literary advisor, directed an adaptation of Marlowe's *Edward II* on which he had collaborated with Lion Feuchtwanger, an established novelist who later became famous for *Jew Süss*. It was a strikingly unusual production. The story goes that Brecht asked Karl Valentin what soldiers going into battle looked like. 'They get the willies, go white' was the answer, so he put the soldiers in white-face, one of the first shock effects of the type later invested with ideological significance and canonized as 'alienation effects'. He was a rising star, and he was sedulously cultivating his career.

Berlin was the mecca of the German theatre in the Twenties, and Brecht visited it in 1920 and 1921 when the idealistic phase of Expressionism was giving way to Black Expressionism, which invested the new loose forms with a harsh and brutal pessimism. Brecht became friendly with one of the most combative of the new shockers, Arnolt Bronnen, and changed Bertold to the snappier Bertolt, just as his new friend had done. He persuaded Bronnen to let him direct his play *Parricide* but the matter ended in shambles when the two stars, Heinrich George and Agnes Straub, walked out quivering with rage and shock respectively at Brecht's requirements. It was only in 1924, when he had two plays accepted in Berlin, *The Jungle of Cities* at Max Reinhardt's Deutsches Theater and *Edward II* at the Prussian State Theatre, that he moved there permanently. He was put on a salary as dramaturg at the Deutsches Theater, but according to Carl Zuckmayer, another aspiring playwright Reinhardt had on the payroll, Brecht only went into the office to pinch coal in his briefcase. Germany was just recovering from the hyper-inflation of 1923.

In Berlin Brecht met Elisabeth Hauptmann and persuaded his publisher that manuscripts would come in faster if he could have her as his secretary. More and more he was taking to discussing work in progress with his friends and trying out new pieces on anybody who dropped in, so frequent rewrites became necessary. Elisabeth Hauptmann was always around to make unobtrusive notes and prepare new drafts at all hours for the next day's work. She had a hand in all of his plays between 1924 and 1933, and it is from her records that we know of Brecht's awakening interest in Marxism in 1926.

From 1924 one of the leading directors in Germany was Erwin Piscator, who had returned from service on the Western Front as a Communist and begun politicizing the German theatre with agitprop plays in 1920. By 1926 he was using film, documentation and constructivist sets to bring out the political and economic context of the plays he staged. Brecht knew him and tried to write a play called *Wheat* when Piscator set up his own company, the Piscatorbühne, in 1927. He abandoned the project when he realised that capitalist commodity trading – the action was set in the Chicago Grain Exchange – made no sense, except for a few speculators. Marxism seemed to offer a means of coming to grips with social processes which otherwise defied dramatic analysis.

Brecht also met Kurt Weill in Berlin. Weill had set plays by Georg Kaiser and Yvan Goll to music, and he was interested in working with Brecht. Elisabeth Hauptmann had begun to translate John Gay's *The Beggar's Opera*, which had been successfully revived in London. Then E.J. Aufricht chanced on Brecht in a café one day when he was looking for a piece with which to open a theatre he had just leased, and Brecht offered to update Gay's ballad opera with Weill for him. His

offer was accepted and he and Weill put the opera together in
the South of France that summer. The rehearsals were
chaotic and dogged by accidents and it came as a surprise to
all concerned when *The Threepenny Opera* became the hit of the
season and a considerable money-spinner for its authors.
With its underworld setting, its police corruption, its
rapacious characters and its risqué songs the piece cocked a
snook at respectable society, and respectable society loved it.
Only later, when he was preparing a film version, did Brecht
seriously try to put political teeth into *The Threepenny Opera*,
for by that time his political views had hardened, not least
after seeing the police opening fire on a peaceful May Day
parade in 1929.

Brecht and Weill and Elisabeth Hauptmann tried unsuccessfully to repeat the formula with *Happy End*, but the real
sequel was in a sense *The Rise and Fall of the City of Mahagonny*
which took Brecht's unlovely modern subject matter and
Weill's jazzy, popular, unmistakably contemporary music
into the genteel confines of Germany's opera houses.

At the time of his biggest popular hit Brecht's attention was
however more and more turning to politics. He devised, for
amateur performance, a number of short *Lehrstücke*, or
teaching plays, as demonstration models of political commit-
ment in action. In the most radical and controversial of these,
The Measures Taken, a Soviet agitator in China has been
liquidated for sympathising openly, against orders, with the
coolies. The play reconstructs the events leading to his death
and makes it clear that the individual must submit absolutely
to Party directives. In *The Exception and the Rule* a bearer
travelling through the desert is shot by his master when he
reaches for his water bottle to share the last drops with him.
A court acquits the master on the grounds that masters can
normally assume that servants want to kill them. In deciding
where the original mistake lay in such an instance, audience
and actors would raise their political consciousness. The
biggest of these directly political pieces was *The Mother*, an

adaptation of Maxim Gorky's novel, which showed the title figure's progress from maternal quietism to socialist activism in pre-revolutionary Russia. Helene Weigel played the lead and Margarete Steffin, who was to be Brecht's next close collaborator, had a bit part. That was in 1932 and the political situation was tense when the play opened. The police eventually banned performances in working-class districts on the pretext that some of the venues were not licensed for theatrical performances, and the play was given as a reading, in which 'alienated' form Brecht found it even more effective.

He had by this time codified his ideas on the epic theatre that was to replace the traditional dramatic or Aristotelian theatre which he regarded as a dream factory that turned out comforting illusions. Epic theatre would be a stimulant rather than a narcotic, and would help change the world. It would tell stories, but in such a way that audiences would be forced to weigh up and judge the events they saw. Smooth, seamless plots would give way to strings of independent incidents moving in jumps and curves, and these 'montages' would keep the audience alert and critical of the way things developed. Brecht believed that characters could be dismantled and reconstructed – he had demonstrated this in *Man Equals Man* – so the classical fixed hero was to give way to figures conditioned by their social situation who changed when that situation changed. At the same time he saw the individual as the agent of social change, so there was to be a constant dialectic or process of reciprocal influence and change. Brecht modified and developed these ideas in later years, but the basic notion remained intact: that theatre had a part to play in bringing about a better, socialist world.

Hitler came to power on 30 January 1933, the Reichstag burnt down on 27 February, and Brecht went into exile the next day. He eventually bought a house in Skovbostrand on the Danish island of Fyn. For the next fourteen years he had neither a theatre nor a public that understood his language. After Hitler's annexation of Austria, only Switzerland, notably the Zurich Schauspielhaus, offered politically unfettered professional facilities for German-language plays.

Brecht now turned to the anti-fascist cause, attending conferences in Paris and London and co-editing a journal that was published in Moscow. He subscribed to the Party line that fascism was the final stage of capitalism, a conspiracy of the rich against the poor which would collapse of its own accord, and his writing in this phase is uninspired, with the happy exception of his poetry. That more private art seemed to prosper in those dark days. He and Kurt Weill wrote an off-beat ballet, *The Seven Deadly Sins*, for Weill's wife, Lotte Lenya. He turned to straight realism, first with *Fear and Misery of the Third Reich*, a string of scenes from life under Hitler, and then with *Senora Carrar's Rifles*, a morale-booster for the Spanish Civil War.

He was however gradually finding his feet in Denmark with his wife and family and Margarete Steffin at his side, eventually joined by Ruth Berlau, a Danish actress who took on the task of promoting his work in Denmark. He was out of Germany, and the working-class voters who were the target of the *Lehrstücke* were out of range, so the political message in his plays became more general and oblique. In 1938 he wrote *Life of Galileo*, the first of a series of masterpieces, which used historical and exotic subjects to deal with contemporary issues. Galileo's cunning, in the first version at least, offered intellectuals in Germany a seventeenth-century recipe for survival in an authoritarian state. *Mother Courage and her Children*, still in the seventeenth century, was a warning against war, which was directed in the first instance at the Danes, lest they should think they could fraternise with the Nazis and come off unscathed. *The Caucasian Chalk Circle* offered a parable on the equitable use of resources from ancient China as a model for what should happen in Europe after Hitler's defeat. The pared-down economy and the schematic figures of the *Lehrstücke* gave way in these plays to a wealth of colour and incident and a parade of some of the most memorable figures in modern theatre, Galileo, Courage, Grusha and Azdak.

Brecht moved to Stockholm in 1939 and to Finland in 1940 where he wrote *The Good Person of Szechwan*, as well as a comedy, *Mr Puntila and his Man Matti*, and a satire, *The Resistible Rise of Arturo Ui*. The last two were aimed at the U.S.A., but were too unconventional to stand much chance on the American commercial stage. In 1941, with Finland threatened by the Germans, he travelled to Moscow. Margarete Steffin had to stay behind there and died of tuberculosis, while the Brecht ménage moved on via Vladivostock to the United States.

In the United States Brecht settled in Santa Monica, close to Hollywood. It was his intention to break into films, but he found working conditions and the prevalent ethos uncongenial. Friends like Fritz Lang and Peter Lorre (whom Brecht had discovered) tried to help, but he could not adapt to the American scene which had been such a fertile source of inspiration in Berlin. His memories of the Theatre Union's efforts to produce *The Mother* in New York in 1935 made him cautious of small-time theatre, but he dreamed of success on Broadway. *The Caucasian Chalk Circle* was conceived as a Broadway vehicle for Luise Rainer, an Austrian who had won two Academy Awards for film roles, and when he revised *Life of Galileo* with Charles Laughton his hope was that Laughton would sweep New York off its feet. Nothing much came of these things, because the American theatre was geared to entertainment, and laughter and tears were not part of the Brecht formula: there, as in Britain, it was to take another ten years before the techniques and something of the spirit of Brecht's theatre began to be assimilated.

Besides being a devastated country, Germany was under military occupation when the war ended and Brecht did not leave the U.S.A. until 1947. By that time McCarthyism was at its height and he appeared before the Committee on Unamerican Activities. He outwitted his investigators with ironic half-truths and skilful innuendo. The Committee thanked him for being an exemplary witness.

Brecht went to Switzerland in 1947, and then, because of visa problems – he had been stateless since 1938 – he returned to Berlin, as he had escaped in 1933, via Prague. He arrived in the Eastern Sector on 22 October 1948 to a warm welcome from the Communist cultural establishment. Brecht needed a German audience and his decision to settle in East Berlin was a natural one, given his unswerving conviction that Communism was the future, its warts necessary but temporary. He was no sycophant though, and observed, when the government announced that the people had let it down in 1953, that perhaps the government should elect another people.

East Berlin treated Brecht lavishly. He was given facilities to direct *Mother Courage* at the Deutsches Theater in 1948, then his own company, the Berliner Ensemble in 1949, and finally his own theatre, the Theater am Schiffbauerdamm in 1954. Brecht was now mainly a director, and it was in these years that he directed the meticulously rehearsed model productions of *Puntila*, *The Mother*, *The Caucasian Chalk Circle* among others, introducing techniques and effects that have since become standard – revealed lighting, uncluttered, spartan sets with a few solid, workmanlike props, well-worn costumes, visible scene-changes, demonstrative, unhistrionic acting, banner captions between scenes, songs – all of which in his hands added up to productions of startling freshness and conviction. Some of these were known as alienation effects designed to make the familiar seem odd and thus stimulate critical appraisal. Stepping out of the action to sing a song could do this in the fifties when plays mainly tried to sustain a consistent illusion, but in the theatre today's innovations are standard practice tomorrow, so new ways constantly have to be found of keeping Brecht's plays sharp and fresh. His reputation has suffered, not least in Britain, from leaden productions which tried so hard to be Brechtian that they forgot the wily old pragmatist's favourite English proverb, the proof of the pudding is in the eating. He spiced his plays to suit the audience's palate, and foreign directors should do so too, with discretion.

In Berlin with Helene Weigel managing the Ensemble, with the assistance of Elisabeth Hauptmann (scripts) and Ruth Berlau (photographic records), and with a bevy of young actresses around him, Brecht should have been happy, but he was under constant strain – from work, conflicting relationships and political irritation (the German Democratic Republic was not quite his kind of Communism). By 1954 his work in Berlin was internationally acclaimed, even in England where Kenneth Tynan was campaigning vigorously for him in the *Observer*. He was preparing the company for a visit to London when he died of a heart attack on 14 August 1956. The visit went ahead and left an unmistakeable mark on the British theatre which, with the Royal Court and the Royal Shakespeare Company in the vanguard, was to change radically under Brecht's posthumous influence.

Fear and Misery of the Third Reich

Brecht left Germany immediately after the Reichstag fire in 1933 and eventually settled on the island of Fyn in Denmark. He continued to work on *The Threepenny Novel* and *The Roundheads and the Peakheads* which he had brought out of Germany, but was soon exercising his mind on the new situation that Hitler's assumption of power had created. In his work up to 1933, even in a directly political piece like *The Mother*, Brecht had concentrated his attack on capitalism and made little direct mention of the new enemy, but as early as the summer of 1933 he was helping Willy Münzenberg prepare his Brown Books documenting the clampdown on racial and political target groups that had followed the Nazi take-over. In Denmark he was host to a stream of visitors from Germany who kept him informed about conditions: what he needed was a form in which this information could be put to work in exile.

Developments in the arts in the Soviet Union at this time were running against people like Brecht, and by 1935 Stalin's imposition of Socialist Realism as the official artistic creed was making his position as Communist writer problematic. The exiled Hungarian critic, Georg Lukacs, who was an authority on German literature, began to apply the criteria of the new proletarian naturalism rigidly, and Brecht, along with all the Expressionists and Soviet luminaries like Shosta-kovitch and Eisenstein, came under fire as a formalist. At the beginning of 1935 Brecht spent two months in Moscow at a meeting convened by his Berlin friend and collaborator, Erwin Piscator, who had been appointed to head MORT, a Moscow-based organisation set up to foster revolutionary theatre on an international scale. Among Piscator's projects was a series of short propaganda films, including one about a German civil servant's wife who received her executed husband's ashes and a bill for his cremation by the same post. In 1934 Brecht had written two poems on everyday fascism, 'The Neighbour' and 'The Chalk Cross', and Piscator's plans may have suggested working these up for the stage (they are, in fact, the basis of scenes 2 and 3 of *Fear and Misery*). He was however still deeply committed to epic theatre, and worked out the first formulation of his theory of 'alienation' while he was in Moscow, but he appears at the same time to have seen the need for short, realistic propaganda plays which would expose the state of society in Germany.

On Brecht's return to Denmark the Spanish Civil War became the new focus of Socialist interest and Brecht received a request for a short Republican piece for 'The Lantern', a semi-amateur theatre group set up in Paris by his Berlin collaborator, the Bulgarian director Slatan Dudow. Brecht obliged with a short realistic play called *Señora Carrar's Rifles*, which was a great success both there and in other countries and later in the German Democratic Republic. It was after this that he informed Dudow of 'a series of little (ten-minute) plays "Spiritual Upsurge of the German People under the Nazi Regime" . . . Minimal cast. As you see, in this way I too am turning to small-scale forms.' It was based on eye-witness accounts and newspaper reports, and Brecht referred to it as a documentary piece. The first five playlets – 'The Spy', 'The Jewish Wife', 'Judicial Process', 'Occupational Disease' and 'The Chalk Cross' – were complete by October 1937 under the title of *Anxiety*. By Spring 1938 the project had nineteen scenes and bore the working title *Fear and Misery of the Third Reich*, and in May eight of these were performed in Paris by Dudow's group (strengthened by Helene Weigel) as *99%*. Later in 1938 Brecht prepared a twenty-seven scene version for an abortive Prague edition, but as finally published in 1945 the piece had the twenty-four scenes of the present edition. An English version was produced in the U.S. the same year, and its title *The Private Life of the Master Race* is still sometimes used in America.

In the final version Brecht tried to organise the scenes chronologically, according to the dates given in the stage directions, starting with the first day of Hitler's regime and ending with the plebiscite in March 1938, a structure which suggests passing time rather than simultaneity, though only one other scene, the bombardment of Almeria, is historically dated. The scenes are also grouped in thematic clusters: the first five show the treachery and brutality of the Nazis in action, scenes six to eight show their impact on the professions, scenes nine and ten on middle-class domestic life, scenes eleven to fifteen on working-class life, and scenes sixteen to nineteen on the lower middle classes (or petite bourgeoisie), while the last five scenes are disparate, though they do bring the action back to the capital after it has ranged over the whole Reich (from Cologne to Breslau and from Lübeck to Karlsruhe with radio voices in the last scene from Vienna).

There would have been great scope for using dialect in performance, but there is no mention of this in any of the reports, an indication that Brecht was not really reverting to realism, far less Socialist Realism, as Lukacs, who to Brecht's chagrin praised the piece, seemed to think. Brecht latterly referred to *Fear and Misery of the Third Reich* as a 'play', in spite of its genesis in small-scale forms, and he thought of it as showing 'behaviour patterns typical of people of different classes under Fascist dictatorship, and not only the "gests" of caution, self-protection, alarm, and so forth but also that of resistance ...' Each scene is a 'gest', which is Brecht's own term meaning that it encapsulates the essence of a specific response, so that the whole thing adds up to a comprehensive catalogue of typical responses. When one compares this with the American version, *The Private Life of the Master Race*, which combines the scenes into three acts and introduces a boy/girl love interest to frame the whole thing, it becomes clear that the overall form of Brecht's final version retains a great measure of the cool abstraction of his earlier work, despite the realism of the individual components. When he wrote the piece Brecht felt that there was little danger of empathy clouding the audience's critical response because it was beyond the range of amateur actors, and the professionals like Weigel were skilled in epic acting anyway. The stanzas of 'The German March-past' at the beginning of each scene also give the play an epic feel.

Nonetheless Brecht is not working in his normal style, as a comparison of 'The Jewish Wife' with other Brechtian departures shows. The Wife takes her leave on the phone with varying degrees of frankness, depending on the intimacy of the other speaker, then rehearses what she will say to her husband, but when he arrives the dialogue lapses into platitudes with which the partners skirt the painful issue but which might well bring a tear to the viewing eye. This is conventional middle-class drama. When Pavel takes his leave after his return from Siberia in *The Mother*, not only is his mother too busy to see to him, he himself wrily draws the audience's attention to her unemotional sense of priorities; and when Grusha decides to leave with the baby in *The*

Caucasian Chalk Circle she expresses no emotion as the Singer describes what is happening. Distancing emotional situations with such devices is Brecht's normal technique.

Max Frisch commented in 1947 that *Fear and Misery of the Third Reich* failed to offer post-war audiences the release that Carl Zuckmayer's melodramatic and highly successful *The Devil's General* provided. The leading East German dramatist, Heiner Müller, on the other hand finds the piece simplistic and over optimistic, especially in a scene like 'The Release', where the tortured Communist whose twisted hand has two fingers missing reticently tells his old friends that they are right to ostracise him. Müller has, incidentally, written a counter-play called *Slaughter* with a corresponding scene which replaces the reticence with mutual accusation, anguish and distrust.

Brecht never considered the play for the Berliner Ensemble and seems to have viewed it after the war as an informative, factual pendant to the satirical presentation of Hitler's career in *The Resistible Rise of Arturo Ui*, with which it might fruitfully be coupled in performance. It still has the power to move and is particularly useful for the amateur groups for whom it was originally intended.

Mother Courage and her Children

By 1938 Brecht had left behind both the political directness of the *Lehrstücke* and the realism of occasional pieces like *Señora Carrar's Rifles* and *Fear and Misery of the Third Reich* and had begun to revitalise and, in more than one sense, revolutionise the historical play, which, since the 'discovery' of Shakespeare in the eighteenth century, had formed the mainstream of German drama. Brecht's mature, epic plays have subjects which are remote either in time, or place, or both from the German present, and yet contain unmistakeable lessons for his German contemporaries and for posterity.

They are his original contribution to the historical play in Germany.

The first of these pieces to be performed was *Mother Courage and her Children* (Zurich, 1941). It was conceived as a warning to his host country Denmark: sitting on the sidelines and making fat profits, as Denmark was, would be out of the question if her aggressive neighbour, Nazi Germany, went to war. By the time Brecht finished *Mother Courage* in 1940 the war had indeed started, but the play remains valid quite apart from its intended context. Brecht himself later defined its message:

> *What is a performance of* Mother Courage and her Children *primarily meant to show?*
> That in wartime the big profits are not made by little people. That war, which is a continuation of business by other means, makes human virtues fatal even to their possessors. That no sacrifice is too great for the struggle against war.

The assumption that war was an integral part of the capitalist system was shared by many Germans in the aftermath of World War I, and in Berlin Brecht had collaborated on several productions by Erwin Piscator that were designed to demonstrate just that. In *Rasputin, the Romanovs, the War and the People that Rose Against Them* Piscator had introduced a scene where three tycoons, British, French and German, successively proclaimed their faith in the justice of the national cause, while projections of belching factory chimneys behind them made it clear that their real motive was profit. Documentary demonstrations like this could show the capitalist system in action and provoke an audience to indignation in the hope that it would espouse the Communist cause; they could even illustrate the system's effect on the proletariat by showing starvation in the slums and death in the trenches. Brecht now wanted to go a stage further and show how the little man – or woman – sometimes contributes to his own misery.

To achieve a measure of detachment he passed over the 1914–1918 War which was still fresh in people's memories and set his play in the Thirty Years' War (1618–1648), which was, until the twentieth century, the most destructive in German history. Historians present it as a religious war between the Protestant north, led in the field by King Gustavus Adolphus of Sweden, and the Catholic south under Emperor Ferdinand I of Austria, led in the field by generals Tilly and Wallenstein. For Brecht the religious element is just camouflage for the war leaders' real motive, profit. The internal chronology of the play follows historical events, but the plot is wholly fictitious and Courage's name is taken from a picaresque novel of the period. Brecht intended the word 'chronicle' in the subtitle to mean the same as 'history' when applied to Shakespeare, but his approach is quite different: Shakespeare, in *King John*, or *Richard III*, or *Henry V*, as his titles suggest, focuses on kings and examines affairs of state, the interplay of politics and the personal motives of the men who control the destinies of nations. Brecht follows the fortunes of a canteen woman and her children and never shows us the leaders; he is not interested in how they run the war, but in how their war affects people at the bottom of the social scale. The plot is a series of business transactions, as if life consisted of nothing else: We see soldiers reduced to pilfering their own stores and raping, murdering and robbing the peasantry; we see peasants selling their last possessions, valuing their cattle more highly than their lives, having their farms bombarded by armies which don't bother to establish which side they are on. The only figure to profit from it all in the end is the prostitute, Yvette, whose looks are ruined in the process by the time she is twenty-five. The only figure to emerge with any moral credit is Kattrin.

At the centre of it all is Mother Courage herself. Her professed aim is to bring her waggon and her children through the war safely. She has been following the Swedish army for 25 years when we meet her in the first scene, and she knows how to handle herself; but her business instincts repeatedly betray her and she loses all three children. Brecht intended her to be an object lesson in misplaced energy. In Marxist terms she belongs to the petite bourgeoisie, a small businesswoman who refuses to give up the delusion that she can make capitalism work for her. When audiences empathised with her at the first performance in Switzerland he rewrote her part to make the conflict between her business and maternal instincts crasser. In the revised version Eilif is recruited behind her back while she is closing a deal, and she refuses to hand over shirts for bandages in scene 5, so the Chaplain has to take them by force. It is still difficult not to sympathise with the spirit which keeps her going, but this is not what Brecht wanted. For him she failed to learn from experience. This is nowhere clearer than at the end of scene 6 when she curses war after Kattrin has been assaulted, and immediately afterwards, at the beginning of scene 7, she jauntily asserts that nobody is going to spoil her war. Business is good and she has sold her one insight for a necklace of silver coins.

Low as she may seem here, Brecht adjudged her behaviour worse in scene 4 when she made the Young Soldier give up his protest, for there she was stifling the spirit revolutions are made of. She abandons her own protest too in this scene because it would be bad for business. Her progress through the play is a process of adopting whatever stance her business interests require in the situations as they arise, and this reveals the false principles which underlie her actions.

Brecht's theatre is intended to help change society. In his analysis the individual's thinking is conditioned by social situation and will change if that changes. The individual is at the same time the agent of social change, so there is a constant dialectic or process of reciprocal influence and development. The difficulty with Mother Courage is that she fails to change as a character, but she still makes Brecht's point. If the play is properly presented the audience will have a sinking feeling as she goes off at the end to catch up with business. Everything that has happened to her in the preceding scenes has demonstrated that there is no life for her in that direction, that all her work and good intentions will, like Eilif's bravery, Swiss Cheese's honesty and Kattrin's generosity, be devoured by the framework she knows, accepts and works within, that of a war of exploitation. That framework, like all forms of exploitation, must be changed, and it suffices if the audience realises this, because the play as a political piece has then made its mark.

Mother Courage is a good example of an epic play with its open-air action covering twelve years and ranging widely over Europe. It uses explanatory scene captions, it breaks the narrative up with songs which comment succinctly on the action, and in Brecht's own production it had even, non-atmospheric lighting and a bare anti-illusionistic set. But most memorably of all it has the first of a series of great characters that Brecht bequeathed to the modern stage.

The Good Person of Szechwan

The Good Person of Szechwan is an important marker in Brecht's career as a playwright. In the first plays conceived in exile, *Señora Carrar's Rifles* (1937) and *Fear and Misery of the Third Reich* (1938) he had bowed to the needs of the hour and adopted straight realism, and when he moved to a larger canvas the framework of historical fact had turned *Life of Galileo* (first version 1938) into a relatively conventional historical drama with few epic characteristics. So when he started in March 1939 to rework a 1927 Berlin project called *Die Ware Liebe* (the pun of the title would be perfectly rendered by *The Good Love* if goods [meaning 'wares'] had a singular in English) his aim was to write an epic play that would come up to his old standard. The subject proved to be intractable and was set aside in September 1939 as a play for the 'theatre of the future' while he wrote the more topical *Mother Courage and her Children*. By the time he returned to it at the beginning of 1940, Hitler's war had forced him to move from Denmark to Sweden, and when he completed it in 1941 he had moved on to Finland.

The finished play illustrates better than any other his claim that the modern dramatist is a scientist, and his plays experiments in social behaviour. In *The Threepenny Opera* the song 'What Keeps Mankind Alive?' offers the proposition 'Food is the first thing. Morals follow on.' This would be a valid maxim for life in Szechwan too, but Brecht is no longer content with social satire larded with trenchant observations, so he sets up an exploratory experiment to establish what the relationship between food and morality, or more precisely money and goodness, really is.

The play is set in China, but it is a China where planes carry the mail, although gods still descend to earth. Brecht wanted to avoid folksiness and encapsulate his experiment in a neutral, foreign ambience. A three-god delegation arrives in Szechwan on a fact-finding mission. For two thousand years, so roughly from the beginning of the Christian era, there have been complaints that no one can survive on earth and remain good. Being good, in spite of the oriental setting, turns out to mean living according to the Ten Commandments. The gods' brief is to find some good people who can be used as a pretext for leaving the world as it is, so the object of Brecht's dramatic experiment is to establish whether or not there is any need for social change. These are not omniscient, all-powerful gods, but bumbling, ill-informed minions who suffer heavy offstage wear and tear in the course of their tour of duty and keep lowering their requirements in a desperate bid to achieve a positive outcome for the anonymous establishment (Heaven Inc.?) that they represent.

When the gods arrive, the only person who will put them up for the night is a penniless prostitute, Shen Teh. They reward her with a thousand silver dollars and she buys a tobacconist's shop, but her kind heart makes her an easy touch for down-and-outs and spongers, and to safeguard her investment she is forced to masquerade as her tough, male cousin Shui Ta. This is intended to be a one-off stop-gap, but when she falls in love with an out-of-work pilot, and he too turns out to be a sponger she again has recourse to Shui Ta. Finally, when she discovers that she is pregnant, she adopts the persona of Shui Ta permanently and sets up a tobacco factory so that *her* child will never need to scavenge in dustbins like the son of the carpenter she has ruined. Shen Teh's disappearance eventually arouses suspicion, and Shui Ta is brought to trial. The gods stand in for the magistrates and Shen Teh reveals herself and explains that everything she did was motivated by the desire to help her neighbours, love her beloved and save her son from going without. The gods take her stated good intentions as their cue for a swift exit on a pink cloud. Their mission accomplished, they are deaf to her complaint that to be good and survive in their world she has to split herself into two separate halves.

This parable works elegantly in general human terms. The incarnation of kindness is confronted by selfishness on all sides: the rich are a scheming lot, and the poor are mean and deceitful. The gods' half-hearted, cynical response at the end is clearly inadequate and the audience is bound to channel its sympathy for Shen Teh into the conclusion that things have to change, so that somehow people can earn a decent living and develop more of their potential without destroying themselves. Brecht's epilogue invites this response.

One of the beauties of the play is that while it works flawlessly for audiences that have no knowledge of or interest in Marxism, it also dismantles readily into Marxist components. The seemingly open ending looks different once Shen Teh's development is analysed in terms of class. She starts among the lumpenproletariat, with only herself to sell, then with the aid of a gift from the gods she moves one rung up the social scale to the petty bourgeoisie, forcing the previous owners of her new shop and the carpenter down the scale in the process. She quickly learns that it is commercial suicide to indulge her natural goodness in commerce, so she invents a business-like cousin to safeguard her investment. This double is a theatrical device which keeps the play firmly in the realm of comedy; there is no question of schizophrenia and the figure remains Shen Teh throughout, as occasional slips of Shui Ta's mask testify ('He' turns to a mirror to straighten 'his' hair when Sun appears in scene 5). Her dual persona serves to externalise an inner conflict between the altruistic moral self and the competitive business self which Brecht saw as inherent in capitalism. Shen Teh is at first reluctant to adopt the business mentality, but gradually her generous impulses become restricted to her family (the unborn child). The tiger in her, the exploitative Shui Ta, takes over, her business empire expands, and she becomes a ruthless capitalist creaming off the surplus value of the labour of a proletariat she has helped to create.

Her lover Sun's predicament can equally be analysed in Marxist terms. He is a trained pilot and could make a living if he could only get a job, but even the job he doesn't get would be on the night mails, which would rob him of the real joy of flying because he would not be able to see the earth below him. So if he weren't unemployed he would be a classic case of alienated labour, unable to see the product of his work.

The germ of *The Good Person of Szechwan* was a piece about prostitution and deprivation in Berlin. Transplanted to China the social structure of the play becomes much less specific, and the flyer becomes a slightly incongruous figure from a more modern world, but the underlying pattern of exploitation remains the same. The gods are not authorised to 'meddle in the sphere of economics', and they refuse to recognize the need for change. Brecht's China turns out on analysis to be a working model of early capitalism in which all generous impulses are subordinated to the profit motive. The development of the play tears Shen Teh apart and leaves her in precisely the same predicament at the end of the play as at the beginning, the need for change is clearly demonstrated, and, in the vocabulary of Brecht's parabolic style, change can only mean revolution. But this is another case where the author's intentions can be subverted by the audience's perceptions, and the implicit revolutionary message can so readily be glossed over that the play is a favourite with teachers and directors looking for a harmless bit of Brecht.

The characters in *The Good Person of Szechwan* are slighter and more schematic than those in *Mother Courage and her Children*. One is reminded of George Grosz's gallery of cartoon figures from the Weimar Republic: the bloated capitalist entertaining girls in good little restaurants, the crippled match-sellers, the scavenging children, the prostitute with the heart of gold. Brecht had trouble rounding out the Good Person to make her plausible, but the intriguing twists in the plot and the wealth of incident compensate for this. *The Good Person of Szechwan* with its songs and interludes, its characters directly addressing the audience, its report punctuated by enactment in Mrs Yang's account of the tobacco factory, and its mask for Shui Ta put Brecht back on the epic standard.

Hugh Rorrison

Fear and Misery of the Third Reich

24 scenes

Collaborator: M. STEFFIN

Translator: JOHN WILLETT

Characters

1 Two SS Officers
2 Man
  Woman
3 SA man
  Cook
  Maidservant
  Chauffeur
  Worker
4 BRÜHL
  DIEVENBACH
  LOHMANN
  Jehovah's Witness
  SS man
5 SS man
  Detainee
  SS Officer
6 Judge
  Inspector
  Prosecutor
  Usher
  Maidservant
  Senior Judge
7 Two patients
  Surgeon
  Sister
  Three assistants
  Nurses
8 Two scientists, X and Y
9 Woman
  Husband
10 Maidservant
  Man
  Wife
  Boy
11 Daughter
  Mother

12 Student
  Young worker
  Group leader
13 Announcer
  Two male workers
  Woman worker
  Gentleman
  SA man
14 Woman
  SA men
  Child
  Worker
  Young woman
15 Man
  Wife
  Released man
16 Old woman
  Two SA men
17 Two bakers
18 Farmer
  Farmer's wife
19 Petit-bourgeois
  Two women
  Young fellow
  Dairywoman
  Butcher's wife
20 Dying man
  Wife
  Pastor
21 Five boys
  Scharführer
22 Two boys
23 Neighbour
  Man
  Wife
24 Woman
  Two workers

The German march-past

When He had ruled five years, and they informed us
That He who claimed to have been sent by God
Was ready for His promised war, the steelworks
Had forged tank, gun and warship, and there waited
Within His hangers aircraft in so great a number
That they, leaving the earth at His command
Would darken all the heavens, then we became determined
To see what sort of nation, formed from what sort of people
In what condition, what sort of thoughts thinking
He would be calling to His colours. We staged a march-past.

See, now they come towards us
A motley sights rewards us
Their banners go before.
To show how straight their course is
They carry crooked crosses
To double-cross the poor.

Some march along like dummies
Others crawl on their tummies
Towards the war He's planned.
One hears no lamentation
No murmurs of vexation
One only hears the band.

With wives and kids arriving
Five years they've been surviving.
Five more is more than they'll last.
A ramshackle collection
They parade for our inspection
As they come marching past.

One big family

First the SS approaches.
Blown up with beer and speeches
They're in a kind of daze.
Their aim is a People imperious
Respected and powerful and serious –
Above all, one that obeys.

The night of January 30th, 1933. Two SS officers lurching down the street.

THE FIRST: Top dogs, that's us. That torchlight procession, impressive, what? Broke one moment, next day running the government. Rags to riches in a single day.
They make water.

THE SECOND: And now it'll be a united nation. I'm expecting the German people to have an unprecedented moral revival.

THE FIRST: Wait till we've coaxed German Man out from among all those filthy subhumans. Hey, what part of Berlin is this? Not a flag showing.

THE SECOND: We've come the wrong way.

THE FIRST: A horrible sight.

THE SECOND: Lot of crooks round here.

THE FIRST: Think it could be dangerous?

THE SECOND: Decent comrades don't live in such slums.

THE FIRST: Not a light to be seen either.

THE SECOND: Nobody at home.

THE FIRST: That lot are. Catch them coming along to watch the birth of the Third Reich. We'd best cover our rear.
Staggering, they set off again, the first following the second.

THE FIRST: Isn't this the bit by the canal?

THE SECOND: Don't ask me.

THE FIRST: Over by the corner's where we cleaned up a
bunch of Marxists. Afterwards they said it was a Catholic
youth club. Pack of lies. Not one of them was wearing a
collar.

THE SECOND: Think he'll really make us a united nation?

THE FIRST: He'll make anything.

He stops, freezes and listens. Somewhere a window has been opened.

THE SECOND: Wozzat?

*He pushes forward the safety catch on his revolver. An old man
in a nightshirt leans out of the window and is heard softly calling
'Emma, are you there?'*

THE SECOND: That's them!

*He rushes round like a maniac, and starts shooting in every
direction.*

THE FIRST *bellows:* Help!

*Behind a window opposite the one where the old man is still stand-
ing a terrible cry is heard. Someone has been hit.*

2

A case of betrayal

> The next to appear are the traitors
> Who've given away their neighbours.
> They know that people know.
> If only the street would forget them!
> They could sleep if their conscience would let them
> But there's so far still to go.

*Breslau 1933. Lower middle-class flat. A man and a woman are
standing by the door listening. They are very pale.*

THE WOMAN: They've got to the ground floor.

THE MAN: Not quite.

THE WOMAN: They've smashed the banisters. He'd already passed out when they dragged him out of his flat.

THE MAN: I simply said the sound of foreign broadcasts didn't come from here.

THE WOMAN: That wasn't all you said.

THE MAN: I said nothing more than that.

THE WOMAN: Don't look at me that way. If you said nothing more, then you said nothing more.

THE MAN: That's the point.

THE WOMAN: Why not go round to the police and make a statement saying nobody called there on Saturday?
Pause.

THE MAN: Catch me going to the police. It was inhuman, the way they were treating him.

THE WOMAN: He asked for it. What's he want to meddle in politics for?

THE MAN: They didn't have to rip his jacket though. Our sort isn't that well off for clothes.

THE WOMAN: What's a jacket more or less?

THE MAN: They didn't have to rip it.

3

The chalk cross

Here come the brown storm troopers
That keen-eyed squad of snoopers
To check where each man stands
Their job's to put the boot in
Then hang around saluting
With bloodstained empty hands.

Berlin 1933. Kitchen of a gentleman's house. The SA man, the cook, the maidservant, the chauffeur.

THE MAIDSERVANT: Did they really only give you half an hour off?

THE SA MAN: Night exercise.

THE COOK: What are all these exercises about?

THE SA MAN: That's an official secret.

THE COOK: Is there a raid on?

THE SA MAN: Like to know, wouldn't you? None of you is going to find out from me. Wild horses wouldn't drag it from me.

THE MAIDSERVANT: So you got to go all the way out to Reinickendorf?

THE SA MAN: Reinickendorf or Rummelsburg or might be Lichtenfelde, why not eh?

THE MAIDSERVANT *somewhat confused:* Won't you have a bit to eat before going off?

THE SA MAN: If you twist my arm. Bring on the field kitchen.

The cook brings in a tray.

No, you don't catch us talking. Always take the enemy by surprise. Zoom in from an unexpected direction. Look at the way the Führer prepares one of his coups. Like trying to see through a brick wall. No way of telling beforehand. For all I know he can't even tell himself. And then wham! – like that. It's amazing what happens. That's what makes people so frightened of us. *He has tucked in his napkin. With knife and fork poised he inquires:* How about if the gentry suddenly pop in, Anna? Me sitting here with a mouth full of sauce. *Exaggerating as though his mouth was full:* Heil Hitler!

THE MAIDSERVANT: Oh, they'll ring for the car first, won't they, Mr Francke?

THE CHAUFFEUR: What d'you say? Oh, of course.

Pacified, the SA man starts turning his attention to the tray.

THE MAIDSERVANT *sitting down beside him:* Don't you feel tired?

THE SA MAN: Bet your life.

THE MAIDSERVANT: But you've got Friday off, haven't you?

THE SA MAN *nods:* If nothing crops up.

THE MAIDSERVANT: Listen. Getting your watch mended was four marks fifty.

THE SA MAN: A bloody scandal.

THE MAIDSERVANT: The watch itself only cost 12 marks.

THE SA MAN: Is that assistant at the hardware shop still as saucy as ever?

THE MAIDSERVANT: Christ alive.

THE SA MAN: You only got to tell me.

THE MAIDSERVANT: I tell you everything anyway. Wearing your new boots are you?

THE SA MAN *not interested:* Yes, what about it?

THE MAIDSERVANT: Minna, you seen Theo's new boots yet?

THE COOK: No.

THE MAIDSERVANT: Let's have a look, then. That's what they're giving them now.

The SA man, his mouth full, stretches out his leg to be inspected. Lovely, aren't they?

The SA man looks around, seeking something.

THE COOK: Something missing?

THE SA MAN: Bit dry here.

THE MAIDSERVANT: Like some beer, love? I'll get it. *She hurries out.*

THE COOK: She'd run her legs off for you, Herr Theo.

THE SA MAN: Yeh, I always do okay. Wham, like that.

THE COOK: You men take a lot for granted, don't you?

THE SA MAN: That's what women want. *Seeing the cook lift a heavy pot.* What are you breaking your back for? Don't you bother, that's my job. *He carries the pot for her.*

THE COOK: That's real good of you. You're always finding things to do for me. Pity other people aren't so considerate. *With a look at the chauffeur.*

THE SA MAN: Don't have to make a song and dance of it. We're glad to help.

There's a knock at the kitchen door.

THE COOK: That'll be my brother. He's bringing a valve for the wireless. *She admits her brother, a worker.* My brother.

THE SA MAN AND THE CHAUFFEUR: Heil Hitler!

The worker mumblers something that could be taken for 'Heil Hitler' at a pinch.

THE COOK: Got the valve, have you?

THE WORKER: Yes.

THE COOK: Want to put it in right away?

The two go out.

THE SA MAN: What's that fellow do?

THE CHAUFFEUR: Out of a job.

THE SA MAN: Come here often?

THE CHAUFFEUR *shrugging his shoulders:* I'm not here that much.

THE SA MAN: Anyhow the old girl's a hundred per cent for Germany.

THE CHAUFFEUR: You bet.

THE SA MAN: But that wouldn't stop her brother being something quite different.

THE CHAUFFEUR: Got any definite reason to suspect him?

THE SA MAN: Me? No. Never. I never suspect anyone. You suspect somebody, see, and it's the same as being sure, almost. And then the fur will fly.

THE CHAUFFEUR *murmurs:* Wham, like that.

THE SA MAN: That's right. *Leaning back, with one eye shut:* Could you understand what he was mumbling? *He imitates the worker's greeting:* Might have been 'Heil Hitler'. Might not. Me and that lot's old pals.

He gives a resounding laugh. The cook and the worker return. She sets food before him.

THE COOK: My brother's that clever with the wireless. And yet he doesn't care a bit about listening to it. If I'd the time I'd always be putting it on. *To the worker:* And you've got more time than you know what to do with, Franz.

THE SA MAN: What's that? Got a wireless and never puts the thing on?

THE WORKER: Bit of music sometimes.

THE COOK: And to think he made himself that smashing set out of twice nothing.

THE SA MAN: How many valves you got then?

THE WORKER *with a challenging stare:* Four.

THE SA MAN: Well, well, no accounting for taste. *To Chauffeur:* Is there?
Maidservant comes back with the beer.

THE MAIDSERVANT: Ice cold.

THE SA MAN *putting his hand on hers in a friendly way:* You're puffed, girl. No call to rush like that, I wouldn't have minded waiting.
She pours the bottle out for him.

THE MAIDSERVANT: Doesn't matter. *Shakes hands with the worker:* Did you bring the valve? Fancy walking all that way here. *To the SA man:* He lives out in Moabit.

THE SA MAN: Hey, where's my beer got to? Somebody's drunk my beer. *To the chauffeur:* Was it you drunk my beer?

THE CHAUFFEUR: No, certainly not. What d'you say that for? Has your beer gone?

THE MAIDSERVANT: But I poured it out for you.

THE SA MAN *to the cook:* You swigged my beer, you did. *Gives a resounding laugh.* Keep your hair on. Little trick they teach you in our squad. How to knock back a beer without being seen or heard. *To the worker:* Did you want to say something?

THE WORKER: That trick's got whiskers.

THE SA MAN: Let's see how you do it then. *He pours him a beer from the bottle.*

THE WORKER: Right. Here I have one beer. *He raises his glass.* And now for the trick. *Calmly and appreciatively he drinks the beer.*

THE COOK: But we all saw you.

THE WORKER *wiping his mouth:* Did you? Then I must have done it wrong.
The chauffeur laughs aloud.

THE SA MAN: What's so funny about that?

THE WORKER: You couldn't have done it any different. How did you do it, then?

THE SA MAN: How can I show you when you've drunk up all my beer?

THE WORKER: Of course. That's right. You can't do that trick without beer. D'you know another trick? You people surely know more than one trick.

THE SA MAN: What d'you mean, 'you people'?

THE WORKER: You young fellows.

THE SA MAN: Oh.

THE MAIDSERVANT: But Theo, Mr Lincke was only joking.

THE WORKER *thinks he had better be conciliatory:* Don't mind, do you?

THE COOK: I'll get you another beer.

THE SA MAN: No call for that. I washed my food down all right.

THE COOK: Herr Theo can take a joke.

THE SA MAN *to the worker:* Why not sit down? We won't bite your head off.

The worker sits down.

Live and let live. And a joke now and then. Why not? Public opinion, that's the one thing we're really strict about.

THE COOK: A good thing you are.

THE WORKER: And how's public opinion these days?

THE SA MAN: Public opinion these days is fine. You with me there?

THE WORKER: Oh yes. It's just that nobody tells anyone what he thinks.

THE SA MAN: Nobody tells anyone? What d'you mean? They tell me all right.

THE WORKER: Really?

THE SA MAN: Well of course they're not going to come along and tell you all their thoughts. You go to them.

THE WORKER: Where?

THE SA MAN: To the public welfare for instance. In the mornings we'll be at the public welfare.

THE WORKER: That's right, now and again you hear somebody grumbling there.

THE SA MAN: You see?

THE WORKER: But that way all you can do is catch them once, then they know you. And after that they'll clam up again.

THE SA MAN: Why should they know me? Shall I show you why they don't? Interested in tricks, aren't you? No reason why I shouldn't show you one, we've got plenty. I always say if they only realised what a lot we've got up our sleeve, and how they'll never survive whatever happens, then perhaps they'd pack it in.

THE MAIDSERVANT: Go on, Theo, tell them how you do it.

THE SA MAN: Right. Let's suppose we're at the public welfare in the Münzstrasse. Let's say you – *looking at the worker* – are in the line ahead of me. But I got to make a few preparations first. *He goes out.*

THE WORKER *winking at the chauffeur*: So now we're getting a chance to see how they do it.

THE COOK: They're going to smell out all the Marxists because they got to be stopped disrupting everything.

THE WORKER: Is that it?

The SA man comes back.

THE SA MAN: I'd be in civvies of course. *To the worker:* OK, start grumbling.

THE WORKER: What about?

THE SA MAN: Go on, you've got something on your chest. Your lot always have.

THE WORKER: Me? No.

THE SA MAN: You're a tough guy, aren't you? Don't tell me you think everything's a hundred per cent.

THE WORKER: Why not?

THE SA MAN: All right, let's call it off. If you won't play the whole thing's off.

THE WORKER: All right then. I'll shoot my mouth off for you. These buggers keep you hanging about as if we'd all the time in the world. Two hours it took me to get here from Rummelsburg.

THE SA MAN: What the hell. Don't tell me the distance from Rummelsburg to the Münzstrasse is any further under Hitler than it was under that racketeering Republic. Come on, you can do better than that.

THE COOK: It's only play acting, Franz, we all know what you say won't be your real opinions.

THE MAIDSERVANT: Don't you see you're just acting a grumbler? Theo won't take it amiss, you can depend on it. He just wants to show us something.

THE WORKER: Right. In that case I'll say. The SA looks very fine, but I think it's shit. Give me the Marxists and the Jews.

THE COOK: Franz! Really!

THE MAIDSERVANT: How can you say that, Mr Lincke?

THE SA MAN *laughing:* For Christ sake! I'd just turn you over to the nearest cop. Not got much imagination, have you? Look, you've got to say something you might be able to wriggle out of. Sort of thing you'd hear in real life.

THE WORKER: All right, then you'll have to give me a hand and provoke me.

THE SA MAN: That went out years ago. Suppose I said 'Our Führer's the greatest man there's ever been, greater than Jesus Christ and Napoleon rolled into on,' all you'd say was 'You bet he is.' So I'd best take the other road and say: 'They're a big-mouthed lot. You know the one about Goebbels and the two fleas? Well, the two fleas had a bet who could get from one side of his mouth to the other quickest. The winner was the one went round the back of his head. It wasn't so far that way.

THE CHAUFFEUR: Ha.

All laugh.

THE SA MAN *to the worker:* Now it's your turn to make a crack.

THE WORKER: I can't cap a story like that bang off. Telling that joke wouldn't stop you being an informer.

THE MAIDSERVANT: He's right, Theo.

THE SA MAN: You're a right bunch of turds. Make me sick, you do. Not a bloody soul got the guts to open his mouth.

THE WORKER: Is that what you really think, or is it what you say at the public welfare?

THE SA MAN: I say it at the public welfare too.

THE WORKER: In that case what I say at the public welfare is Look before you leap. I'm a coward. I don't carry a gun.

THE SA MAN: Right, brother, if you're going to be so careful about looking, let me tell you you can look and look, then all of a sudden you're in the voluntary labour service.

THE WORKER: And if you don't look?

THE SA MAN: Then you'll be in it just the same. Sure. It's voluntary, see? Voluntary's good, don't you think?

THE WORKER: That's where it might be possible for some daring fellow to make a joke or two about the Voluntary Labour Service suppose both of you were standing at the Public Welfare and you gave him one of those looks with your blue eyes. I wonder what he could say. Maybe: another fifteen went off yesterday. Funny how they get them to do it, when you think it's all voluntary and folk are paid no more for doing something than for doing nothing though they must need to eat more. Then I heard the one about Dr Ley and the cat and of course I saw the whole thing. You know that story?

THE SA MAN: No, we don't.

THE WORKER: Well, Dr Ley went on this little Strength Through Joy trip, strictly on business, and he met one of those former Weimar party bosses – I'm not up in all their names, anyway it might have been in a concentration camp though Dr Ley's got much too much sense to visit one of those – and the old boss asked him how'd he get the workers to swallow all the things they usedn't to put up with at any price. Dr Ley pointed to a cat lying in the sun and said: suppose you wanted to give that cat a mouthful of mustard and make her swallow it whether she wanted or not. How would you do it? Boss takes the mustard and smears it over the cat's chops; of course it spits it back in his face, no question of swallowing, just a lot of bloody scratches. No, old boy, says Dr Ley in his endearing way, you got the wrong approach. Now watch me. He takes the mustard with a practised follow-through and sticks it abracadabra up the wretched beast's arsehole. *To the ladies:* Excuse my French, but that's part of the story. – Numbed and stunned by the frightful pain, cat instantly sets to licking out the lot. There you are, my dear fellow, says the triumphant Dr Ley, she's eating it. And voluntarily at that!
They laugh.

THE WORKER: Yes, it's very funny.

THE SA MAN: That's got things going. Voluntary Labour Service, that's a favourite subject. Trouble is: nobody bothers to dig his toes in. Oh, they can make us eat shit and we'll still say thank you for it.

THE WORKER: I'm not so sure about that. There am I the other day on the Alexanderplatz wondering whether to volunteer for the Voluntary Labour Service spontaneouslike or wait till they shove me in. Over from the grocer's on the corner comes a skinny little woman, must be some proletarian's wife. Half a mo, says I, what are the proletarians doing in the Third Reich when we've got national unity and even Baron Thyssen is in it? No, says she, not when they've gone and put up the price of marge. From fifty pfennigs to one mark. You trying to tell me that's national unity? Better mind out, ma, says I, what you're saying to me, I'm patriotic to the backbone. All bones and no meat, says she, and chaff in the bread. She was that worked up. I just stand there mumbling: best get butter then. It's better for you. Mustn't skimp on your food, cause that saps the people's strength and we can't afford that what with so many enemies encircling us even in the top civil service . . . we been warned. No, says she, we're all of us Nazis so long as we got breath in our bodies, what mayn't be long now in view of the war menace. Only the other day I got to offer my best sofa to the Winter Aid, says she, cause I hear Goering's having to sleep on the floor he's that worried about our raw materials, and in the office they say they'd rather have a piano – you know, for Strength Through Joy. And no proper flour to be had. I takes my sofa away from the Winter Aid People and goes to the second-hand dealer round the corner, I been meaning to buy half a pound of butter for some time. And at the dairy they tell me: no butter today, comrade, would you like some guns? I say, give me, says she. I say: come on what d'you want guns for, ma? On an empty stomach? No, says she, if I'm going to be hungry they should be shot, the whole lot of them starting with Hitler at the top . . . Come on, says I, come on, exclaims I appalled . . . With Hitler at the top we'll conquer France, says she. Now we're getting our petrol from wool. And the wool? says I. The wool, says she: these days that's made from petrol. Wool's another thing we need. Any time a bit of good stuff from the old days reaches the Winter Aid the lot that run the place grab it for themselves, says she. If Hitler only knew, says they, but he knows nothing the poor lamb, never went to secondary school they say. I was struck dumb by so much subversiveness. You just stay here, young lady, says I, I got to make a call at police headquarters. But when I come back with an officer what d'you think, she's cleared off. *Stops play-acting.* What d'you say to that, eh?

THE SA MAN *still acting:* Me? What do I say? Well, I might give a reproachful look. You went straight round to the police, I might say. Can't risk talking freely when you're around.

THE WORKER: I should think not. Not with me. You confide in me, you'll be done. I know my duty as a comrade: any time my own mother mutters something to me about the price of margarine or something I go straight to the local SA office. I'll denounce my own brother for grumbling about the voluntary labour service. As for my girl, when she tells me 'Heil Hitler' she's got pregnant at a work camp then I have them bring her in: we can't have abortions because if we made exceptions for our nearest and dearest the Third Reich would run out of manpower, and the Third Reich's what we love best. – Was that more like it? Did I act all right?

THE SA MAN: I guess that'll do. *Goes on acting.* You'll be okay, go and draw your benefit, we've all understood, eh brothers? But you can count on me, my friend, 'nuff said, mum's the word. *He slaps him on the shoulder. No longer acting:* Right, then in you go into the office and they'll pick you up bang off.

THE WORKER: What, without you leaving the line and following me in?

THE SA MAN: Yeh.

THE WORKER: And without you giving someone a wink, which might look fishy?

THE SA MAN: Without me winking.

THE WORKER: How's it done then?

THE SA MAN: Ha, you'd like to know that trick. Well, stand up, and show us your back. *He turns him round by the shoulders, so that everyone can see his back. Then to the maidservant:* Seen it?

THE MAIDSERVANT: Look, he's got a white cross on it.

THE COOK: Right between his shoulders.

THE CHAUFFEUR: So he has.

THE SA MAN: And how did he get it? *Shows the palm of his*

hand. See, just a little white chalk cross and there's its impression large as life.

The worker takes off his jacket and looks at the cross.

THE WORKER: Nice work.

THE SA MAN: Not bad, eh? I always have my chalk on me. Ah, you have to use your loaf, things don't always go according to the book. *With satisfaction:* Well, so it's off to Reinickendorf. *Corrects himself:* That's where my aunt lives, you know. You lot don't seem very enthusiastic. *To the maidservant:* What are you gawping like that for, Anna? Missed the whole point of the trick, I suppose?

THE MAIDSERVANT: Of course not. Think I'm silly or something?

THE SA MAN *as if the whole joke has gone sour, stretches his hand out to her:* Wipe it off.

She washes his hand with a rag.

THE COOK: You've got to use those sort of methods so long as they keep on trying to undermine everything our Führer has built up and what makes other people so envious of us.

THE CHAUFFEUR: What was that? Oh yes, quite so. *Looks at his watch.* Well, time to wash the car again. Heil Hitler! *Exit.*

THE SA MAN: What kind of a fellow's that?

THE MAIDSERVANT: Keeps himself to himself. Not a bit political.

THE WORKER: Well, Minna, I'd better be off. No hard feelings about the beer, eh? And let me say I'm surer than ever that no one's going to complain about the Third Reich and get away with it. That's set my mind at rest. Me, I don't ever come across that sort of subversive element. I'd gladly confront them if I did. Only I'm not quite so quick to the punch as you. *Clearly and distinctly:* All right, Minna, thanks a lot and Heil Hitler!

THE OTHERS: Heil Hitler!

THE SA MAN: Take a tip from me and don't be quite so innocent. It attracts attention. No call to have to watch your mouth with me, I can take a joke now and again. All right: Heil Hitler!

The worker goes.

THE SA MAN: Bit sudden the way those two cleared out. Something's put ants in their pants. I shouldn't have said that about Reinickendorf. They're waiting to pounce on that sort of thing.

THE MAIDSERVANT: There's something else I wanted to ask you, Theo.

THE SA MAN: Fire away, any time.

THE COOK: I'm off to put out the laundry. I was young once too. *Exit.*

THE SA MAN: What is it?

THE MAIDSERVANT: But I shan't ask unless I can see you won't mind; otherwise I'll say nothing.

THE SA MAN: Spit it out, then.

THE MAIDSERVANT: It's just that ... I don't like saying ... well, I need 20 marks from our account.

THE SA MAN: Twenty marks?

THE MAIDSERVANT: There you are, you *do* mind.

THE SA MAN: Twenty marks out of our savings account, can't expect me to give three cheers. What do you want it for?

THE MAIDSERVANT: I'd rather not say.

THE SA MAN: So. You're not saying. That's a laugh.

THE MAIDSERVANT: I know you won't agree with me, Theo, so I'd sooner not give my reasons yet awhile.

THE SA MAN: Well, if you don't trust me ...

THE MAIDSERVANT: Of course I trust you.

THE SA MAN: So you want to give up having a joint savings account?

THE MAIDSERVANT: How can you say that? If I take out twenty marks I'll still have ninety-seven marks left.

THE SA MAN: No need to do sums for my benefit. I know how much there is. I just think you're wanting to break it off, probably because you're flirting with someone else. Perhaps you'll be wanting to check our statement too.

THE MAIDSERVANT: I'm not flirting with anyone else.

THE SA MAN: Then tell me what it's for.

THE MAIDSERVANT: You don't want to let me have it.

THE SA MAN: How am I to tell it isn't for something wrong?

THE MAIDSERVANT: It's not anything wrong, and if I didn't need it I wouldn't call for it, you must know that.

THE SA MAN: I don't know nothing. All I know is the whole business strikes me as rather fishy. Why should you suddenly need twenty marks? It's quite a bit of money. You pregnant?

THE MAIDSERVANT: No.

THE SA MAN: Sure?

THE MAIDSERVANT: Yes.

THE SA MAN: If I thought for a minute you were planning anything illegal, if I caught a whiff of that kind of thing, I'd be down like a ton of bricks, let me tell you. You might just have heard that any interference with our burgeoning fruit is the worst crime you can commit. If the German people stopped multiplying itself it would be all up with our historic mission.

THE MAIDSERVANT: But Theo, I don't know what you're talking about. It's nothing like that, I'd have told you if it was because you'd be involved too. But if that's what you're thinking then let me tell you. It's just I want to help Frieda buy a winter coat.

THE SA MAN: And why can't your sister buy her coats for herself?

THE MAIDSERVANT: How could she on her disability pension, it's twenty-six marks eighty a month.

THE SA MAN: What about our Winter Aid? But that's just it, you've no confidence in our National Socialist state. I can tell that anyway from the sort of conversations that go on in this kitchen. Do you think I didn't see what a long face you pulled at my experiment?

THE MAIDSERVANT: What do you mean by a long face?

THE SA MAN: You pulled one all right. Just like our friends who cleared out so suddenly.

THE MAIDSERVANT: If you really want to know what I think, I don't like that kind of thing.

THE SA MAN: And what is it you don't like, may I ask?

THE MAIDSERVANT: The way you catch those poor down and outs by dressing up and playing tricks and all that. My father's unemployed too.

THE SA MAN: Ha, that's all I needed to hear. As if talking to that fellow Lincke hadn't already set me thinking.

THE MAIDSERVANT: Do you mean to say you're going to nail him for what he did just to please you and with all of us egging him on?

THE SA MAN: I'm not saying nothing. As I already told you. And if you've anything against what I'm doing as part of my duty then let me say just look in *Mein Kampf* and you'll see how the Führer himself didn't think it beneath him to test the people's attitude of mind, and it was actually his job for a while when he was in the army and it was all for Germany and the consequences were tremendously important.

THE MAIDSERVANT: If that's your line, Theo, then I'd just like to know if I can have the twenty marks. That's all.

THE SA MAN: Then all I can say to you is I'm not in the mood to have anything taken off me.

THE MAIDSERVANT: What do you mean, taken off you? Whose money is it, yours or mine?

THE SA MAN: That's a nice way to be speaking about our joint money all of a sudden. I suppose that's why we purged the Jews from the life of our nation, so we could have our own kith and kin suck our blood instead?

THE MAIDSERVANT: How can you say things like that on account of twenty marks?

THE SA MAN: I've plenty of expenses. My boots alone set me back twenty-seven marks.

THE MAIDSERVANT: But weren't they issued to you?

THE SA MAN: That's what we thought. And that's why I took the better kind, the ones with gaiters. Then they demanded payment and we were stung.

THE MAIDSERVANT: Twenty-seven marks for boots? So what other expenses were there?

THE SA MAN: What d'you mean, other expenses?

THE MAIDSERVANT: Didn't you say you had lots of expenses?

THE SA MAN: Forgotten what they were. Anyway I'm not here to be cross-examined. Keep your hair on, I'm not going to swindle you. And as for the twenty marks I'll think it over.

THE MAIDSERVANT *weeping:* Theo, I just can't believe you'd tell me the money was all right and it wasn't true. Oh now I don't know what to think. Surely there's twenty marks left in the savings bank out of all that money?

THE SA MAN *slapping her on the shoulder:* But nobody's suggesting for a minute that there's nothing left in our savings bank. Out of the question. You know you can rely on me. You trust something to me, it's like locking it in the safe. Well, decided to trust Theo again, have you?

She weeps without replying.

THE SA MAN: It's just nerves, you've been working too hard. Well, time I went off to that night exercise. I'll be coming for you on Friday, then. Heil Hitler! *Exit.*

The maidservant tries to suppress her tears and walks distractedly up and down the kitchen. The cook comes back with a basket of linen.

THE COOK: What's wrong? Had a quarrel? Theo's such a splendid boy. Pity there aren't more like him. Nothing serious, is it?

THE MAIDSERVANT *still weeping:* Minna, can't you go out to your brother's and tell him to watch out for himself?

THE COOK: What for?

THE MAIDSERVANT: Just watch out, I mean.

THE COOK: On account of tonight? You can't be serious. Theo would never do such a thing.

THE MAIDSERVANT: I don't know what to think any longer, Minna. He's changed so. They've completely ruined him. He's keeping bad company. Four years we've been going out together, and now it seems to me just as though ... I even feel like asking you to look at my shoulder and see if there's a white cross on it.

4

Peat-bog soldiers

> With storm troopers parading
> These men carry on debating
> What Lenin and Kautsky meant
> Till, clutching the tomes they've cited
> They're forcibly united
> By joint imprisonment.

Esterwegen concentration camp, 1934. Some prisoners are mixing cement.

BRÜHL *softly to Dievenbach:* I'd steer clear of Lohmann; he talks.

DIEVENBACH *aloud:* Oi, Lohmann, here's Brühl saying I should steer clear of you; you talk.

BRÜHL: Bastard.

LOHMANN: That's good coming from you, you bloody Judas. Why did Karl get given solitary?

BRÜHL: Nothing to do with me. Was it me got cigarettes from God knows where?

THE JEHOVAH'S WITNESS: Look out.

The SS sentry up on the embankment goes by.

THE SS MAN: Someone was talking here. Who was it? *Nobody answers.* If that happens just once more it'll be solitary confinement for the lot of you, get me? Now sing! *The prisoners sing verse 1 of the 'Song of the Peat-bog Soldiers'. The SS man moves on.*

> 'See, whichever way one gazes
> Naught but boggy heath lies there.
> Not one bird his sweet voice raises
> In those oak trees gaunt and bare.
>> We are the peat-bog soldiers
>> With shovels on our shoulders
>> We march.'

THE JEHOVAH'S WITNESS: Why do you people carry on quarreling even now?

DIEVENBACH: Don't you worry, Jehovah, you wouldn't understand. *Indicating Brühl:* Yesterday his party voted for Hitler's foreign policy in the Reichstag. And he – *indicating Lohmann* – thinks Hitler's foreign policy means war.

BRÜHL: Not with us around.

LOHMANN: Last war we had you were around all right.

BRÜHL: Anyway the German armed forces are too weak.

LOHMANN: Still, your lot did at least bring Hitler a battle-cruiser as part of the wedding deal.

THE JEHOVAH'S WITNESS *to Dievenbach:* What were you? Communist or Social-democrat?

DIEVENBACH: I kept outside all that.

LOHMANN: But you're inside now all right, inside a camp I mean.

THE JEHOVAH'S WITNESS: Look out.

The SS man appears again. He watches them, Slowly Brühl starts singing the third verse of the 'Song of the Peat-bog soldiers'. The SS man moves on.

'Back and forth the guards keep pacing
Not a soul can get away.
Shots for those who try escaping
Thick barbed wire for those who stay.
  We are the peat-bog soldiers
  With shovels on our shoulders
  We march.'

LOHMANN *hurls his shovel from him:* When I think I'm only in here because your lot sabotaged the united front I could bash your bloody brains out right now.

BRÜHL: Ha! 'Like your brother must I be/Or you'll turn and clobber me' – is that it? United front indeed. Softly softly catchee monkey: would have suited you nicely to sneak all our members away, wouldn't it?

LOHMANN: When you'd rather have Hitler sneak them away, like now. You traitors!

BRÜHL *furiously takes his shovel and brandishes it at Lohmann,*

who holds his own shovel at the ready: I'll teach you
something you won't forget!

THE JEHOVAH'S WITNESS: Look out.

*He hastily starts singing the last verse of the 'Song of the Peat-
bog soldiers'.*

*The SS man reappears and the others join in as they resume
mixing their cement.*

'We've no use for caterwauling.
Sunshine follows after rain.
One day soon you'll hear us calling:
Homeland, you are ours again.
        And then we peat-bog soldiers
        Will rise, throw back our shoulders
        And march.'

THE SS MAN: Which of you shouted 'Traitors'?

Nobody answers.

THE SS MAN: You people never learn, do you? *To Lohmann:*
Which?

Bohmann stares at Brühl and says nothing.

THE SS MAN *to Dievenbach:* Which?

Dievenbach says nothing.

THE SS MAN *to the Jehovah's Witness:* Which?

The Jehovah's Witness says nothing.

THE SS MAN *to Brühl:* Which?

Brühl says nothing.

THE SS MAN: I shall count up to five, then it'll be solitary
confinement for the whole lot of you till you turn blue.

*He waits for five seconds. They all stand in silence staring straight
ahead.*

THE SS MAN: So it's solitary.

5

Servants of the people

The camps are run by warders
Narks, butchers and marauders —
The people's servants they
They'll crush you and assail you
And flog you and impale you
For negligible pay.

Oranienburg Concentration Camp 1934. A small yard between the huts. In the darkness a sound of flogging. As it gets light an SS man is seen flogging a detainee. An SS officer stands in the background smoking; with his back to the scene. Then he goes off.

THE SS MAN *sits down on a barrel, exhausted:* Work on.
The detainee rises from the ground and starts unsteadily cleaning the drains.
Why can't you say no when they ask if you're a communist, you cunt? It means the lash for you and I have to stay in barracks. I'm so fucking tired. Why can't they give the job to Klapproth? He enjoys this sort of thing. Look, if that bastard comes round again — *he listens* — you're to take the whip and flog the ground hard as you can, right?

THE DETAINEE: Yes, sir.

THE SS MAN: But only because you buggers have flogged me out, right?

THE DETAINEE: Yes, sir.

THE SS MAN: Here he comes.
Steps are heard outside, and the SS man points to the whip. The detainee picks it up and flogs the ground. This doesn't sound authentic, so the SS man idly points to a nearby basket which the detainee then flogs. The steps outside come to a stop. The SS man abruptly rises in some agitation, snatches the whip and begins beating the detainee.

THE DETAINEE *softly:* Not my stomach.

The SS man hits him on the bottom. The SS officer looks in.

THE SS OFFICER: Flog his stomach.

The SS man beats the detainee's stomach.

6

Judicial process

> The judges follow limply.
> They were told that justice is simply
> What serves our People best.
> They objected: how are we to know that?
> But they'll soon be interpreting it so that
> The whole people is under arrest.

Augsburg 1934. Consultation room in a court building. A milky January morning can be seen through the window. A spherical gas lamp is still burning. The district judge is just putting on his robes. There is a knock.

THE JUDGE: Come in.

Enter the police inspector.

THE INSPECTOR: Good morning, your honour.

THE JUDGE: Good morning, Mr Tallinger. It's about the case of Häberle, Schünt and Gaunitzer. I must admit the whole affair is a bit beyond me.

THE INSPECTOR:?

THE JUDGE: I understand from the file that the shop where the incident occurred – Arndt's the jeweller's – is a Jewish one?

THE INSPECTOR:?

THE JUDGE: And presumably Häberle, Schünt and Gaunitzer are still members of Storm Troop 7?

The inspector nods.

THE JUDGE: Which means that the Troop saw no reason to discipline them?

The inspector shakes his head.

THE JUDGE: All the same, I take it the Troop must have instituted some kind of inquiry in view of the disturbance which the incident caused in the neighbourhood?

The inspector shrugs his shoulders.

THE JUDGE: I would appreciate it, Tallinger, if you would give me a brief summary before we go into court. Would you?

THE INSPECTOR *mechanically:* On 2 December 1933 at 0815 hours SA men Häberle, Schünt and Gaunitzer forced their way into Arndt's jewellers in the Schlettowstrasse and after a brief exchange of words wounded Mr Arndt age 54 on the head. The material damage amounted to a total of eleven thousand two hundred and thirty-four marks. Inquiries were instituted by the criminal investigation department on 7 December 1933 and led to . . .

THE JUDGE: Come on, Tallinger, that's all in the files. *He points irritably at the charge sheet, which consists of a single page.* This is the flimsiest and sloppiest made-out indictment I've ever seen, not that the last few months have been much of a picnic, let me tell you. But it does say that much. I was hoping you might be able to tell me a bit about the background.

THE INSPECTOR: Yes, your honour.

THE JUDGE: Well, then?

THE INSPECTOR: There isn't any background to this case, your honour, so to speak.

THE JUDGE: Tallinger, are you trying to tell me it's all clear as daylight?

THE INSPECTOR *grinning:* Clear as daylight: no.

THE JUDGE: Various items of jewellery are alleged to have vanished in the course of the incident. Have they been recovered?

THE INSPECTOR: Not to my knowledge: no.

THE JUDGE: ?

THE INSPECTOR: Your honour, I've got a family.

THE JUDGE: So have I, Tallinger.

THE INSPECTOR: Yes, sir.

Pause.

THE INSPECTOR: This Arndt fellow is a Jew, you know.

THE JUDGE: So one would infer from the name.

THE INSPECTOR: Yes, sir, There's been a rumour for some time in the neighbourhood that there was a case of racial profanation.

THE JUDGE *begins to get a glimmer:* Indeed. Involving whom?

THE INSPECTOR: Arndt's daughter. She's nineteen and supposed to be pretty.

THE JUDGE: Was there any official follow-up?

THE INSPECTOR *reluctantly:* Well, no. The rumour died a natural death.

THE JUDGE: Who set it going?

THE INSPECTOR: The landlord of the building. A certain Mr von Miehl.

THE JUDGE: I suppose he wanted the Jewish shop out of his building?

THE INSPECTOR: That's what we thought. But then he seems to have changed his line.

THE JUDGE: At least that would explain why there was a certain amount of resentment against Arndt round there. Leading these young people to act from a kind of upsurge of national feeling . . .

THE INSPECTOR *firmly:* I wouldn't say that, your honour.

THE JUDGE: What wouldn't you say?

THE INSPECTOR: That Häberle, Schünt and Gaunitzer will try to get much mileage out of the racial profanation business.

THE JUDGE: Why not?

THE INSPECTOR: As I told you, there hasn't been any official mention of the name of the Aryan involved. It could be anyone. Anywhere there's a bunch of Aryans you might find him, you get me? And where d'you find those bunches of Aryans? In other words the SA don't want this dragged up.

THE JUDGE *impatiently:* Why tell me about it, then?

THE INSPECTOR: Because you said you'd got a family. To

stop you dragging it up. Any of the local witnesses might mention it.

THE JUDGE: I see. But I can't see much else.

THE INSPECTOR: The less the better, if you want my personal opinion.

THE JUDGE: It's easy for you to say that. I have to deliver a judgement.

THE INSPECTOR *vaguely:* That's right . . .

THE JUDGE: So we're left with a direct provocation on Arndt's part, or else there's no way of explaining what happened.

THE INSPECTOR: Just what I'd say myself, your honour.

THE JUDGE: Then how were those SA people provoked?

THE INSPECTOR: According to their statements: partly by Arndt himself and partly by some unemployed man he'd got in to sweep the snow. Apparently they were on their way to have a beer together and as they passed the shop there were Wagner the unemployed man and Arndt himself standing in the doorway and shouting vulgar terms of abuse at them.

THE JUDGE: I don't suppose they have any witnesses, have they?

THE INSPECTOR: Oh, they have. The landlord – you know, von Miehl – said he was at the window and saw Wagner provoking the SA men. And Arndt's partner, a man called Stau, was round at Troop HQ the same afternoon and admitted in front of Häberle, Schünt and Gaunitzer that Arndt had always talked disparagingly about the SA, to him too.

THE JUDGE: Oh, so Arndt's got a partner? Aryan?

THE INSPECTOR: Aryan: what else? Can you really see him taking on a Jew as his front man?

THE JUDGE: But the partner wouldn't go and give evidence against him?

THE INSPECTOR *slyly:* Who's to say?

THE JUDGE *irritated:* What do you mean? There's no way the firm can claim damages if it can be proved that Arndt provoked Häberle, Schünt and Gaunitzer to assault him.

THE INSPECTOR: What makes you think Stau's interested in claiming damages?

THE JUDGE: I don't get you. Surely he's a partner?

THE INSPECTOR: That's it.

THE JUDGE: ?

THE INSPECTOR: We've found out – unofficially of course and off the record – that Stau's a regular visitor to Troop HQ. He used to be in the SA and may still be. Probably that's what made Arndt make him a partner. What's more, Stau's already been mixed up in a similar affair, where the SA dropped in on someone. They picked the wrong man that time and it took quite a bit of effort to get it all swept under the mat. Of course that's not to say that in our particular case Stau ... Well, anyhow he's someone to be careful of. I hope you'll treat this as completely confidential, given what you said about your family earlier.

THE JUDGE *shaking his head:* I don't quite see how it can be in Mr Stau's interest for his business to lose more than eleven thousand marks.

THE INSPECTOR: Yes, the jewellery has disappeared. Anyhow Häberle, Schünt and Gaunitzer haven't got it. And they haven't fenced it either.

THE JUDGE: Indeed.

THE INSPECTOR: Stau naturally can't be expected to keep Arndt on as his partner if Arndt can be shown to have acted in a provocative way. And any loss he has caused will have to made up to Stau, see?

THE JUDGE: Yes, I do indeed see. *For a moment he looks thoughtfully at the inspector, who resumes his blank official expression.* Yes, then I suppose the long and the short of it will be that Arndt provoked the SA men. It seems that the fellow had made himself generally disliked. Didn't you tell me that the goings-on in his own family had already led the landlord to complain? Ah well, I know this shouldn't really be dragged up, but anyway we can take it that there will be relief in those quarters if he moves out shortly. Thank you very much, Tallinger, you've been a great help.

The judge gives the inspector a cigar. The inspector leaves. In the doorway he meets the official prosecutor, who is just entering.

THE PROSECUTOR *to the judge:* Can I have a word with you?

THE JUDGE *as he peels an apple for his breakfast:* You can indeed.

THE PROSECUTOR: It's about the case of Häberle, Schünt and Gaunitzer.

THE JUDGE *otherwise occupied:* Yes?

THE PROSECUTOR: It seems quite a straightforward case on the face of it . . .

THE JUDGE: Right. I really don't see why your department decided to prosecute, if you don't mind my saying so.

THE PROSECUTOR: What do you mean? The case has caused a deplorable stir in the neighbourhood. Even members of the party have thought it ought to be cleared up.

THE JUDGE: I simply see it as a plain case of Jewish provocation, that's all.

THE PROSECUTOR: Oh, rubbish, Goll! Don't imagine our indictments can be dismissed so lightly just because they seem a bit tersely expressed these days. I could have guessed you'd blithely settle for the most obvious interpretation. Better not make a boob of this. It doesn't take long to get transferred to the Silesian backwoods. And it's not all that cosy there these days.

THE JUDGE *puzzled, stops eating his apple:* I don't understand that one little bit. Are you seriously telling me you propose to let the Jew Arndt go free?

THE PROSECUTOR *expansively:* You bet I am. The fellow had no idea of provoking anyone. Are you suggesting that because he's Jewish he can't expect justice in the courts of the Third Reich? That's some pretty queer opinions you're venting there, Goll.

THE JUDGE *irritably:* I was venting no opinions whatever. I simply concluded that Häberle, Schünt and Gaunitzer were provoked.

THE PROSECUTOR: But can't you see it wasn't Arndt who provoked them but that unemployed fellow, what's his damn name, the one clearing the snow, yes, Wagner?

THE JUDGE: There's not one single word about that in your indictment, my dear Spitz.

THE PROSECUTOR: Of course not. It merely came to the attention of the Prosecutor's office that those SA men had

made an assault on Arndt. Which meant that we were
officially bound to take action. But if witness von Miehl
should testify in court that Arndt wasn't in the street at
all during the dispute, whereas that unemployed fellow,
what's his damn name, yes, Wagner, was hurling insults
at the SA, then it will have to be taken into account.

THE JUDGE *tumbling to earth:* Is that what von Miehl is
supposed to be saying? But he's the landlord who wants
to get Arndt out of his building. He's not going to give
evidence for him.

THE PROSECUTOR: Come on, what have you got against
von Miehl? Why shouldn't he tell the truth under oath?
Perhaps you don't realise that, quite apart from the fact
that he's in the SS, von Miehl has pretty good contacts in
the Ministry of Justice? My advice to you, Goll old man,
is to treat him as a man of honour.

THE JUDGE: That's what I'm doing. After all, you can't
call it exactly a dishonourable these days not to want a
Jewish shop in one's building.

THE PROSECUTOR *generously:* If the fellow pays his rent . . .

THE JUDGE *diplomatically:* I believe he's supposed to have
reported him already on another matter . . .

THE PROSECUTOR: So you're aware of that? But who
told you it was in order to get the fellow out? Particularly as the complaint was withdrawn? That suggests
something more like a particularly close understanding,
wouldn't you say? My dear Goll, how can you be so naïf?

THE JUDGE *now getting really annoyed:* My dear Spitz, it's not
that simple. The partner I thought would want to cover
him wants to report him, and the landlord who reported
him wants to cover him. You have to know the ins and outs.

THE PROSECUTOR: What do we draw our pay for?

THE JUDGE: Shockingly mixed-up business. Have a
Havana?

*The prosecutor takes a Havana and they smoke in silence. Then
the judge gloomily reflects.*

THE JUDGE: But suppose it's established in court that
Arndt never provoked anybody, then he can go on and
sue the SA for damages.

THE PROSECUTOR: To start with he can't sue the SA but
only Häberle, Schünt and Gaunitzer, who haven't a penny
that's if he doesn't simply have to make do with that
unemployed fellow, what's his damn name ... got it,
Wagner. *With emphasis:* Secondly he may think twice
before suing members of the SA.

THE JUDGE: Where is he at the moment?

THE PROSECUTOR: In hospital.

THE JUDGE: And Wagner?

THE PROSECUTOR: In a concentration camp.

THE JUDGE *with a certain relief:* Oh well, in those circumstances I don't suppose Arndt will be wanting to sue the
SA. And Wagner won't be particularly keen to make a
big thing of his innocence. But the SA aren't going to be
all that pleased if the Jew gets off scot free.

THE PROSECUTOR: The SA will have proof in court that
they were provoked. By the Jew or by the Marxist, it's all
the same to them.

THE JUDGE *still dubious:* Not entirely. After all the dispute
between the SA and the unemployed man did result in
damage to the shop. Storm Troop 7 isn't altogether in the
clear.

THE PROSECUTOR: Oh well, you can't have everything.
You'll never be able to satisfy all parties. As for which
you should aim to satisfy, that's a matter for your sense of
patriotism, my dear Goll. All I can say is that patriotic
circles – by which I mean the highest quarters of the SS –
are looking to the German judiciary to show a bit more
backbone.

THE JUDGE *with a deep sigh:* The process of law is getting a
bit complicated these days, my dear Spitz, you must admit.

THE PROSECUTOR: Of course. But you have an excellent
remark by our Minister of Justice to guide you. Justice is
what serves the German people best.

THE JUDGE *apathetically:* Mm yes.

THE PROSECUTOR: Mustn't let it get you down, that's all.
He gets up. So now you've got the background. Should be
plain sailing. See you later, my dear Goll.
He leaves. The judge is not at all happy. He stands by the window

for a while. Then he leafs aimlessly through his papers. Finally he presses the bell. A court usher enters.

THE JUDGE: Go and find Detective-Inspector Tallinger in the witnesses' room and bring him back here. Discreetly. *Exit the usher. Then the inspector reappears.*

THE JUDGE: Tallinger, you nearly landed me in the cart with your idea of treating this as a case of provocation on Arndt's part. Apparently Mr von Miehl is all set to swear that it was Wagner the unemployed man who did the provoking and not Arndt.

THE INSPECTOR *giving nothing away:* So they say, your honour.

THE JUDGE: What's that mean: 'so they say'?

THE INSPECTOR: That Wagner shouted the offensive remarks.

THE JUDGE: Isn't it true?

THE INSPECTOR *offended:* Your honour, whether it's true or not it's not something we can . . .

THE JUDGE *firmly:* Listen to me, Detective-Inspector Tallinger. This is a German court you're in. Has Wagner admitted that or has he not?

THE INSPECTOR: Your honour, I didn't go to the concentration camp myself, if you want to know. The official report of his deposition – Wagner's supposed to have got something wrong with his kidneys – says that he admitted it. It's only that . . .

THE JUDGE: There you are, he did admit it. It's only that what?

THE INSPECTOR: He served in the war and was wounded in the neck, and according to Stau, you know, Arndt's partner, he can't talk above a whisper. So how von Miehl could have heard him from the first floor hurling insults isn't entirely . . .

THE JUDGE: I imagine it will be said that you don't need a voice in order to tell someone to 'get stuffed', as they put it. You can do it with a simple gesture. It's my impression the Prosecutor's department want to provide the SA with some way out of that sort. More precisely, of that sort and no other.

THE INSPECTOR: Yes, your honour.

THE JUDGE: What is Arndt's statement?

THE INSPECTOR: That he had no part in it and just hurt his head falling down the stairs. That's all we can get out of him.

THE JUDGE: The fellow's probably quite innocent and got into it accidentally, like Pontius Pilate and the Creed.

THE INSPECTOR *gives up:* Yes, your honour.

THE JUDGE: And it should be good enough for the SA if their men get off.

THE INSPECTOR: Yes, your honour.

THE JUDGE: Don't stand there saying 'yes, your honour' like a damn metronome.

THE INSPECTOR: Yes, your honour.

THE JUDGE: What are you trying to tell me? Don't get on your high horse now, Tallinger. You must make allowances for my being a bit on edge. I realise you're an honest man. And when you advised me you must have had something at the back of your mind?

THE INSPECTOR *being a kindly soul, plunges in:* Hasn't it struck you that our deputy prosecutor might simply be after your job and is putting the skids under you, sir? That's what they're saying. – Look at it this way, your honour: you find the Jew not guilty. He never provoked a soul. Wasn't around. Got his head bashed in by pure accident, some quarrel between a different lot of people. Then after a while, back he comes to the shop. No way Stau can prevent it. And the shop is about eleven thousand marks short. Stau will be just as hit by this loss, because now he can't claim the eleven thousand back from Arndt. So Stau, from what I know of his sort, is going to tackle the SA about his jewels. He can't approach them in person because being in partnership with a Jew counts as being sold out to Judah. But he'll have people who can. Then it will come out that the SA go pinching jewels in an upsurge of national feeling. You can guess for yourself how Storm Troop 7 is going to look at your verdict. And the man in the street won't understand anyway. Because how can it be possible for a Jew to win a case against the SA under the Third Reich?

For some while there has been noise off. It now becomes quite loud.

THE JUDGE: What's that shocking noise? Just a minute, Tallinger. *He rings. The usher comes in.* What's that din, man?

THE USHER: The courtroom's full. And now they're jammed so tight in the corridors that nobody can get through. And there are some people from the SA there who say they've got to get through because they've orders to attend.

Exit the usher, while the judge just looks scared.

THE INSPECTOR *continuing:* Those people are going to be a bit of a nuisance to you, you know. I'd advise you to concentrate on Arndt and not stir up the SA.

THE JUDGE *sits brokenly, holding his head in his hands. In a weary voice:* All right, Tallinger, I'll have to think it over.

THE INSPECTOR: That's the idea, your honour.

He leaves. The judge gets up with difficulty and rings insistently. Enter the usher.

THE JUDGE: Just go over and ask Judge Fey of the High Court if he'd mind looking in for a moment.

The usher goes. Enter the judge's maidservant with his packed breakfast.

THE MAIDSERVANT: You'll be forgetting your own head next, your honour. You're a terrible man. What did you forget this time? Try and think. The most important thing of all! *She hands him the packet.* Your breakfast! You'll be going off again and buying those rolls hot from the oven and next thing we'll have another stomach-ache like last week. Because you don't look after yourself properly.

THE JUDGE: That'll do, Marie.

THE MAIDSERVANT: Had a job getting through, I did. The whole building's full of brownshirts on account of the trial. But they'll get it hot and strong today, won't they, your honour? Like at the butcher's folk were saying 'good thing there's still some justice left'. Going and beating a business man up! Half the SA used to be criminals; it's common knowledge in the neighbourhood. If we didn't have justice they'd be making away with the cathedral. After the rings, they were; that Häberle's got a girl friend who was on the game till six months ago. And they attacked Wagner, him with the neck wound and no job, when he was shovelling snow with everyone looking on. They're quite open about it, just terrorising the neighbourhood, and if anybody says anything they lay for him and beat him senseless.

THE JUDGE: All right, Marie. Just run along now.

THE MAIDSERVANT: I told them in the butcher's: his honour will show them where they get off, right? All the decent folk are on your side, that's a fact, your honour. Only don't eat your breakfast too quickly, it might do you harm. It's so bad for the health, and now I'll be off and not hold you up, you'll have to be going into court, and don't get worked up in court or perhaps you'd better eat first, it'll only take a few minutes and they won't matter and you shouldn't eat when your stomach's all tensed up. Because you should take better care of yourself. Your health's your most precious possession, but now I'll be off, there's no need to tell you and I can see you're raring to get on with the case and I've got to go to the grocer's still.

Exit the maidservant. Enter Judge Fey of the High Court, an elderly judge with whom the district judge is friends.

THE SENIOR JUDGE: What's up?

THE JUDGE: I've got something I'd like to discuss with you if you've a moment. I'm sitting on a pretty ghastly case this morning.

THE SENIOR JUDGE: *sitting down:* I know, the SA case.

THE JUDGE *stops pacing around:* How d'you know about that?

THE SENIOR JUDGE: It came up in discussion yesterday afternoon. A nasty business.

The judge starts again nervously pacing up and down.

THE JUDGE: What are they saying over your side?

THE SENIOR JUDGE: You aren't envied. *Intrigued:* What'll you do?

THE JUDGE: That's just what I'd like to know. I must say I didn't realise this case had become so famous.

THE SENIOR JUDGE: *slightly amazed:* Indeed?

THE JUDGE: That partner is said to be a rather disagreeable customer.

THE SENIOR JUDGE: So I gather. Not that von Miehl is much of a humanitarian either.

THE JUDGE: Is anything known about him?

THE SENIOR JUDGE: Enough to go on with. He's got those sort of contacts.

Pause.

THE JUDGE: Very high ones?

THE SENIOR JUDGE: Very high.

Pause.

THE SENIOR JUDGE: *cautiously:* Suppose you leave the Jew out of it and acquit Häberle, Schünt and Gaunitzer on the ground that the unemployed man provoked them before he dodged back into the shop, I imagine the SA might find that all right? Arndt won't sue the SA in any case.

THE JUDGE *anxiously:* There's Arndt's partner. He'll go to the SA and ask for his valuables back. And then, you know, Fey, I'll have the whole SA leadership gunning for me.

THE SENIOR JUDGE *after considering this argument, which apparently has taken him by surprise:* But suppose you don't leave the Jew out of it, then von Miehl will bring bigger guns to bear, to put it mildly. Perhaps you didn't realise he's being pressed by his bank? Arndt's his lifebelt.

THE JUDGE *appalled:* Pressed by his bank!

There is a knock.

THE SENIOR JUDGE: Come in!

Enter the usher.

THE USHER: Your honour, I really don't know what to do about keeping seats for the Chief State Prosecutor and President Schönling of the High Court. If only their honours would let one know in time.

THE SENIOR JUDGE *since the judge says nothing:* Clear two seats and don't interrupt us.

Exit the usher.

THE JUDGE: That's something I could have done without.

THE SENIOR JUDGE: Whatever happens, von Miehl can't afford to abandon Arndt and let him be ruined. He needs him.

THE JUDGE *crushed:* Someone he can milk.

THE SENIOR JUDGE: I said nothing of the sort, my dear Goll. And it seems to me quite extraordinary that you should imply I did. Let me make it crystal clear that I've not said one word against Mr von Miehl. I regret having to do so, Goll.

THE JUDGE *getting worked up:* But Fey, you can't take it that way. Not in view of our mutual relationship.

THE SENIOR JUDGE: What on earth do you mean, 'our mutual relationship'? I can't interfere in your cases. You have to choose for yourself whose toes you are going to tread on, the SA or the Ministry of Justice; either way it's your decision and nobody else's. These days everybody's his own best friend.

THE JUDGE: Of course I'm my own best friend. But what do I advise myself to do?

He stands by the door, listening to the noise outside.

THE SENIOR JUDGE: A bad business.

THE JUDGE *agitatedly:* I'll do anything, my God, can't you see my position? You've changed so. I'll give my judgement this way or that way, whatever way they want me to, but I've got to know first what they want me to do. If one doesn't know that, there's no justice left.

THE SENIOR JUDGE: I wouldn't go round shouting that there's no justice left if I were you, Goll.

THE JUDGE: Oh God, what have I said now? That's not what I meant. I just mean that with so many conflicting interests . . .

THE SENIOR JUDGE: There are no conflicting interests in the Third Reich.

THE JUDGE: Of course not. I wasn't saying there were. Don't keep weighing every single word of mine on your scales.

THE SENIOR JUDGE: Why shouldn't I? I am a judge.

THE JUDGE *who is breaking into a sweat:* But Fey, if every word uttered by every judge had to be weighed like that! I'm prepared to go over everything in the most careful and conscientious possible way, but I have to be told what kind of a decision will satisfy higher considerations. If I allow the

Jew to have stayed inside the shop then I'll upset the landlord – I mean the partner; I'm getting muddled – and if the
provocation came from the unemployed man then it'll be
the landlord who – yes, but von Miehl would rather – Look,
they can't pack me off to the backwoods in Silesia, I've got
a hernia and I'm not getting embroiled with the SA, Fey,
after all I've a family. It's easy for my wife to say I should
just find out what actually happened. I'd wake up in hospital
if nothing worse. Do I talk about assault? No, I'll talk
about provocation. So what's wanted? I shan't condemn the
SA of course but only the Jew or the unemployed man,
only which of the two should I condemn? How do I decide
between unemployed man and Jew or between partner and
landlord. Whatever happens I'm not going to Silesia, Fey,
I'd rather a concentration camp, the whole thing's impossible. Don't look at me like that. I'm not in the dock.
I'm prepared to do absolutely anything.

THE SENIOR JUDGE *who has got to his feet:* Being prepared
isn't enough, my dear fellow.

THE JUDGE: But how am I to make my decision?

THE SENIOR JUDGE: Usually a judge goes by what his
conscience tells him, Judge Goll. Let that be your guide.
It has been a pleasure.

THE JUDGE: Yes, of course: to the best of my heart and
conscience. But here and now; what's my choice to be,
Fey? What?

*The senior judge has left. The judge looks wordlessly after him.
The telephone rings.*

THE JUDGE *picks up the receiver:* Yes? – Emmy? – What
have they put off? Our skittles session? – Who was it
rang? – Priesnitz, the one who's just taken his finals?
Where did he get the message? – What I'm talking about?
I've got a judgement to deliver.

*He hangs up. The usher enters. The noise in the corridors becomes
obtrusive.*

THE USHER: Häberle, Schünt, Gaunitzer, your honour.

THE JUDGE *collecting his papers:* One moment.

THE USHER: I've put the President of the High Court at
the press table. He was quite happy about it. But the Chief

State Prosecutor refused to take a seat among the witnesses. He wanted to be on the bench, I think. Then you'd have had to preside from the dock, your honour! *He laughs foolishly at his own joke.*

THE JUDGE: Whatever happens I'm not doing that.

THE USHER: This way out, your honour. But where's your folder got to with the indictment?

THE JUDGE *utterly confused:* Oh yes, I'll need that. Or I won't know who's being accused, will I? What the devil are we to do with the Chief State Prosecutor?

THE USHER: But your honour, that's your address book you've picked up. Here's the file.

He pushes it under the judge's arm. Wiping the sweat off his face, the judge goes distractedly out.

7

Occupational disease

And as for the physicians
The State gives them positions
And pays them so much a piece.
Their job is to keep mending
The bits the police keep sending
Then send it all back to the police.

Berlin 1934. A ward in the Charité Hospital. A new patient has been brought in. Nurses are busy writing his name on the slate at the head of his bed. Two patients in neighbouring beds are talking.

THE FIRST PATIENT: Know anything about him?

THE SECOND: I saw them bandaging him downstairs. He was on a stretcher quite close to me. He was still conscious then, but when I asked what he'd got he didn't answer. His whole body's one big wound.

THE FIRST: No need to ask then, was there?

THE SECOND: I didn't see till they started bandaging him.

ONE OF THE NURSES: Quiet please, it's the professor.

Followed by a train of assistants and nurses the surgeon enters the ward. He stops by one of the beds and pontificates.

THE SURGEON: Gentlemen, we have here a quite beautiful case showing how essential it is to ask questions and keep on searching for the deeper causes of the disease if medicine is not to degenerate into mere quackery. This patient has all the symptoms of neuralgia and for a considerable time he received the appropriate treatment. In fact however he suffers from Raynaud's Disease, which he contracted in the course of his job as a worker operating pneumatically powered tools; that is to say, gentlemen, an occupational disease. We have now begun treating him correctly. His case will show you what a mistake it is to treat the patient as a mere component of the clinic instead of asking where he has come from, how did he contract his disease and what he will be going back to once treatment is concluded. There are three things a good doctor has to be able to do. What are they? The first?

THE FIRST ASSISTANT: Ask questions.

THE SURGEON: The second?

THE SECOND ASSISTANT: Ask questions.

THE SURGEON: And the third?

THE THIRD ASSISTANT: Ask questions, sir.

THE SURGEON: Correct. Ask questions. Particularly concerning . . .?

THE THIRD ASSISTANT: The social conditions, sir.

THE SURGEON: The great thing is never to be shy of looking into the patient's private life – often a regrettably depressing one. If someone is forced to follow some occupation that is bound in the long run to destroy his body, so that he dies in effect to avoid starving to death, one doesn't much like hearing about it and consequently doesn't ask.

He and his followers move on to the new patient.

What has this man got?

The sister whispers in his ear.
Oh, I see.
He gives him a cursory examination with evident reluctance.
Dictates: Contusions on the back and thighs. Open wounds on the abdomen. Further symptoms?

THE SISTER *reads out:* Blood in his urine.

THE SURGEON: Diagnosis on admission?

THE SISTER: Lesion to left kidney.

THE SURGEON: Get him X-rayed. *Starts to turn away.*

THE THIRD ASSISTANT *who has been taking down his medical history:* How was that incurred, sir?

THE SURGEON: What have they put?

THE SISTER: Falling downstairs, it says here.

THE SURGEON *dictating:* A fall down the stairs. Why are his hands tied that way, Sister?

THE SISTER: The patient has twice torn his dressings off, professor.

THE SURGEON: Why?

THE FIRST PATIENT *sotto voce:* Where has the patient come from and where is he going back to?
All heads turn in his direction.

THE SURGEON *clearing his throat:* If this patient seems disturbed give him morphine. *Moves on to the next bed:* Feeling better now? It won't be long before you're fit as a fiddle. *He examines the patient's neck.*

ONE ASSISTANT *to another:* Worker. Brought in from Oranienburg.

THE OTHER ASSISTANT *grinning:* Another case of occupational disease, I suppose.

8

The physicists

Enter the local Newtons
Dressed up like bearded Teutons –
Not one of them hook-nosed.
Their science will end up barbarian
For they'll get an impeccably Aryan
State-certified physics imposed.

*Göttingen 1935. Institute for Physics. Two scientists, X and Y. Y
has just entered. He has a conspiratorial look.*

Y: I've got it.

X: What?

Y: The answer to what we asked Mikovsky in Paris.

X: About gravity waves?

Y: Yes.

X: What about it?

Y: Guess who's written giving just what we wanted.

X: Go on.

*Y takes a scrap of paper writes a name and passes it to X. As
soon as X has read it Y takes it back, tears it into small pieces
and throws it into the stove.*

Y: Mikovsky passed our questions on to him. This is his
answer.

X *grabs for it greedily:* Give me. *He suddenly holds himself back.*
Just suppose we were caught corresponding with him like
this . . .

Y: We absolutely mustn't be.

X: Well, without it we're stuck. Come on, give me.

Y: You won't be able to read. I used my own shorthand, it's
safer. I'll read it out to you.

X: For God's sake be careful.

Y: Is Rollkopf in the lab today? *He points to the right.*

X: *pointing to the left:* No, but Reinhardt is. Sit over here.

Y *reads:* The problem concerns two arbitrary countervariant
vectors *psi* and *nu* and a countervariant vector *t*. This is
used to form the elements of a mixed tensor of the second
degree whose structure can be expressed by
$\Sigma^{-k} = C^{-l}_{bi}$.

X *who has been writing this down, suddenly gives him a sign to shut
up:* Just a minute.

*He gets up and tiptoes over to the wall, left. Having evidently
heard nothing suspicious he returns. Y goes on reading aloud, with
other similar interruptions. These lead them to inspect the telephone, suddenly open the door etc.*

Y: Where matter is passive, incoherent and not acting on
itself by means of tensions $T = \mu$ will be the only component of the tensional energy depth that differs from o.
Hence a static gravitational field is created whose equa-
tion, taking into account the constant proportionality
factor $8\pi x$ will be $\Delta f = 4\pi x \mu$. Given a suitable choice of
spatial coordinates the degree of variation from $c^2 df^2$ will
be very slight . . .

*A door slams somewhere and they try to hide their notes. Then
this seems to be unnecessary. From this point on they both become
engrossed in the material and apparently oblivious of the danger of
what they are doing.*

Y *reads on:* . . . by comparison however with the passive
mass from which the field originates the masses concerned are very small, and the motion of the bodies
implicated in the gravitational field is brought within this
static field by means of a geodetic world line. As such
this satisfies the variational principle $\delta \int ds = o$ where the
ends of the relevant portion of the world line remain fixed.

X: But what's Einstein got to say about . . .

*Y's look of horror makes X aware of his mistake so that he sits
there paralysed with shock. Y snatches the notes which he has been
taking down and hides away all the papers.*

Y *very loudly, in the direction of the left hand wall:* What a typical
piece of misplaced Jewish ingenuity. Nothing to do with
physics.

*Relieved, they again bring out their notes and silently resume work,
using the utmost caution.*

9

The Jewish wife

> Over there we can see men coming
> Whom He's forced to relinquish their women
> And coupled with blondes in their place.
> It's no good their cursing and praying
> For once He catches them racially straying
> He'll whip them back into the Race.

Frankfurt 1935. It is evening. A woman is packing suitcases. She is choosing what to take. Now and again she removes something from her suitcase and returns it to its original place in the room in order to pack another item instead. For a long while she hesitates whether to take a large photograph of her husband that stands on the chest of drawers. Finally she leaves the picture where it is. The packing tires her and for a time she sits on a suitcase leaning her head on her hand. Then she gets to her feet and telephones.

THE WOMAN: This is Judith Keith. Hullo, is that you, doctor? Good evening. I just wanted to ring up and say you'll have to be looking for another bridge partner; I'm going away. – No, not long, but anyway a few weeks – I want to go to Amsterdam. – Yes, it's said to be lovely there in spring. – I've got friends there. – No, plural, believe it or not. – Who will you get for a fourth? – Come on, we haven't played for a fortnight. – That's right, Fritz had a cold too. It's absurd to go on playing bridge when it's as cold as this, I always say. – But no, doctor, how could I? – Anyway Thekla had her mother there. – I know. – What put that idea into my head? – No, it was nothing sudden, I kept putting it off, and now I've really got to . . . Right, we'll have to cancel our cinema date, remember me to Thekla. – Ring him up on a Sunday sometimes, could you perhaps? – Well, au revoir! – Yes, of course I will. – Goodbye.
She hangs up and calls another number.

This is Judith Keith. Can I speak to Frau Schöck? –
Lotte? – I just wanted to say goodbye. I'm going away
for a bit. – No, nothing's wrong, it's just that I want
to see some new faces. – I really meant to say that Fritz
has got the Professor coming here on Tuesday evening,
and I wondered if you could both come too, I'm off
tonight as I said. – Tuesday, that's it. – No, I only
wanted to tell you I'm off tonight, there's no connec-
tion, I just thought you might be able to come then. –
Well, let's say even though I shan't be there, right? –
Yes, I know you're not that sort, but what about it,
these are unsettled times and everybody's being so careful, so you'll come? – It depends on Max? He'll manage
it, the Professor will be there, tell him. – I must ring
off now. – Goodbye then.

She hangs up and calls another number.

That you, Gertrud? It's Judith. I'm so sorry to disturb
you. – Thanks, I just wanted to ask if you could see that
Fritz is all right, I'm going away for a few months. –
Being his sister, I thought you . . . Why not? – Nobody'd
think that, anyway not Fritz. – Well, of course he knows
we don't . . . get on all that well, but . . . Then he can
simply call you if you prefer it that way. – Yes, I'll tell
him that. – Everything's fairly straight, of course the flat's
on the big side. – You'd better leave his workroom to Ida
to deal with, she knows what's to be done. – I find her
pretty intelligent, and he's used to her. – And there's another thing, I hope you don't mind my saying so, but he
doesn't like talking before meals, can you remember that?
I always used to watch myself. – I don't want to argue
about that just now, it's not long till my train goes and I
haven't finished packing, you know. – Keep an eye on his
suits and remind him to go to his tailor, he's ordered a
new overcoat, and do see that his bedroom's properly
heated, he likes sleeping with the window open and it's
too cold. – No, I don't think he needs to toughen himself
up, but I must ring off now. – I'm very grateful to you,
Gertrud, and we'll write to each other, won't we? –
Goodbye.

She hangs up and calls another number.

Anna? It's Judith; look, I'm just off. – No, there's no way out, things are getting too difficult. – Too difficult! – Well, no, it isn't Fritz's idea, he doesn't know yet, I simply packed my things. – I don't think so. – I don't think he'll say all that much. It's all got too difficult for him, just in every day matters. – That's something we haven't arranged. – We just never talked about it, absolutely never. – No, he hasn't altered, on the contrary. – I'd be glad if you and Kurt could look after him a bit, to start with. – Yes, specially Sundays, and try to make him give up this flat. – It's too big for him. – I'd like to have come and said goodbye to you, but it's your porter, you know. – So, goodbye; no, don't come to the station, it's a bad idea. – Goodbye, I'll write. – That's a promise.

She hangs up without calling again. She has been smoking. Now she sets fire to the small book in which she has been looking up the numbers. She walks up and down two or three times. Then she starts speaking. She is rehearsing the short speech which she proposes to make to her husband. It is evident that he is sitting in a particular chair.

Well, Fritz, I'm off. I suppose I've waited too long, I'm awfully sorry, but . . .

She stands there thinking, then starts in a different way.

Fritz, you must let me go, you can't keep . . . I'll be your downfall, it's quite clear; I know you aren't a coward, you're not scared of the police, but there are worse things. They won't put you in a camp, but they'll ban you from the clinic any day now. You won't say anything at the time, but it'll make you ill. I'm not going to watch you sitting around in the flat pretending to read magazines, it's pure selfishness on my part, my leaving, that's all. Don't tell me anything . . .

She again stops. She makes a fresh start.

Don't tell me you haven't changed; you have! Only last week you established quite objectively that the proportion of Jewish scientists wasn't all that high. Objectivity is always the start of it, and why do you keep telling me I've never been such a Jewish chauvinist as now? Of course

I'm one. Chauvinism is catching. Oh, Fritz, what has happened to us?

She again stops. She makes a fresh start.

I never told you I wanted to go away, have done for a long time, because I can't talk when I look at you, Fritz. Then it seems to me there's no point in talking. It has all been settled already. What's got into them, d'you think? What do they really want? What am I doing to them? I've never had anything to do with politics. Did I vote Communist? But I'm just one of those bourgeois housewives with servants and so on, and now all of a sudden it seems only blondes can be that. I've often thought lately about something you told me years back, how some people were more valuable than others, so one lot were given insulin when they got diabetes and the others weren't. And this was something I understood, idiot that I was. Well, now they've drawn a new distinction of the same sort, and this time I'm one of the less valuable ones. Serves me right.

She again stops. She makes a fresh start.

Yes, I'm packing. Don't pretend you haven't noticed anything the last few days. Nothing really matters, Fritz, except just one thing: if we spend our last hour together without looking at each other's eyes. That's a triumph they can't be allowed, the liars who force everyone else to lie. Ten years ago when somebody said no one would think I was Jewish, you instantly said yes, they would. And that's fine. That was straightforward. Why take things in a roundabout way now? I'm packing so they shan't take away your job as senior physician. And because they've stopped saying good morning to you at the clinic, and because you're not sleeping nowadays. I don't want you to tell me I mustn't go. And I'm hurrying because I don't want to hear you telling me I must. It's a matter of time. Principles are a matter of time. They don't last for ever, any more than a glove does. There are good ones which last a long while. But even they only have a certain life. Don't get the idea that I'm angry. Yes, I am. Why should I always be understanding? What's wrong with the shape of my nose and the colour of my hair? I'm to leave the town where I was born just so they don't have to go short of butter. What sort of people are you, yourself included? You work out the quantum theory and the Trendelenburg test, then allow a lot of semi-barbarians to tell you you're to conquer the world but you can't have the woman you want. The artificial lung, and the dive-bomber! You are monsters or you pander to monsters. Yes, I know I'm being unreasonable, but what good is reason in a world like this? There you sit watching your wife pack and saying nothing. Walls have ears, is that it? But you people say nothing. One lot listens and the other keeps silent. To hell with that. I'm supposed to keep silent too. If I loved you I'd keep silent. I truly do love you. Give me those underclothes. They're suggestive. I'll need them. I'm thirty-six, that isn't too old, but I can't do much more experimenting. The next time I settle in a country things can't be like this. The next man I get must be allowed to keep me. And don't tell me you'll send me money; you know you won't be allowed to. And you aren't to pretend it's just a matter of four weeks either. This business is going to last rather more than four weeks. You know that, and so do I. So don't go telling me 'After all it's only for two or three weeks' as you hand me the fur coat I shan't need till next winter. And don't let's speak about disaster. Let's speak about disgrace. Oh, Fritz!

She stops. A door opens. She hurriedly sees to her appearance. The husband comes in.

THE HUSBAND: What are you doing? Tidying up?

THE WOMAN: No.

THE HUSBAND: Why are you packing?

THE WOMAN: I want to get away.

THE HUSBAND: What are you talking about?

THE WOMAN: We did mention the possibility of my going away for a bit. It's no longer very pleasant here.

THE HUSBAND: That's a lot of nonsense.

THE WOMAN: Do you want me to stay, then?

THE HUSBAND: Where are you thinking of going?

THE WOMAN: Amsterdam. Just away.

THE HUSBAND: But you've got nobody there.

THE WOMAN: No.

THE HUSBAND: Why don't you wish to stay here? There's absolutely no need for you to go so far as I'm concerned.

THE WOMAN: No.

THE HUSBAND: You know I haven't changed, you do, don't you, Judith?

THE WOMAN: Yes.

He embraces her. They stand without speaking among the suitcases.

THE HUSBAND: And there's nothing else makes you want to go?

THE WOMAN: You know that.

THE HUSBAND: It might not be such a bad idea, I suppose. You need a breather. It's stifling in this place. I'll come and collect you. As soon as I get across the frontier, even if it's only for two days, I'll start feeling better.

THE WOMAN: Yes, why don't you?

THE HUSBAND: Things can't go on like this all that much longer. Something's bound to change. The whole business will die down again like an inflammation – it's a disaster, it really is.

THE WOMAN: Definitely. Did you run into Schöck?

THE HUSBAND: Yes, just on the stairs, that's to say. I think he's begun to be sorry about the way they dropped us. He was quite embarrassed. In the long run they can't completely sit on filthy intellectuals like us. And they won't be able to run a war with a lot of spineless wrecks. People aren't all that standoffish if you face up to them squarely. What time are you off, then?

THE WOMAN: Nine-fifteen.

THE HUSBAND: And where am I to send money to?

THE WOMAN: Let's say poste restante, Amsterdam main Post-Office.

THE HUSBAND: I'll see they give me a special permit. Good God, I can't send my wife off with ten marks a month. It's all a lousy business.

THE WOMAN: If you can come and collect me it'll do you a bit of good.

THE HUSBAND: To read a paper with something in it for once.

THE WOMAN: I rang Gertrud. She'll see you're all right.

THE HUSBAND: Quite unnecessary. For two or three weeks.

THE WOMAN *who has again begun packing:* Do you mind handing me my fur coat?

THE HUSBAND *handing it to her:* After all it's only for two or three weeks.

10

The spy

Here come the worthy schoolteachers
The Youth Movement takes the poor creatures
And makes them all thrust out their chest.
Every schoolboy's a spy. So now marking
Is based not on knowledge, but narking
And on who knows whose weaknesses best.

They educate traducers
To set hatchet-men and bruisers
On their own parents' tail.
Denounced by their sons as traitors
To Himmler's apparatus
The fathers go handcuffed to gaol.

Cologne 1935. A wet Sunday afternoon. The man, the wife and the boy have finished lunch. The maidservant enters.

THE MAIDSERVANT: Mr and Mrs Klimbtsch are asking if you are at home.

THE MAN *snarls:* No.

The maidservant goes out.

THE WIFE: You should have gone to the phone yourself. They must know we couldn't possibly have gone out yet.

THE MAN: Why couldn't we?

THE WIFE: Because it's raining.

THE MAN: That's no reason.

THE WIFE: Where could we have gone to? That's the first thing they'll ask.

THE MAN: Oh, masses of places.

THE WIFE: Let's go then.

THE MAN: Where to?

THE WIFE: If only it wasn't raining.

THE MAN: And where'd we go if it wasn't raining?

THE WIFE: At least in the old days you could go and meet someone.

Pause.

THE WIFE: It was a mistake you not going to the phone. Now they'll realise we don't want to have them.

THE MAN: Suppose they do?

THE WIFE: Then it wouldn't look very nice, our dropping them just when everyone else does.

THE MAN: We're not dropping them.

THE WIFE: Why shouldn't they come here in that case?

THE MAN: Because Klimbtsch bores me to tears.

THE WIFE: He never bored you in the old days.

THE MAN: In the old days . . . All this talk of the old days gets me down.

THE WIFE: Well anyhow you'd never have cut him just because the school inspectors are after him.

THE MAN: Are you telling me I'm a coward?

Pause.

THE MAN: All right, ring up and tell them we've just come back on account of the rain.

The wife remains seated.

THE WIFE: What about asking the Lemkes to come over?

THE MAN: And have them go on telling us we're slack about civil defence?

THE WIFE *to the boy:* Klaus-Heinrich, stop fiddling with the wireless.

The boy turns his attention to the newspapers.

THE MAN: It's a disaster, its raining like this. It's quite intolerable, living in a country where it's a disaster when it rains.

THE WIFE: Do you really think it's sensible to go round making remarks like that?

THE MAN: I can make what remarks I like between my own four walls. This is my home, and I shall damn well say . . .

He is interrupted. The maidservant enters with coffee things. So long as she is present they remain silent.

THE MAN: Have we got to have a maid whose father is the block warden?

THE WIFE: We've been over that again and again. The last thing you said was that it had its advantages.

THE MAN: What aren't I supposed to have said? If you mentioned anything of the sort to your mother we could land in a proper mess.

THE WIFE: The things I talk about to my mother . . .

Enter the maidservant with the coffee.

THE WIFE: That's all right, Erna. You can go now, I'll see to it.

THE MAIDSERVANT: Thank you very much, ma'am.

THE BOY *looking up from his paper:* Is that how vicars always behave, dad?

THE MAN: How do you mean?

THE BOY: Like it says here.

THE MAN: What's that you're reading?

Snatches the paper from his hands.

THE BOY: Hey, our group leader said it was all right for us to know about anything in that paper.

THE MAN: I don't have to go by what your group leader says. It's for me to decide what you can or can't read.

THE WIFE: There's ten pfennigs, Klaus-Heinrich, run over and get yourself something.

THE BOY: But it's raining.

He hangs round the window, trying to make up his mind.

THE MAN: If they go on reporting these cases against priests I shall cancel the paper altogether.

THE WIFE: Which are you going to take, then? They're all reporting them.

THE MAN: If all the papers are full of this kind of filth I'd sooner not read a paper at all. And I wouldn't be any worse informed about what's going on in the world.

THE WIFE: There's something to be said for a bit of a clean-up.

THE MAN: Clean-up, indeed. The whole thing's politics.

THE WIFE: Well, it's none of our business anyway. After all, we're protestants.

THE MAN: It matters to our people all right if it can't hear the word vestry without being reminded of dirt like this.

THE WIFE: But what do you want them to do when this kind of thing happens?

THE MAN: What do I want them to do? Suppose they looked into their own back yard. I'm told it isn't all so snowy white in that Brown House of theirs.

THE WIFE: But that only goes to show how far our people's recovery has gone, Karl.

THE MAN: Recovery! A nice kind of recovery. If that's what recovery looks like, I'd sooner have the disease any day.

THE WIFE: You're so on edge today. Did something happen at the school?

THE MAN: What on earth could have happened at school? And for God's sake don't keep saying I'm on edge, it makes me feel on edge.

THE WIFE: We oughtn't to keep on quarrelling so, Karl. In the old days . . .

THE MAN: Just what I was waiting for. In the old days. Neither in the old days nor now did I wish to have my son's imagination perverted for him.

THE WIFE: Where has he got to, anyway?

THE MAN: How am I to know?

THE WIFE: Did you see him go?

THE MAN: No.

THE WIFE: I can't think where he can have gone. *She calls:* Klaus-Heinrich!

She hurries out of the room, and is heard calling. She returns.

THE WIFE: He really has left.

THE MAN: Why shouldn't he?

THE WIFE: But it's raining buckets.

THE MAN: Why are you so on edge at the boy's having left?

THE WIFE: You remember what we were talking about?

THE MAN: What's that got to do with it?

THE WIFE: You've been so careless lately.

THE MAN: I have certainly not been careless, but even if I had what's that got to do with the boy's having left?

THE WIFE: You know how they listen to everything.

THE MAN: Well?

THE WIFE: Well. Suppose he goes round telling people? You know how they're always dinning it into them in the Hitler Youth. They deliberately encourage the kids to repeat everything. It's so odd his going off so quietly.

THE MAN: Rubbish.

THE WIFE: Didn't you see when he went?

THE MAN: He was hanging round the window for quite a time.

THE WIFE: I'd like to know how much he heard.

THE MAN: But he must know what happens to people who get reported.

THE WIFE: What about that boy the Schmulkes were telling us about? They say his father's still in a concentration camp. I wish we knew how long he was in the room.

THE MAN: The whole thing's a load of rubbish.

He hastens to the other rooms and calls the boy.

THE WIFE: I just can't see him going off somewhere without saying a word. It wouldn't be like him.

THE MAN: Mightn't he be with a school friend?

THE WIFE: Then he'd have to be at the Mummermanns'. I'll give them a ring. (She telephones)

THE MAN: It's all a false alarm, if you ask me.

THE WIFE *telephoning*: Is that Mrs Mummermann? It's Mrs Furcke here. Good afternoon. Is Klaus-Heinrich with you? He isn't? – Then where on earth can the boy be? – Mrs Mummermann do you happen to know if the Hitler Youth place is open on Sunday afternoons? – It is? – Thanks a lot, I'll ask them.

She hangs up. They sit in silence.

THE MAN: What do you think he overheard?

THE WIFE: You were talking about the paper. You shouldn't have said what you did about the Brown House. He's so patriotic about that kind of thing.

THE MAN: What am I supposed to have said about the Brown House?

THE WIFE: You remember perfectly well. That things weren't all snowy white in there.

THE MAN: Well, nobody can take that as an attack, can they? Saying things aren't all white, or snowy white rather, as I qualified it – which makes a difference, quite a substantial one at that – well, it's more a kind of jocular remark like the man in the street makes in the vernacular, sort of, and all it really means is that probably not absolutely everything even there is always exactly as the Führer would like it to be. I quite deliberately emphasised that this was only 'probably' so by using the phrase, as I very well remember, 'I'm *told*' things aren't *all* – and that's another obvious qualification – so snowy white there. 'I'm told'; that doesn't mean its necessarily so. How could I say things aren't snowy white? I haven't any proof. Wherever there are human beings there are imperfections. That's all I was suggesting, and in very qualified form. And in any case there was a certain occasion when the Führer himself expressed the same kind of criticisms a great deal more strongly.

THE WIFE: I don't understand you. You don't need to talk to me in that way.

THE MAN: I'd like to think I don't. I wish I knew to what extent you gossip about all that's liable to be said between these four walls in the heat of the moment. Of course I wouldn't dream of accusing you of casting ill-considered aspersions on your husband, any more than I'd think my boy capable for one moment of doing anything to harm his own father. But doing harm and doing it wittingly are unfortunately two very different matters.

THE WIFE: You can stop that right now! What about the kind of things you say yourself? Here am I worrying myself silly whether you made that remark about life in Nazi Germany being intolerable before or after the one about the Brown House.

THE MAN: I never said anything of the sort.

THE WIFE: You're acting absolutely as if I were the police. All I'm doing is racking my brains about what the boy may have overheard.

THE MAN: The term Nazi Germany just isn't in my vocabulary.

THE WIFE: And that stuff about the warden of our block and how the papers print nothing but lies, and what you were saying about civil defence the other day – when does the boy hear a single constructive remark? That just doesn't do any good to a child's attitude of mind, it's simply demoralising, and at a time when the Führer keeps stressing that Germany's future lies in Germany's youth. He really isn't the kind of boy to rush off and denounce one just like that. It makes me feel quite ill.

THE MAN: He's vindictive, though.

THE WIFE: What on earth has he got to be vindictive about?

THE MAN: God knows, but there's bound to be something. The time I confiscated his tree-frog perhaps.

THE WIFE: But that was a week ago.

THE MAN: It's that kind of thing that sticks in his mind, though.

THE WIFE: What did you confiscate it for, anyway?

THE MAN: Because he wouldn't catch any flies for it. He was letting the creature starve.

THE WIFE: He really is run off his feet, you know.

THE MAN: There's not much the frog can do about that.

THE WIFE: But he never came back to the subject, and I gave him ten pfennigs only a moment ago. He only has to want something and he gets it.

THE MAN: Exactly. I call that bribery.

THE WIFE: What do you mean by that?

THE MAN: They'll simply say we were trying to bribe him to keep his mouth shut.

THE WIFE: What do you imagine they could do to you?

THE MAN: Absolutely anything. There's no limit. My God! And to think I'm supposed to be a teacher. An educator of our youth. Our youth scares me stiff.

THE WIFE: But they've nothing against you.

THE MAN: They've something against everyone. Everyone's suspect. Once the suspicion's there, one's suspect.

THE WIFE: But a child's not a reliable witness. A child hasn't the faintest idea what it's talking about.

THE MAN: So you say. But when did they start having to have witnesses for things?

THE WIFE: Couldn't we work out what you could have meant by your remarks? Then he could just have mis-understood you.

THE MAN: Well, what did I say? I can't even remember. It's all the fault of that damned rain. It puts one in a bad mood. Actually I'm the last person to say anything against the moral resurgence the German people is going through these days. I foresaw the whole thing as early as the winter of 1932.

THE WIFE: Karl, there just isn't time to discuss that now. We must straighten everything out right away. There's not a minute to spare.

THE MAN: I don't believe Karl-Heinrich's capable of it.

THE WIFE: Let's start with the Brown House and all the filth.

THE MAN: I never said a word about filth.

THE WIFE: You said the paper's full of filth and you want to cancel it.

THE MAN: Right, the paper. But not the Brown House.

THE WIFE: Couldn't you have been saying that you won't stand for such filth in the churches? And that you think the people now being tried could quite well be the same as used to spread malicious rumours about the Brown House suggesting things weren't all that snowy white there? And that they ought to have started looking into their own place instead? And what you were telling the boy was that he should stop fiddling with the wireless and read the paper because you're firmly of the opinion that the youth of the Third Reich should have a clear view of what's happening round about them.

THE MAN: It wouldn't be any use.

THE WIFE: Karl, you're not to give up now. You should be strong, like the Führer keeps on . . .

THE MAN: I'm not going to be brought before the law and have my own flesh and blood standing in the witness box and giving evidence against me.

THE WIFE: There's no need to take it like that.

THE MAN: It was a great mistake our seeing so much of the Klimbtsches.

THE WIFE: But nothing whatever has happened to him.

THE MAN: Yes, but there's talk of an inquiry.

THE WIFE: What would it be like if everybody got in such a panic as soon as there was talk of an inquiry?

THE MAN: Do you think our block warden has anything against us?

THE WIFE: You mean, supposing they asked him? He got a box of cigars for his birthday the other day and his Christmas box was ample.

THE MAN: The Gauffs gave him fifteen marks.

THE WIFE: Yes, but they were still taking a socialist paper in 1932, and as late as May 1933 they were hanging out the old nationalist flag.

The phone rings.

THE MAN: That's the phone.

THE WIFE: Shall I answer it?

THE MAN: I don't know.

THE WIFE: Who could be ringing us?

THE MAN: Wait a moment. If it rings again, answer it.

They wait. It doesn't ring again.

THE MAN: We can't go on living like this!

THE WIFE: Karl!

THE MAN: A Judas, that's what you've borne me. Sitting at the table listening, gulping down the soup we've given him and noting down whatever his father says, the little spy.

THE WIFE: That's a dreadful thing to say.

Pause.

THE WIFE: Do you think we ought to make any kind of preparations?

THE MAN: Do you think he'll bring them straight back with him?

THE WIFE: Could he really?

THE MAN: Perhaps I'd better put on my Iron Cross.

THE WIFE: Of course you must, Karl.

He gets it and puts it on with shaking hands.

THE WIFE: But they've nothing against you at school, have they?

THE MAN: How's one to tell? I'm prepared to teach whatever they want taught; but what's that? If only I could tell . . . How am I to know what they want Bismarck to have been like? When they're taking so long to publish the new text books. Couldn't you give the maid another ten marks? She's another who's always listening.

THE WIFE *nodding:* And what about the picture of Hitler; shouldn't we hang it above your desk? It'd look better.

THE MAN: Yes, do that.

The wife starts taking down the picture.

THE MAN: Suppose the boy goes and says we deliberately rehung it, though, it might look as if we had a bad conscience.

The wife puts the picture back on its old hook.

THE MAN: Wasn't that the door?

THE WIFE: I didn't hear anything.

THE MAN: It was.

THE WIFE: Karl!

She embraces him.

THE MAN: Keep a grip on yourself. Pack some things for me.

The door of the flat opens. Man and wife stand rigidly side by side in the corner of the room. The door opens and enter the boy, a paper bag in his hand. Pause.

THE BOY: What's the matter with you people?

THE WIFE: Where have you been?

The boy shows her the bag, which contains chocolate.

THE WIFE: Did you simply go out to buy chocolate?

THE BOY: Wherever else? Obvious, isn't it?

He crosses the room munching, and goes out. His parents look enquiringly after him.

THE MAN: Do you suppose he's telling the truth?

The wife shrugs her shoulders.

I I

The black shoes

These widows and orphans you're seeing
Have heard Him guaranteeing
A great time by and by.
Meanwhile they must make sacrifices
As the shops all put up their prices.
That great time is pie in the sky.

Bitterfeld, 1935. Kitchen in a working-class flat. The mother is peeling potatoes. Her thirteen-year-old daughter is doing homework.

THE DAUGHTER: Mum, am I getting my two pfennigs?
THE MOTHER: For the Hitler Youth?
THE DAUGHTER: Yes.
THE MOTHER: I haven't any money left.
THE DAUGHTER: But if I don't bring my two pfennigs a week I won't be going to the country this summer. And our teacher said Hitler wants town and country to get to know each other. Town people are supposed to get closer to the farmers. But I'll have to bring along my two pfennigs.
THE MOTHER: I'll try to find some way of letting you have them.
THE DAUGHTER: Oh lovely, mum. I'll give a hand with the 'taters. It's lovely in the country, isn't it? Proper meals there. Our gym teacher was saying I've got a potato belly.
THE MOTHER: You've nothing of the kind.
THE DAUGHTER: Not right now. Last year I had. A bit.
THE MOTHER: I might be able to get us some offal.
THE DAUGHTER: I get my roll at school; that's more than you do. Bertha was saying when she went to the country last year they had bread and goose dripping. Meat too sometimes. Lovely, isn't it?

THE MOTHER: Of course.

THE DAUGHTER: And all that fresh air.

THE MOTHER: Didn't she have to do some work too?

THE DAUGHTER: Of course. But lots to eat. Only the farmer was a nuisance, she said.

THE MOTHER: What'd he do?

THE DAUGHTER: Oh, nothing. Just kept pestering her.

THE MOTHER: Aha.

THE DAUGHTER: Bertha's bigger than me, though. A year older.

THE MOTHER: Get on with your homework.

Pause, then:

THE DAUGHTER: But I won't have to wear those old black shoes from the welfare, will I?

THE MOTHER: You won't be needing them. You've got your other pair, haven't you?

THE DAUGHTER: Just that those have got a hole.

THE MOTHER: Oh dear, when it's so wet.

THE DAUGHTER: I'll put some paper in, that'll do it.

THE MOTHER: No, it won't. If they've gone they'll have to be resoled.

THE DAUGHTER: That's so expensive.

THE MOTHER: What've you got against the welfare pair?

THE DAUGHTER: I can't stand them.

THE MOTHER: Because they look so clumsy?

THE DAUGHTER: So you think so too.

THE MOTHER: Of course they're older.

THE DAUGHTER: Have I *got* to wear them?

THE MOTHER: If you can't stand them you needn't wear them.

THE DAUGHTER: I'm not being vain, am I?

THE MOTHER: No. Just growing up.

Pause, then:

THE DAUGHTER: Then can I have my two pfennigs, Mum? I do so want to go.

THE MOTHER *slowly:* I haven't the money for that.

12

Labour service

By sweeping away class barriers
The poor are made fetchers and carriers
In Hitler's Labour Corps.
The rich serve a year alongside them
To show that no conflicts divide them.
Some pay would please them more.

*The Lüneburger Heide, 1935. A Labour Service column at work.
A young worker and a student are digging together.*

THE STUDENT: What did they put that stocky little fellow
from Column 3 in clink for?

THE YOUNG WORKER *grinning:* The group leader was
saying we'll learn what it's like to work and he said, under
his breath like, he'd as soon learn what it's like to get a
pay packet. They weren't pleased.

THE STUDENT: Why say something like that?

THE YOUNG WORKER: Because he already knows what it's
like to work, I should think. He was down the pits at
fourteen.

THE STUDENT: Look out, Tubby's coming.

THE YOUNG WORKER: If he looks our way I can't just dig
out half a spit.

THE STUDENT: But I can't shovel away more than I'm doing.

THE YOUNG WORKER: If he cops me there'll be trouble.

THE STUDENT: No more cigarettes from me, then.

THE YOUNG WORKER: He'll cop me sure enough.

THE STUDENT: And you want to go on leave, don't you?
Think I'm going to pay you if you can't take a little risk
like that?

THE YOUNG WORKER: You've already had your money's
worth and more.

THE STUDENT: But I'm not going to pay you.

THE GROUP LEADER *comes and watches them:* Well, Herr Doktor, now you can see what working is really like, can't you?

THE STUDENT: Yes, Herr Group Leader.

The young worker digs half a spit of earth. The student pretends to be shovelling like mad.

THE GROUP LEADER: You owe it all to the Führer.

THE STUDENT: Yes, Herr Group Leader.

THE GROUP LEADER: Shoulder to shoulder and no class barriers; that's his way. The Führer wants no distinctions made in his labour camps. Never mind who your dad is. Carry on! *He goes.*

THE STUDENT: I don't call that half a spit.

THE YOUNG WORKER: Well, I do.

THE STUDENT: No cigarettes for today. Better remember there are an awful lot of people want cigarettes just as much as you.

THE YOUNG WORKER *slowly:* Yes, there are an awful lot of people like me. That's something we often forget.

13

Workers' playtime

> Then the media, a travelling circus
> Come to interview the workers
> With microphone in hand
> But the workers can't be trusted
> So the interview is adjusted
> To fit what Goebbels has planned.

Leipzig 1934. Foreman's office in a factory. A radio announcer bearing a microphone is chatting to three workers; a middle-aged worker, an old worker and a woman worker. In the background are a gentleman from the office and a stocky figure in SA uniform.

THE ANNOUNCER: Here we are with flywheels and driving belts in full swing all around us, surrounded by our
comrades working as busily as ants, joyously doing their
bit to provide our beloved fatherland with everything it
requires. This morning we are visiting the Fuchs spin-
ning mills. And in spite of the hard toil and the tensing
of every muscle here we see nothing but joyous and
contented faces on all sides. But let us get our comrades to
speak for themselves. (To the old worker) I understand
you've been working here for twenty-one years, Mr . . .

THE OLD WORKER: Sedelmaier.

THE ANNOUNCER: Mr Sedelmaier. Tell me, Mr Sedelmaier, how is it that we see nothing but these happy,
joyous faces in every side?

THE OLD WORKER after a moment's thought: There's a lot of
jokes told.

THE ANNOUNCER: Really? Right, so a cheerful jest or two
makes work seem child's play, what? The deadly menace
of pessimism is unknown under National Socialism, you
mean. Different in the old days, wasn't it?

THE OLD WORKER: Aye.

THE ANNOUNCER: That rotten old Weimar republic didn't
give the workers much to laugh about you mean. What
are we working for, they used to ask.

THE OLD WORKER: Aye, that's what some of them say.

THE ANNOUNCER: I didn't quite get that. Oh, I see, you're
referring to the inevitable grouses, but they're dying out
now they see that kind of thing's a waste of time because
everything's booming in the Third Reich now there's a
strong hand on the helm once again. That's what you feel
too, – to the woman worker – isn't it, Miss . . .

THE WOMAN WORKER: Schmidt.

THE ANNOUNCER: Miss Schmidt. And which of these steel
mammoths enjoys your services?

THE WOMAN WORKER reciting: And then we also work at
decorating our place of work which gives us great
pleasure. Our portrait of the Führer was purchased thanks
to voluntary contributions and we are very proud of him.
Also of the geranium plants which provide a magical

touch of colour in the greyness of our working environ-
ment, by suggestion of Miss Kinze.

THE ANNOUNCER: So you decorate your place of work
with flowers, the sweet offspring of the fields. And I imagine there've been a good few other changes in this factory since Germany's destiny took its new turning?

GENTLEMAN FROM THE OFFICE *prompting:* Wash rooms.

THE WOMAN WORKER: The wash rooms were the personal
idea of Mr Bäuschle our managing director for which we
would like to express our heartfelt thanks. Anybody who
wants to wash can do so in these fine washrooms so long
as there isn't too much of a crowd fighting for the basins.

THE ANNOUNCER: Everybody wants to be first, what?
So there's always a jolly throng?

THE WOMAN WORKER: Only six taps for 552 of us. So
there are lots of quarrels. It's disgraceful how some of
them behave.

THE ANNOUNCER: But it's all sorted out perfectly
happily. And now we are going to hear a few words from
Mr – if you'd be so good as to tell me your name?

THE WORKER: Mahn.

THE ANNOUNCER: Mr Mahn. Right, Mr Mahn, would
you tell us what moral effect the great increase in the
workforce here has had on your fellow workers?

THE WORKER: How do you mean?

THE ANNOUNCER: Well, are all of you happy to see the
wheels turning and plenty of work for everybody?

THE WORKER: You bet.

THE ANNOUNCER: And everybody once more able to
take his wage packet home at the end of the week, that's
not to be sneezed at either.

THE WORKER: No.

THE ANNOUNCER: Things weren't always like that. Under
that rotten old republic many a comrade had to plod his
weary way to the public welfare and live on charity.

THE WORKER: 18 marks 50. No deductions.

THE ANNOUNCER *with a forced laugh:* Ha. Ha. A capital
joke! Not much to deduct, was there?

THE WORKER: No. Nowadays they deduct more.

The gentleman from the office moves forward uneasily, as does the stocky man in SA uniform.

THE ANNOUNCER: So there we are, everybody's once again got bread and work under National Socialism. You're absolutely right, Mr – what did you say your name was? Not a single wheel is idle, not a single shaft needs to rust up in Adolf Hitler's Germany. *He roughly pushes the worker away from the microphone.* In joyful cooperation the intellectual worker and the manual worker are tackling the reconstruction of our beloved German Fatherland. Heil Hitler!

14

The box

> The coffins the SA carry
> Are sealed up tight, to bury
> Their victims' raw remains.
> Here's one who wouldn't give in
> He fought for better living
> That we might lose our chains.

Essen 1934. Working-class flat. A woman with two children. A young worker and his wife, who are calling on them. The woman is weeping. Steps can be heard on the staircase. The door is open.

THE WOMAN: He simply said they were paying starvation wages, that's all. And it's true. What's more, our elder girl's got lung trouble and we can't afford milk. They couldn't possibly have harmed him, could they?
The SA men bring in a big box and put it on the floor.

SA MAN: Don't make a song and dance about it. Anybody can catch pneumonia. Here are the papers, all present and correct. And don't you go doing anything silly, now.

The SA men leave.

A CHILD: Mum, is dad in there?

THE WORKER *who has gone over to the box:* That's zinc it's made of.

THE CHILD: Please can we open it?

THE WORKER *in a rage:* You bet we can. Where's your toolbox?

THE YOUNG WOMAN: Don't you open it, Hans. It'll only make them come for you.

THE WORKER: I want to see what they did to him. They're frightened of people seeing that. That's why they used zinc. Leave me alone!

THE YOUNG WOMAN: I'm not leaving you alone. Didn't you hear them?

THE WORKER: Don't you think we ought to just have a look at him?

THE WOMAN *taking her children by the hand and going up to the zinc box:* There's still my brother, they might come for him, Hans. And they might come for you too. The box can stay shut. We don't need to see him. He won't be forgotten.

15

Release

> Questioned in torture cellars
> These men were no tale-tellers.
> They held out all through the night.
> Let's hope they didn't go under
> But their wives and friends must wonder
> What took place at first light.

Berlin, 1936. Working-class kitchen. Sunday morning. Man and wife. Sound of military music in the distance.

THE MAN: He'll be here any minute.

THE WIFE: None of you know anything against him, after all.

THE MAN: All we know is that they let him out of the concentration camp.

THE WIFE: So why don't you trust him?

THE MAN: There've been too many cases. They put so much pressure on them in there.

THE WIFE: How's he to convince you?

THE MAN: We'll find out where he stands all right.

THE WIFE: Might take time.

THE MAN: Yes.

THE WIFE: And he might be a first-rate comrade.

THE MAN: He might.

THE WIFE: It must be dreadful for him when he sees everybody mistrusting him.

THE MAN: He knows it's necessary.

THE WIFE: All the same.

THE MAN: I can hear something. Don't go away while we're talking.

There is a ring. The man opens the door, the released man enters.

THE MAN: Hullo, Max.

The released man silently shakes hands with the man and his wife.

THE WIFE: Would you like a cup of coffee with us? We're just going to have some.

THE RELEASED MAN: If it's not too much trouble.

Pause.

THE RELEASED MAN: You got a new cupboard.

THE WIFE: It's really an old one, cost eleven marks fifty. Ours was falling to pieces.

THE RELEASED MAN: Ha.

THE MAN: Anything doing in the street?

THE RELEASED MAN: They're collecting.

THE WIFE: We could do with a suit for Willi.

THE MAN: Hey, I'm not out of work.

THE WIFE: That's just why we could do with a suit for you.

THE MAN: Don't talk such nonsense.

THE RELEASED MAN: Work or no work, anybody can do with something.

THE MAN: You found work yet?

THE RELEASED MAN: They say so.

THE MAN: At Siemens?

THE RELEASED MAN: There or some other place.

THE MAN: It's not as hard as it was.

THE RELEASED MAN: No.

Pause.

THE MAN: How long you been inside?

THE RELEASED MAN: Six months

THE MAN: Meet anyone in there?

THE RELEASED MAN: No one I knew. *Pause.* They're sending them to different camps these days. You could land up in Bavaria.

THE MAN: Ha.

THE RELEASED MAN: Things haven't changed much outside.

THE MAN: Not so as you'd notice.

THE WIFE: We live a very quiet life, you know. Willi hardly ever sees any of his old friends, do you, Willi?

THE MAN: Ay, we keep pretty much to ourselves.

THE RELEASED MAN: I don't suppose you ever got them to shift those rubbish bins from the hallway?

THE WIFE: Goodness, you remember that? Ay, he says he can't find anywhere else for them.

THE RELEASED MAN *as the wife is pouring him a cup of coffee:* Just give me a drop. I don't want to stay long.

THE MAN: Got any plans?

THE RELEASED MAN: Selma told me you looked after her when she was laid up. Thanks very much.

THE WIFE: It was nothing. We'd have told her to come over in the evening more, only we've not even got the wireless.

THE MAN: Anything they tell you is in the paper anyway.

THE RELEASED MAN: Not that there's much in the old rag.

THE WIFE: As much as there is in the *Völkischer Beobachter*, though.

THE RELEASED MAN: And in the *Völkischer Beobachter* there's just as much as there is in the old rag, eh?

THE MAN: I don't read that much in the evenings. Too tired.

THE WIFE: Here, what's wrong with your hand? All screwed up like that and two fingers missing?

THE RELEASED MAN: Oh, I had a fall.

THE MAN: Good thing it was your left one.

THE RELEASED MAN: Ay, that was a bit of luck. I'd like a word with you. No offence meant, Mrs Mahn.

THE WIFE: None taken. I've just got to clean the stove.
She gets to work on the stove. The released man watches her, a thin smile on his lips.

THE MAN: We've got to go out right after dinner. Has Selma quite recovered?

THE RELEASED MAN: All but for her hip. Doing washing is bad for her. Tell me ... *He stops short and looks at them. They look at him. He says nothing further.*

THE MAN *hoarsely:* What about a walk round the Alexanderplatz before dinner? See what's doing with their collection?

THE WIFE: We could do that, couldn't we?

THE RELEASED MAN: Sure.
Pause.

THE RELEASED MAN *quietly:* Hey, Willi, you know I've not changed.

THE MAN *lightly:* Course you haven't. They might have a band playing there. Get yourself ready, Anna. We've finished our coffee. I'll just run a comb through my hair.
They go into the next room. The released man remains seated. He has picked up his hat. He is aimlessly whistling. The couple return, dressed to go out.

THE MAN: Come on then, Max.

THE RELEASED MAN: Very well. But let me just say: I find it entirely right.

THE MAN: Good, then let's go.
They go out together.

16

Charity begins at home

With banners and loud drumming
The Winter Aid come slumming
Into the humblest door.
They've marched round and collected
The crumbs the rich have rejected
And brought them to the poor.

Their hands, more used to beatings
Now offer gifts and greetings.
They conjure up a smile.
Their charity soon crashes
Their food all turns to ashes
And chokes the uttered 'Heil!'

Karlsruhe 1937. An old woman's flat. She is standing at a table with her daughter while the two SA men deliver a parcel from the Winter Aid Organisation.

THE FIRST SA MAN: Here you are, Ma, a present from the Führer.

THE SECOND SA MAN: So you can't say he's not looking after you properly.

THE OLD WOMAN: Thanks very much, thanks very much. Look, Erna, potatoes. And a woollen sweater. And apples.

THE FIRST SA MAN: And a letter from the Führer with something in it. Go on, open it.

THE OLD WOMAN *opening the letter:* Five marks! What d'you say to that, Erna?

THE SECOND SA MAN: Winter Aid.

THE OLD WOMAN: You must take an apple, young man, and you too, for bringing these things to me, and up all those stairs too. It's all I got to offer you. And I'll take one myself.

She takes a bite at an apple. All eat apples with the exception of the young woman.

THE OLD WOMAN: Go on, Erna, you take one too, don't just stand there. That shows you things aren't like your husband says.

THE FIRST SA MAN: What does he say, then?

THE YOUNG WOMAN: He doesn't say anything. The old lady's wandering.

THE OLD WOMAN: Of course it's just his way of talking, you know, it don't mean any harm, just the way they all talk. How prices have gone up a bit much lately. *Pointing at her daughter with the apple:* And she got her account book and actually reckoned food had cost her 123 marks more this year than last. Didn't you, Erna? *She notices that the SA man seems to have taken this amiss.* But of course it's just because we're rearming, isn't it? What's the matter, I said something wrong?

THE FIRST SA MAN: Where do you keep your account book, young woman?

THE SECOND SA MAN: And who are you in the habit of showing it to?

THE YOUNG WOMAN: It's at home. I don't show it to no one.

THE OLD WOMAN: You can't object if she keeps accounts, how could you?

THE FIRST SA MAN: And if she goes about spreading alarm and despondency; are we allowed to object then?

THE SECOND SA MAN: What's more I don't remember her saying 'Heil Hitler' all that loudly when we came in. Do you?

THE OLD WOMAN: But she *did* say 'Heil Hitler' and I say the same. 'Heil Hitler'!

THE SECOND SA MAN: Nice nest of Marxists we've stumbled on here, Albert. We'd better have a good look at those accounts. Just you come along and show us where you live.

He seizes the young woman by the arm.

THE OLD WOMAN: But she's in her third month. You can't ... that's no way for you to behave. After bring-

ing the parcel and taking the apples. Erna! But she *did*
say 'Heil Hitler', what am I to do, Heil Hitler! Heil
Hitler!

She vomits up the apple. The SA lead her daughter off.

THE OLD WOMAN *continuing to vomit:* Heil Hitler!

17

Two bakers

> Now come the master bakers
> Compelled to act as fakers
> And made to use their art
> On substitute ingredients –
> Spuds, bran and blind obedience.
> It lands them in the cart.

*Landsberg, 1936. Prison yard. Prisoners are walking in a circle.
Now and again two of them talk quietly to each other downstage.*

THE ONE: So you're a baker too, new boy?

THE OTHER: Yes. Are you?

THE ONE: Yes. What did they get you for?

THE OTHER: Look out!

They again walk round the circle.

THE OTHER: Refusing to mix potatoes and bran in my
bread. And you? How long've you been in?

THE ONE: Two years.

THE OTHER: And what did they get you for? Look out!

They again walk round the circle.

THE ONE: Mixing bran in my bread. Two years ago they
still called that adulteration.

THE OTHER: Look out!

18

The farmer feeds his sow

You'll notice in our procession
The farmer's sour expression:
They've underpriced his crop.
But what his pigs require
Is milk, whose price has gone higher.
It makes him blow his top.

Aichach, 1937. A farmyard. It is night. The farmer is standing by the pigsty giving instructions to his wife and two children.

THE FARMER: I wasn't having you mixed up in this, but you found out and now you'll just have to shut your trap. Or else your Dad'll go off to Landsberg gaol for the rest of his born days. There's nowt wrong in our feeding our cattle when they're hungry. God doesn't want any beast to starve. And soon as she's hungry she squeals and I'm not having a sow squealing with hunger on my farm. But they won't let me feed her. Cause the State says so. But I'm feeding her just the same, I am. Cause if I don't feed her she'll die on me, and I shan't get any compensation for that.

THE FARMER'S WIFE: Too right. Our grain's our grain. And those buggers have no business telling us what to do. They got the Jews out but the State's the worst Jew of them all. And the Reverend Father saying 'Thou shalt not muzzle the ox that treadeth out the corn.' That's his way of telling us go ahead and feed our cattle. It weren't us as made their four year plan, and we weren't asked.

THE FARMER: That's right. They don't favour the farmers and the farmers don't favour them. I'm supposed to deliver over my grain and pay through the nose for my cattle feed. So that that spiv can buy guns.

THE FARMER'S WIFE: You stand by the gate, Toni, and

you, Marie, run into the pasture and soon as you see anyone coming give us a call.

The children take up their positions. The farmer mixes his pig-swill and carries it to the sty, looking cautiously around him. His wife looks cautiously too.

THE FARMER *pouring the swill into the sow's trough:* Go on, have a good feed, love. Heil Hitler! When a beast's hungry there ain't no State.

19

The old militant

Behold several million electors.
One hundred per cent in all sectors
Have asked to be led by the nose.
They didn't get real bread and butter
They didn't get warm coats or fodder
They *did* get the leader they chose.

Calw (Württemberg), 1938. A square with small shops. In the background a butcher's, in the foreground a dairy. It is a dark winter's morning. The butcher's is not open yet. But the dairy's lights are on and there are a few customers waiting.

A PETIT-BOURGEOIS: No butter again today, what?

THE WOMAN: It'll be all I can afford on my old man's pay, anyway.

A YOUNG FELLOW: Stop grumbling, will you? Germany needs guns, not butter, no question about that. He spelled it out.

THE WOMAN *backing down:* Quite right too.

Silence.

THE YOUNG FELLOW: D'you think we could have reoccupied the Rhineland with butter? Everyone was for doing it the way we did, but catch them making any sacrifices.

A SECOND WOMAN: Keep your hair on. All of us are making some.

THE YOUNG FELLOW *mistrustfully:* What d'you mean?

THE SECOND WOMAN *to the first:* Don't you give something when they come round collecting?

The first woman nods.

THE SECOND WOMAN: There you are. She's giving. And so are we. Voluntary-like.

THE YOUNG FELLOW: That's an old story. Not a penny to spare when the Führer needs a bit of backing, as it were, for his mighty tasks. It's just rags, what they give the Winter Aid. They'd give 'em the moths if they could get away with it. We know the kind we got to deal with. That factory owner in number twelve went and gave us a pair of worn-out riding boots.

THE PETIT-BOURGEOIS: No foresight, that's the trouble.

The dairywoman comes out of her shop in a white apron.

THE DAIRYWOMAN: Won't be long now. *To the second woman:* Morning, Mrs Ruhl. Did you hear they came for young Lettner last night?

THE SECOND WOMAN: What, the butcher?

THE DAIRYWOMAN: Right, his son.

THE SECOND WOMAN: But he was in the SA.

THE DAIRYWOMAN: Used to be. The old fellow's been in the party since 1929. He was away at a livestock sale yesterday or they'd have taken him off too.

THE SECOND WOMAN: What're they supposed to have done?

THE DAIRYWOMAN: Been overcharging for meat. He was hardly getting nothing on his quota and had to turn customers away. Then they say he started buying on the black market. From the Jews even.

THE YOUNG FELLOW: Bound to come for him, weren't they?

THE DAIRYWOMAN: Used to be one of the keenest of the lot, he did. He shopped old Zeisler at number seventeen for not taking the *Völkischer Beobachter*. An old militant, that's him.

THE SECOND WOMAN: He'll get a surprise when he comes back.

THE DAIRYWOMAN: *If* he comes back.

THE PETIT-BOURGEOIS: No foresight, that's the trouble.

THE SECOND WOMAN: Looks as if they won't open at all today.

THE DAIRYWOMAN: Best thing they can do. The police only have to look round a place like that and they're bound to find something, aren't they? With stock so hard to get. We get ours from the cooperative, no worries so far. *Calling out:* There'll be no cream today. *General murmur of disappointment.* They say Lettners raised a mortgage on the house. They counted on its being cancelled or something.

THE PETIT-BOURGEOIS: They can't start cancelling mortgages. That'd be going a bit too far.

THE SECOND WOMAN: Young Lettner was quite a nice fellow.

THE DAIRYWOMAN: Old Lettner was always the crazy one. Went and shoved the boy in the SA, just like that. When he'd sooner have been going out with a girl, if you ask me.

THE YOUNG FELLOW: What d'you mean, crazy?

THE DAIRYWOMAN: Crazy, did I say? Oh, he always went crazy if anyone said anything against the Idea, in the old days. He was always speaking about the Idea, and down with the selfishness of the individual.

THE PETIT-BOURGEOIS: They're opening up after all.

THE SECOND WOMAN: Got to live, haven't they?

A stout woman comes out of the butcher's shop, which is now half-lit. She stops on the pavement and looks down the street for something. Then she turns to the diary woman.

THE BUTCHER'S WIFE: Good morning, Mrs Schlichter. Have you seen our Richard? He should have been here with the meat well before now.

The dairywoman doesn't reply. All of them just stare at her. She understands, and goes quickly back into the shop.

THE DAIRYWOMAN: Act as though nothing's happened. It all blew up day before yesterday when the old man made such a stink you could hear him shouting right across the square. They counted that against him.

THE SECOND WOMAN: I never heard a word about that, Mrs Schlichter.

THE DAIRYWOMAN: Really? Didn't you know how he refused to hang that plaster ham they brought him in his shop window? He'd gone and ordered it cause they insisted, what with him hanging nothing in his window all week but the slate with the prices. He said: I've got nothing left for the window. When they brought that dummy ham, along with a side of veal, what's more, so natural you'd think it was real, he shouted he wasn't hanging any make-believe stuff in his window as well as a lot more I wouldn't care to repeat. Against the government, all of it, after which threw the stuff into the road. They had to pick it up out of the dirt.

THE SECOND WOMAN: Ts, ts, ts, ts.

THE PETIT-BOURGEOIS: No foresight, that's the trouble.

THE SECOND WOMAN: How can people lose control like that?

THE DAIRYWOMAN: Particularly such a smooth operator.
At this moment someone turns on a second light in the butcher's shop.

THE DAIRYWOMAN: Look at that!
She points excitedly at the half-lit shop window.

THE SECOND WOMAN: There's something in the window.

THE DAIRYWOMAN: It's old Lettner. In his coat too. But what's he standing on? *Suddenly calls out:* Mrs Lettner!

THE BUTCHER'S WIFE: What is it?
The dairywoman points speechlessly at the shop window. The butcher's wife glances at it, screams and falls down in a faint. The second woman and the dairywoman hurry over to her.

THE SECOND WOMAN *back over her shoulder:* He's hung himself in his shop window.

THE PETIT-BOURGEOIS: There's a sign round his neck.

THE FIRST WOMAN: It's the slate. There's something written on it.

THE SECOND WOMAN: It says 'I voted for Hitler'.

20

The Sermon on the Mount

> The Church's Ten Commandments
> Are subject to amendments
> By order of the police.
> Her broken head is bleeding
> For new gods are succeeding
> Her Jewish god of peace

Lübeck 1937. A fisherman's kitchen. The fisherman is dying. By his bed stand his wife and, in SA uniform, his son. The pastor is there.

THE DYING MAN: Tell me: is there really anything afterwards?

THE PASTOR: Are you then troubled by doubts?

THE WIFE: He's kept on saying these last four days that there's so much talking and promising you don't know what to believe. You mustn't think badly of him, your Reverence.

THE PASTOR: Afterwards cometh eternal life.

THE DYING MAN: And that'll be better?

THE PASTOR: Yes.

THE DYING MAN: It's got to be.

THE WIFE: He's taken it out of himself, you know.

THE PASTOR: Believe me, God knows it.

THE DYING MAN: You think so? *After a pause:* Up there, I suppose a man'll be able to open his mouth for once now and again?

THE PASTOR *slightly confused:* It is written that faith moveth mountains. You must believe. You will find it easier then.

THE WIFE: Your Reverence, you mustn't think he doesn't believe. He always took Communion. *To her husband, urgently:* Here's his Reverence thinking you don't believe. But you do believe, don't you?

THE DYING MAN: Yes ...

Silence.

THE DYING MAN: There's nothing else then.

THE PASTOR: What are you trying to say by that? There's nothing else then?

THE DYING MAN: Just; there's nothing else then. Eh? I mean, suppose there had been anything?

THE PASTOR: But what could there have been?

THE DYING MAN: Anything at all.

THE PASTOR: But you have had your dear wife and your son.

THE WIFE: You had us, didn't you?

THE DYING MAN: Yes ...

Silence.

THE DYING MAN: I mean: if life had added up to anything ...

THE PASTOR: I'm not quite sure I understand you. You surely don't mean that you only believe because your life has been all toil and hardship?

THE DYING MAN *looks round until he catches sight of his son:* And is it going to be better for them?

THE PASTOR: For youth, you mean? Let us hope so.

THE DYING MAN: If the boat had had a motor ...

THE WIFE: You mustn't worry about that now.

THE PASTOR: It is not a moment to be thinking of such things.

THE DYING MAN: I've got to.

THE WIFE: We'll manage all right.

THE DYING MAN: But suppose there's a war?

THE WIFE: Don't speak about that now. *To the pastor:* These last times he was always talking to the boy about war. They didn't agree about it.

The pastor looks at the son.

THE SON: He doesn't believe in our future.

THE DYING MAN: Tell me: up there, does *he* want war?

THE PASTOR *hesitating:* It says: Blessed are the peacemakers.

THE DYING MAN: But if there's a war ...

THE SON: The Führer doesn't want a war!

The dying man makes a wide gesture of the hand, as if shoving that away.

THE DYING MAN: So if there's a war . . .
The son wants to say something.

THE WIFE: Keep quiet now.

THE DYING MAN *to the pastor, pointing at his son:* You tell him that about the peacemakers.

THE PASTOR: We are all in the hand of God, you must not forget.

THE DYING MAN: You telling him?

THE WIFE: But his Reverence can't do anything to stop war, be reasonable. Better not talk about it nowadays, eh, your Reverence?

THE DYING MAN: You know: they're a swindling lot. I can't buy a motor for my boat. Their aeroplanes get motors all right. For war, for killing. And when it's stormy like this I can't bring her in. because I haven't a motor. Those swindlers! War's what they're after! *He sinks back exhausted.*

THE WIFE *anxiously fetches a cloth and a bowl of water, and wipes away his sweat:* You mustn't listen. He doesn't know what he's saying.

THE PASTOR: You should calm yourself, Mr Claasen.

THE DYING MAN: You telling him about the peacemakers?

THE PASTOR *after a pause:* He can read for himself. It's in the Sermon on the Mount.

THE DYING MAN: He says it's all written by a Jew and it doesn't apply.

THE WIFE: Don't start on that again! He doesn't mean it like that. That's what he hears the others saying.

THE DYING MAN: Yes. *To the Pastor:* Does it apply?

THE WIFE *with an anxious glance at her son:* Don't make trouble for his Reverence, Hannes. You shouldn't ask that.

THE SON: Why shouldn't he ask that?

THE DYING MAN: Does it apply or not?

THE PASTOR: It is also written: Render therefore unto Caesar the things which are Caesar's; and unto God the things that are God's.
The dying man sinks back. His wife lays the damp cloth on his forehead.

21

The motto

Their boys learn it's morally healthy
To lay down one's life for the wealthy:
It's a lesson that's made very clear.
It's far harder than spelling or figures
But their teachers are terrible floggers
So they're fearful of showing fear.

Chemnitz, 1937. Meeting room of the Hitler Youth. A squad of boys, mostly with gas masks slung round their necks. A small group are looking at a boy with no mask who is sitting by himself on a bench and helplessly moving his lips as if learning something.

THE FIRST BOY: He still hasn't got one.

THE SECOND BOY: His old lady won't buy him one.

THE FIRST BOY: But she must know he'll get into trouble.

THE THIRD BOY: If she ain't got the cash ...

THE FIRST BOY: And old Fatty's got a down on him in any case.

THE SECOND BOY: He's back to learning it: 'The Motto'.

THE FOURTH BOY: That's four weeks he's been trying to learn it, and it's just a couple of verses.

THE THIRD BOY: He's known it off for ages.

THE SECOND BOY: He only gets stuck cause he's frightened.

THE FOURTH BOY: That's terribly funny, don't you think?

THE FIRST BOY: Devastating. *He calls:* D'you know it, Pschierer?
The fifth boy looks up, distracted, gets the meaning and nods. Then he goes on learning.

THE SECOND BOY: Old Fatty only keeps on at him cause he's got no gasmask

THE THIRD BOY: The way he tells it, it's because he wouldn't go to the pictures with him.

THE FOURTH BOY: That's what I heard too. D'you think it's true?

THE SECOND BOY: Could be, why not? I wouldn't go to the pictures with Fatty either. But he wouldn't start anything with me. My old man wouldn't half kick up a stink.

THE FIRST BOY: Look out, here's Fatty.

The boys come to attention in two ranks. Enter a somewhat corpulent Scharführer. The Hitler salute.

THE SCHARFÜHRER: From the right, number!

They number.

THE SCHARFÜHRER: Gasmasks – on!

The boys put on their gasmasks. Some of them have not got one. They simply go through the motions of the drill.

THE SCHARFÜHRER: We'll start with 'The Motto'. Who's going to recite it for us? *He looks round as if unable to make up his mind, then suddenly:* Pschierer! You do it so nicely.

The fifth boy steps forward and stands to attention in front of the others.

THE SCHARFÜHRER: Can you do it, maestro?

THE FIFTH BOY: Yes, sir!

THE SCHARFÜHRER: Right, get cracking! Verse number one!

THE FIFTH BOY:

Thou shalt gaze on death unblinking –
Saith the motto for our age –
Sent into the fray unflinching
Heedless of the battle's rage.

THE SCHARFÜHRER: Don't wet your pants now. Carry on! Verse number two!

THE FIFTH BOY:

Victory is ours for gaining.
Beat, stab, shoot . . .

He has got stuck, and repeats these words. One or two of the boys find it difficult not to burst out laughing.

THE SCHARFÜHRER: So once again you haven't learnt it?

THE FIFTH BOY: Yes, sir!

THE SCHARFÜHRER: I bet you learn something different at home, don't you? *Shouts:* Carry on!

THE FIFTH BOY:

Beat, stab, shoot them so they fall.
Be a German . . . uncomplaining, uncomplaining
Be a German uncomplaining
Die for this . . . die for this, and give your all.

THE SCHARFÜHRER: Now what's so difficult about that?

22

News of the bombardment of Almeria gets to the barracks

> The soldiers in His armed forces
> Get full meat and pudding courses
> And can also ask for more.
> It helps them to face the firing
> And not to think of enquiring
> Who He is fighting for.

Berlin, 1937. Corridor in a barracks. Looking around them nervously, two working-class boys are carrying away something wrapped in brown paper.

THE FIRST BOY: Aren't half worked up today, are they?

THE SECOND BOY: They say it's cause war could break out. Over Spain.

THE FIRST BOY: White as a sheet, some of them.

THE SECOND BOY: Cause we bombarded Almeria. Last night.

THE FIRST BOY: Where's that?

THE SECOND BOY: In Spain, silly. Hitler telegraphed for a German warship to bombard Almeria right away. As a punishment. Cause they're reds down there, and reds have got to be scared shitless of the Third Reich. Now it could lead to war.

THE FIRST BOY: And now they're scared shitless too.

THE SECOND BOY: Right. Scared shitless, that's them.

THE FIRST BOY: What do they want to go bombarding for if they're white as a sheet and scared shitless cause it could lead to war?

THE SECOND BOY: They just started bombarding cause Hitler wants it that way.

THE FIRST BOY: Whatever Hitler wants they want too. The whole lot are for Hitler. Cause he's built up our new armed forces.

THE SECOND BOY: You got it.

Pause.

THE FIRST BOY: Think we can sneak out now?

THE SECOND BOY: Better wait, or we'll run into one of those Lieutenants. Then he'll confiscate everything and they'll be in trouble.

THE FIRST BOY: Decent of them to let us come every day.

THE SECOND BOY: Oh, they ain't millionaires any more than us, you know. They know how it is. My old lady only gets ten marks a week, and there are three of us. It's just enough for potatoes.

THE FIRST BOY: Smashing nosh they get here. Meatballs today.

THE SECOND BOY: How much d'they give you this time?

THE FIRST BOY: One dollop, as usual. Why?

THE SECOND BOY: They gave me two this time.

THE FIRST BOY: Let's see. They only gave one.

The second boy shows him.

THE FIRST BOY: Did you say anything to them?

THE SECOND BOY: No. Just 'good morning' as usual.

THE FIRST BOY: I don't get it. And me too, 'Heil Hitler' as usual.

THE SECOND BOY: Funny. They gave me two dollops.

THE FIRST BOY: Why d'they suddenly do that. I don't get it.

THE SECOND BOY: Nor me. Coast's clear now.

They quickly run off.

23

Job creation

> He sees that jobs are provided.
> The poor go where they are guided:
> He likes them to be keen.
> They're allowed to serve the nation.
> Their blood and perspiration
> Can fuel His war machine.

Spandau, 1937. A worker comes home and finds a neighbour there.

THE NEIGHBOUR: Good evening, Mr Fenn. I just came to
see if your wife could lend me some bread. She's popped
out for a moment.

THE MAN: That's all right, Mrs Dietz. What d'you think of
the job I got?

THE NEIGHBOUR: Ah, they're all getting work. At the
new factory, aren't you? You'll be turning out bombers
then?

THE MAN: And how.

THE NEIGHBOUR: They'll be needed in Spain these days.

THE MAN: Why specially Spain?

THE NEIGHBOUR: You hear such things about the stuff
they're sending. A disgrace, I call it.

THE MAN: Best mind what you say.

THE NEIGHBOUR: You joined them now too?

THE MAN: I've not joined nothing. I get on with my work.
Where's Martha gone?

THE NEIGHBOUR: I'd best warn you, I suppose. It could
be something nasty. Just as I came in the postman was
here, and there was some kind of letter got your wife all
worked up. Made me wonder if I shouldn't ask the
Schiermanns to lend me that bread.

THE MAN: Cor. *He calls:* Martha!
Enter his wife. She is in mourning.

THE MAN: What are you up to? Who's dead then?

THE WIFE: Franz. We got a letter.
She hands him a letter.

THE NEIGHBOUR: For God's sake! What happened to him?

THE MAN: It was an accident.

THE NEIGHBOUR *mistrustfully:* But wasn't he a pilot?

THE MAN: Yes.

THE NEIGHBOUR: And he had an accident?

THE MAN: At Stettin. In the course of a night exercise with
troops, it says here.

THE NEIGHBOUR: He won't have had no accident. Tell
me another.

THE MAN: I'm only telling you what it says here. The letter's
from the commandant.

THE NEIGHBOUR: Did he write to you lately? From Stettin?

THE MAN: Don't get worked up, Martha. It won't help.

THE WIFE *sobbing:* No, I know.

THE NEIGHBOUR: He was such a nice fellow, that brother of yours. Like me to make you a pot of coffee?

THE MAN: Yes, if you would, Mrs Dietz.

THE NEIGHBOUR *looking for a pot:* That sort of thing's always a shock.

THE WIFE: Go on, have your wash, Herbert. Mrs Dietz won't mind.

THE MAN: There's no hurry.

THE NEIGHBOUR: So he wrote to you from Stettin?

THE MAN: That's where the letters always came from.

THE NEIGHBOUR *gives a look:* Really? I suppose he'd gone south with the others?

THE MAN: What do you mean, gone south?

THE NEIGHBOUR: Way south to sunny Spain.

THE MAN *as his wife again bursts into sobs:* Pull yourself together, Martha. You shouldn't say that sort of thing, Mrs Dietz.

THE NEIGHBOUR: I just wonder what they'd tell you in Stettin if you went and tried to collect your brother.

THE MAN: I'm not going to Stettin.

THE NEIGHBOUR: They always sweep things under the mat. They think it's heroic of them not to let anything come out. There was a fellow in the boozer bragging about how clever they are at covering up their war. When one of your bombers gets shot down and the blokes inside jump out with parachutes, the other bombers machine-gun them down in midair – their own blokes – so's they can't tell the Reds where they've come from.

THE WIFE *who is feeling sick:* Get us some water, will you, Herbert, I'm feeling sick.

THE NEIGHBOUR: I really didn't mean to upset you, it's just the way they cover it all up. They know it's criminal all right and that their war can't stand being exposed. Same in this case. Had an accident in the course of an exercise! What are they exercising at? A war, that's what!

THE MAN: Don't talk so loudly in here, d'you mind? *To his wife:* How are you feeling?

THE NEIGHBOUR: You're another of them keeps quiet about it all. There's your answer, in that letter.

THE MAN: Just shut up, would you?

THE WIFE: Herbert!

THE NEIGHBOUR: So now it's 'shut up, would you?'. Because you got a job. Your brother-in-law got one too, didn't he? Had an 'accident' with one of the same things you're making in that factory.

THE MAN: I don't like that, Mrs Dietz. Me working on 'one of the same things'! What are all the rest of them working on? What's your husband working on? Electric bulbs, isn't it? I suppose they're not for war. Just to give light. But what's the light for? To light tanks, eh? Or a battleship? Or one of those same things? He's only making light bulbs, though. My God, there's nothing left that's not for war. How am I supposed to find a job if I keep telling myself 'not for war!'? D'you want me to starve?

THE NEIGHBOUR *subduedly:* I'm not saying you got to starve. Of course you're right to take the job. I'm just talking about those criminals. A nice kind of job creation, I don't think.

THE MAN *seriously:* And better not go around in black like that, Martha. They don't like it.

THE NEIGHBOUR: The questions it makes people ask: that's what they don't like.

THE WIFE *calmly:* You'd rather I took it off?

THE MAN: Yes, if I'm not to lose my job any minute.

THE WIFE: I'm not taking it off.

THE MAN: What d'you mean?

THE WIFE: I'm not taking it off. My brother's dead. I'm going into mourning.

THE MAN: If you hadn't got it because Rosa bought it when Mother died, you wouldn't be able to go into mourning.

THE WIFE *shouting:* Don't anyone tell me I'm not going into mourning! If they can slaughter him I have a right to cry, don't I? I never heard of such a thing. It's the most inhuman thing ever happened! They're criminals of the lowest kind!

THE NEIGHBOUR *while the man sits speechless with horror:* But Mrs Fenn!

THE MAN *hoarsely:* If you're going to talk like that we could do more than lose our job.

THE WIFE: Let them come and get me, then! They've concentration camps for women too. Let them just put me in one of those because I dare to mind when they kill my brother! What was he in Spain for?

THE MAN: Shut up about Spain!

THE NEIGHBOUR: That kind of talk could get us into trouble, Mrs Fenn.

THE WIFE: Are we to keep quiet just because they might take your job away? Because we'll die of starvation if we don't make bombers for them? And die just the same if we do? Exactly like my Franz? They created a job for him too. Three foot under. He could as well have had that here.

THE MAN *holding a hand over her mouth:* Shut up, will you? It doesn't help.

THE WIFE: What does help then? Do something that does!

24

Consulting the People

> And as the column passes
> We call with urgent voices:
> Can none of you say No?
> You've got to make them heed you.
> This war to which they lead you
> Will soon be your death-blow.

Berlin. March 13th, 1938. A working-class flat, with two men and a woman. The constricted space is blocked by a flagpole. A great noise of jubilation from the radio, with church bells and the sound of aircraft. A voice is saying 'And now the Führer is about to enter Vienna.'

THE WOMAN: It's like the sea.

THE OLDER WORKER: Aye, it's one victory after another for that fellow.

THE YOUNGER WORKER: And us that gets defeated.

THE WOMAN: That's right.

THE YOUNGER WORKER: Listen to them shouting. Like they're being given a present.

THE OLDER WORKER: They are. An invasion.

THE YOUNGER WORKER: And then it's what they call 'consulting the People'. 'Ein Volk, ein Reich, ein Führer!' 'A single people, a single empire, a single leader.' 'Willst du das, Deutscher?' 'You're German, are you in favour?' And us not able to put out the least little leaflet about this referendum. Here, in a working-class district like Neukölln.

THE WOMAN: How d'you mean, not able?

THE YOUNGER WORKER: Too dangerous.

THE OLDER WORKER: And just when they've caught Karl. How are we to get the addresses?

THE YOUNGER WORKER: We'd need someone to do the writing too.

THE WOMAN *points at the radio:* He had a hundred thousand men to launch his attack. We need one man. Fine. If he's the only one who's got what's needed, then he'll score the victories.

THE YOUNGER WORKER *in anger:* So we can do without Karl.

THE WOMAN: If that's the way you people feel then we may as well split up.

THE OLDER WORKER: Comrades, there's no use kidding ourselves. Producing a leaflet's getting harder and harder, that's a fact. It's no good acting as if we just can't hear all that victory din – *pointing at the radio. To the woman:* You've got to admit, anyone hearing that sort of thing might think they're getting stronger all the time. It really does sound like a single people, wouldn't you say?

THE WOMAN: It sounds like twenty thousand drunks being stood free beer.

THE YOUNGER WORKER: For all you know we might be the only people to say so.

THE WOMAN: Right. Us and others like us.

The woman smoothes out a small crumpled piece of paper.

THE OLDER WORKER: What have you got there?

THE WOMAN: It's a copy of a letter. There's such a din I
can read it out. *She reads:*

'DEAR SON: TOMORROW I SHALL HAVE CEASED TO BE. EXECU-
TIONS ARE USUALLY AT SIX A.M. I'M WRITING NOW BECAUSE I
WANT YOU TO KNOW I HAVEN'T CHANGED MY OPINIONS, NOR
HAVE I APPLIED FOR A PARDON BECAUSE I DIDN'T COMMIT ANY
CRIME. I JUST SERVED MY COUNTRY. AND IF IT LOOKS AS
THOUGH I GOT NOWHERE LIKE THAT IT ISN'T SO. EVERY MAN TO
HIS POST, SHOULD BE OUR MOTTO. OUR TASK IS VERY DIFFICULT,
BUT IT'S THE GREATEST ONE THERE IS — TO FREE THE HUMAN
RACE FROM ITS OPPRESSORS. TILL THAT'S DONE LIFE HAS NO
OTHER VALUE. LET THAT OUT OF OUR SIGHTS AND THE WHOLE
HUMAN RACE WILL RELAPSE INTO BARBARISM. YOU'RE STILL
QUITE YOUNG BUT IT WON'T HURT YOU TO REMEMBER ALWAYS
WHICH SIDE YOU ARE ON. STICK WITH YOUR OWN CLASS, THEN
YOUR FATHER WON'T HAVE SUFFERED HIS UNHAPPY FATE IN
VAIN, BECAUSE IT ISN'T EASY. LOOK AFTER YOUR MOTHER,
YOUR BROTHERS AND SISTERS TOO, YOU'RE THE ELDEST. BETTER
BE CLEVER. GREETINGS TO YOU ALL YOUR LOVING FATHER.'

THE OLDER WORKER: There aren't really that few of us
after all.

THE YOUNGER WORKER: What's to go in the referendum
leaflet, then?

THE WOMAN *thinking:* Best thing would be just one word:
NO!

Mother Courage and her Children

A Chronicle of the Thirty Years War

Translator: JOHN WILLETT

Characters

MOTHER COURAGE
KATTRIN, *her dumb daughter*
EILIF, *the elder son*
SWISS CHEESE, *the younger son*
THE RECRUITER
THE SERGEANT
THE COOK
THE GENERAL
THE CHAPLAIN
THE ARMOURER
YVETTE POTTIER
THE MAN WITH THE PATCH
ANOTHER SERGEANT
THE ANCIENT COLONEL
A CLERK
A YOUNG SOLDIER
AN OLDER SOLDIER
A PEASANT
THE PEASANT'S WIFE
THE YOUNG MAN
THE OLD WOMAN
ANOTHER PEASANT
HIS WIFE
THE YOUNG PEASANT
THE ENSIGN
Soldiers
A Voice

Spring 1624. The Swedish Commander-in-Chief Count Oxenstierna is raising troops in Dalecarlia for the Polish campaign. The canteen woman Anna Fierling, known under the name of Mother Courage, loses one son

Country road near a town.
A sergeant and a recruiter stand shivering.

RECRUITER: How can you muster a unit in a place like this? I've been thinking about suicide, Sergeant. Here am I, got to find our commander four companies before the twelfth of the month, and people round here are so nasty I can't sleep nights. S'pose I get hold of some bloke and shut my eye to his pigeon chest and varicose veins, I get him proper drunk, he signs on the line, I'm just settling up, he goes for a piss, I follow him to the door because I smell a rat; bob's your uncle, he's off like a flea with the itch. No notion of word of honour, loyalty, faith, sense of duty. This place has shattered my confidence in the human race, sergeant.

SERGEANT: It's too long since they had a war here; stands to reason. Where's their sense of morality to come from? Peace – that's just a mess; takes a war to restore order. Peacetime, the human race runs wild. People and cattle get buggered about, who cares? Everyone eats just as he feels inclined, a hunk of cheese on top of his nice white bread, and a slice of fat on top of the cheese. How many young blokes and good horses in that town there, nobody knows; they never thought of counting. I been in places ain't seen a war for nigh seventy years: folks hadn't got names to them, couldn't tell one another apart. Takes a war to get proper nominal rolls and inventories – shoes in bundles and corn in bags, and man and beast properly numbered and carted off, cause it stands to reason: no order, no war.

RECRUITER: Too true.

SERGEANT: Same with all good things, it's a job to get a war going. But once it's blossomed out there's no holding it; folk start fighting shy of peace like punters what can't stop for fear of having to tot up what they lost. Before that it's war they're fighting shy of. It's something new to them.

RECRUITER: Hey, here's a cart coming. Two tarts with two young fellows. Stop her, sergeant. If this one's a flop I'm not standing around in your spring winds any longer, I can tell you.

Sound of a jew's-harp. Drawn by two young fellows, a covered cart rolls in. On it sit Mother Courage and her dumb daughter Kattrin.

MOTHER COURAGE: Morning, sergeant.

SERGEANT *blocking the way*: Morning, all And who are you?

MOTHER COURAGE: Business folk. *Sings*:

You captains, tell the drums to slacken
And give your infanteers a break:
It's Mother Courage with her waggon
Full of the finest boots they make.
With crawling lice and looted cattle
With lumbering guns and straggling kit –
How can you flog them into battle
Unless you get them boots that fit?

The new year's come. The watchmen shout.
The thaw sets in. The dead remain.
Wherever life has not died out
It staggers to its feet again.

Captains, how can you make them face it –
Marching to death without a brew?

Courage has rum with which to lace it
And boil their souls and bodies through.
Their musket primed, their stomach hollow –
Captains, your men don't look so well.
So feed them up and let them follow
While you command them into hell.
    The new year's come. The watchmen shout.
    The thaw sets in. The dead remain.
    Wherever life has not died out
    It staggers to its feet again.

SERGEANT: Halt! Who are you with, you trash?

THE ELDER SON: Second Finnish Regiment.

SERGEANT: Where's your papers?

MOTHER COURAGE: Papers?

THE YOUNGER SON: What, mean to say you don't know Mother Courage?

SERGEANT: Never heard of her. What's she called Courage for?

MOTHER COURAGE: Courage is the name they gave me because I was scared of going broke, sergeant, so I drove me cart right through the bombardment of Riga with fifty loaves of bread aboard. They were going mouldy, it was high time, hadn't any choice really.

SERGEANT: Don't be funny with me. Your papers.

MOTHER COURAGE *pulling a bundle of papers from a tin box and climbing down off the cart*: That's all my papers, sergeant. You'll find a whole big missal from Altötting in Bavaria for wrapping gherkins in, and a road map of Moravia, the Lord knows when I'll ever get there, might as well chuck it away, and here's a stamped certificate that my horse hasn't got foot-and-mouth, only he's dead worse luck, cost fifteen florins he did – not me luckily. That enough paper for you?

SERGEANT: You pulling my leg? I'll knock that sauce out of you. S'pose you know you got to have a licence.

MOTHER COURAGE: Talk proper to me, do you mind, and don't you dare say I'm pulling your leg in front of my unsullied children, 'tain't decent, I got no time for you. My honest face, that's me licence with the Second Regiment, and if it's too difficult for you to read there's nowt I can do about it. Nobody's putting a stamp on that.

RECRUITER: Sergeant, methinks I smell insubordination in this individual. What's needed in our camp is obedience.

MOTHER COURAGE: Sausage, if you ask me.

SERGEANT: Name.

MOTHER COURAGE: Anna Fierling.

SERGEANT: You all called Fierling then?

MOTHER COURAGE: What d'you mean? It's me's called Fierling, not them.

SERGEANT: Aren't all this lot your children?

MOTHER COURAGE: You bet they are, but why should they all have to be called the same, eh? *Pointing to her elder son:* For instance, that one's called Eilif Nojocki – Why? his father always claimed he was called Kojocki or Mojocki or something. The boy remembers him clearly, except that the one he remembers was someone else, a Frenchie with a little beard. Aside from that he's got his father's wits; that man knew how to snitch a peasant's pants off his bum without him noticing. This way each of us has his own name, see.

SERGEANT: What, each one different?

MOTHER COURAGE: Don't tell me you ain't never come across that.

SERGEANT: So I s'pose he's a Chinaman? *Pointing to the younger son.*

MOTHER COURAGE: Wrong. Swiss.

SERGEANT: After the Frenchman?

MOTHER COURAGE: What Frenchman? I never heard tell of no Frenchman. You keep muddling things up, we'll be hanging around here till dark. A Swiss, but called Fejos, and the name has nowt to do with his father. He was called something quite different and was a fortifications engineer, only drunk all the time.

Swiss Cheese beams and nods; dumb Kattrin too is amused.

SERGEANT: How in hell can he be called Fejos?

MOTHER COURAGE: I don't like to be rude, sergeant, but you ain't got much imagination, have you? Course he's called Fejos, because when he arrived I was with a Hungarian, very decent fellow, had terrible kidney trouble though he never touched a drop. The boy takes after him.

SERGEANT: But he wasn't his father . . .

MOTHER COURAGE: Took after him just the same. I call him Swiss Cheese. *Pointing to her daughter:* And that's Kattrin Haupt, she's half German.

SERGEANT: Nice family, I must say.

MOTHER COURAGE: Aye, me cart and me have seen the world.

SERGEANT: I'm writing all this down. *He writes.* And you're from Bamberg in Bavaria; how d'you come to be here?

MOTHER COURAGE: Can't wait till war chooses to visit Bamberg, can I?

RECRUITER *to Eilif:* You two should be called Jacob Ox and Esau Ox, pulling the cart like that. I s'pose you never get out of harness?

EILIF: Ma, can I clobber him one? I wouldn't half like to.

MOTHER COURAGE: And I says you can't; just you stop where you are. And now two fine officers like you, I bet you could use a good pistol, or a belt buckle, yours is on its last legs, sergeant.

SERGEANT: I could use something else. Those boys are healthy as young birch trees, I observe: chests like barrels, solid leg muscles. So why are they dodging their military service, may I ask?

MOTHER COURAGE *quickly:* Nowt doing, sergeant. Yours is no trade for my kids.

RECRUITER: But why not? There's good money in it, glory

too. Flogging boots is women's work. *To Eilif:* Come here, let's see if you've muscles in you or if you're a chicken.

MOTHER COURAGE: He's a chicken. Give him a fierce look, he'll fall over.

RECRUITER: Killing a young bull that happens to be in his way. *Wants to lead him off.*

MOTHER COURAGE: Let him alone, will you? He's nowt for you folk.

RECRUITER: He was crudely offensive and talked about clobbering me. The two of us are going to step into that field and settle it man to man.

EILIF: Don't you worry, mum, I'll fix him.

MOTHER COURAGE: Stop there! You varmint! I know you, nowt but fights. There's a knife down his boot. A slasher, that's what he is.

RECRUITER: I'll draw it out of him like a milk-tooth. Come along, sonny.

MOTHER COURAGE: Sergeant, I'll tell the colonel. He'll have you both in irons. The lieutenant's going out with my daughter.

SERGEANT: No rough stuff, chum. *To Mother Courage:* What you got against military service? Wasn't his own father a soldier? Died a soldier's death, too? Said it yourself.

MOTHER COURAGE: He's nowt but a child. You want to take him off to slaughterhouse, I know you lot. They'll give you five florins for him.

RECRUITER: First he's going to get a smart cap and boots, eh?

EILIF: Not from you.

MOTHER COURAGE: Let's both go fishing, said angler to worm. *To Swiss Cheese:* Run off, call out they're trying to kidnap your brother. *She pulls a knife:* Go on, you kidnap him, just try. I'll slit you open, trash. I'll teach you to make war with him. We're doing an honest trade in ham and linen, and we're peaceable folk.

SERGEANT: Peaceable I don't think; look at your knife. You should be ashamed of yourself; put that knife away, you old harridan. A minute back you were admitting you live off the war, how else should you live, what from? But how's anyone to have war without soldiers?

MOTHER COURAGE: No need for it to be my kids.

SERGEANT: Oh, you'd like war to eat the pips but spit out the apple? It's to fatten up your kids, but you won't invest in it. Got to look after itself, eh? And you called Courage, fancy that. Scared of the war that keeps you going? Your sons aren't scared of it, I can see that.

EILIF: Take more than a war to scare me.

SERGEANT: And why? Look at me: has army life done all that badly by me? Joined up at seventeen.

MOTHER COURAGE: Still got to reach seventy.

SERGEANT: I don't mind waiting.

MOTHER COURAGE: Under the sod, eh?

SERGEANT: You trying to insult me, saying I'll die?

MOTHER COURAGE: S'pose it's true? S'pose I can see the mark's on you? S'pose you look like a corpse on leave to me? Eh?

SWISS CHEESE: She's got second sight, Mother has.

RECRUITER: Go ahead, tell the sergeant's fortune, might amuse him.

MOTHER COURAGE: Gimme helmet. *He gives it to her.*

SERGEANT: It don't mean a bloody sausage. Anything for a laugh though.

MOTHER COURAGE *taking out a sheet of parchment and tearing it up*: Eilif, Swiss Cheese and Kattrin, may all of us be torn apart like this if we lets ourselves get too mixed up in the war. *To the Sergeant:* Just for you I'm doing it for free. Black's for death. I'm putting a big black cross on this slip of paper.

SWISS CHEESE: Leaving the other one blank, see?

MOTHER COURAGE: Then I fold them across and shake

them. All of us is jumbled together like this from our mother's womb, and now draw a slip and you'll know. *The Sergeant hesitates.*

RECRUITER *to Eilif*: I don't take just anybody, they all know I'm choosey, but you got the kind of fire I like to see.

SERGEANT *fishing in the helmet*: Too silly. Load of eyewash.

SWISS CHEESE: Drawn a black cross, he has. Write him off.

RECRUITER: They're having you on; not everybody's name's on a bullet.

SERGEANT *hoarsely*: You've put me in the shit.

MOTHER COURAGE: Did that yourself the day you became a soldier. Come along, let's move on now. 'Tain't every day we have a war, I got to get stirring.

SERGEANT: God damn it, you can't kid me. We're taking that bastard of yours for a soldier.

EILIF: Swiss Cheese'd like to be a soldier too.

MOTHER COURAGE: First I've heard of that. You'll have to draw too, all three of you. *She goes to the rear to mark crosses on further slips.*

RECRUITER *to Eilif*: One of the things they say against us is that it's all holy-holy in the Swedish camp; but that's a malicious rumour to do us down. There's no hymn-singing but Sundays, just a single verse, and then only for those got voices.

MOTHER COURAGE *coming back with the slips, which she drops into the sergeant's helmet*: Trying to get away from their ma, the devils, off to war like calves to salt-lick. But I'm making you draw lots, and that'll show you the world is no vale of joys with 'Come along, son, we need a few more generals'. Sergeant, I'm so scared they won't get through the war. Such dreadful characters, all three of them. *She hands the helmet to Eilif.* Hey, come on, fish out your slip. *He fishes one out, unfolds it. She snatches it from him.* There you are, it's a cross. Oh, wretched mother that I am, o pain-racked giver of birth! Shall he die? Aye, in the springtime of life he is doomed. If he becomes a soldier he shall bite the dust, it's plain to see. He is too foolhardy, like his dad was. And if he ain't sensible he'll go the way of all flesh, his slip proves it. *Shouts at him*: You going to be sensible?

EILIF: Why not?

MOTHER COURAGE: Sensible thing is stay with your mother, never mind if they poke fun at you and call you chicken, just you laugh.

RECRUITER: If you're pissing in your pants I'll make do with your brother.

MOTHER COURAGE: I told you laugh. Go on, laugh. Now you draw, Swiss Cheese. I'm not so scared on your account, you're honest. *He fishes in the helmet.* Oh, why look at your slip in that strange way? It's got to be a blank. There can't be any cross on it. Surely I'm not going to lose *you*. *She takes the slip.* A cross? What, you too? Is that because you're so simple, perhaps? O Swiss Cheese, you too will be sunk if you don't stay utterly honest all the while, like I taught you from childhood when you brought the change back from the baker's. Else you can't save yourself. Look, sergeant, that's a black cross, ain't it?

SERGEANT: A cross, that's right. Can't think how I come to get one. I always stay in the rear. *To the Recruiter:* There's no catch. Her own family get it too.

SWISS CHEESE: I get it too. But I listen to what I'm told.

MOTHER COURAGE *to Kattrin*: And now you're the only one I know's all right, you're a cross yourself; got a kind heart you have. *Holds the helmet up to her on the cart, but takes the slip out herself.* No, that's too much. That can't be right; must have made a mistake shuffling. Don't be too kind-hearted, Kattrin, you'll have to give it up, there's a cross above your path too. Lie doggo, girl, it can't be that hard once you're born dumb, Right, all of you know now. Look out for yourselves, you'll need to. And now up we get and on we go. *She climbs on to the cart.*

RECRUITER *to the sergeant*: Do something.

SERGEANT: I don't feel very well.

RECRUITER: Must of caught a chill taking your helmet off in that wind. Involve her in a deal. *Aloud:* Might as well have a look at that belt-buckle, sergeant. After all, our friends here have to live by their business. Hey, you people, the sergeant wants to buy that belt-buckle.

MOTHER COURAGE: Half a florin. Two florins is what a belt like that's worth. *Climbs down again.*

SERGEANT: 'Tain't new. Let me get out of this damned wind and have a proper look at it. *Goes behind the cart with the buckle.*

MOTHER COURAGE: Ain't what I call windy.

SERGEANT: I s'pose it might be worth half a florin, it's silver.

MOTHER COURAGE *joining him behind the cart*: It's six solid ounces.

RECRUITER *to Eilif*: And then we men'll have one together. Got your bounty money here, come along. *Eilif stands undecided.*

MOTHER COURAGE: Half a florin it is.

SERGEANT: It beats me. I'm always at the rear. Sergeant's the safest job there is. You can send the others up front, cover themselves with glory. Me dinner hour's properly spoiled. Shan't be able to hold nowt down, I know.

MOTHER COURAGE: Mustn't let it prey on you so's you can't eat. Just stay at the rear. Here, take a swig of brandy, man. *Gives him a drink.*

RECRUITER *has taken Eilif by the arm and is leading him away up stage*: Ten florins bounty money, then you're a gallant fellow fighting for the king and women'll be after you like flies. And you can clobber me for free for insulting you. *Exeunt both.*

Dumb Kattrin leans down from the cart and makes hoarse noises.

MOTHER COURAGE: All right, Kattrin, all right. Sergeant's just paying. *Bites the half-florin.* I got no faith in any kind of money. Burnt child, that's me, sergeant. This coin's good, though. And now let's get moving. Where's Eilif?

SWISS CHEESE: Went off with the recruiter.

MOTHER COURAGE *stands quite still, then*: You simpleton. *To Kattrin*: 'Tain't your fault, you can't speak, I know.

SERGEANT: Could do with a swig yourself, ma. That's life. Plenty worse things than being a soldier. Want to live off war, but keep yourself and family out of it, eh?

MOTHER COURAGE: You'll have to help your brother pull now, Kattrin.

Brother and sister hitch themselves to the cart and start pulling. Mother Courage walks alongside. The cart rolls on.

SERGEANT *looking after them*:

Like the war to nourish you?
Have to feed it something too.

2

In the years 1625 and 1626 Mother Courage crosses Poland in the train of the Swedish armies. Before the fortress of Wallhof she meets her son again. Successful sale of a capon and heyday of her dashing son

The general's tent.

Beside it, his kitchen. Thunder of cannon. The cook is arguing with Mother Courage, who wants to sell him a capon.

THE COOK: Sixty hellers for a miserable bird like that?

MOTHER COURAGE: Miserable bird? This fat brute? Mean

to say some greedy old general – and watch your step if you got nowt for his dinner – can't afford sixty hellers for him?

THE COOK: I can get a dozen like that for ten hellers just down the road.

MOTHER COURAGE: What, a capon like this you can get just down the road? In time of siege, which means hunger that tears your guts. A rat you might get: 'might' I say because they're all being gobbled up, five men spending best part of day chasing one hungry rat. Fifty hellers for a giant capon in time of siege!

THE COOK: But it ain't us having the siege, it's t'other side. We're conducting the siege, can't you get that in your head?

MOTHER COURAGE: But we got nowt to eat too, even worse than them in the town. Took it with them, didn't they? They're having a high old time, everyone says. And look at us! I been to the peasants, there's nowt there.

THE COOK: There's plenty. They're sitting on it.

MOTHER COURAGE *triumphantly*: They ain't. They're bust, that's what they are. Just about starving. I saw some, were grubbing up roots from sheer hunger, licking their fingers after they boiled some old leather strap. That's way it is. And me got a capon here and supposed to take forty hellers for it.

THE COOK: Thirty, not forty. I said thirty.

MOTHER COURAGE: Here, this ain't just any old capon. It was such a gifted beast, I been told, it could only eat to music, had a military march of its own. It could count, it was that intelligent. And you say forty hellers is too much? General will make mincemeat of you if there's nowt on his table.

THE COOK: See what I'm doing? *He takes a piece of beef and puts his knife to it.* Here I got a bit of beef, I'm going to roast it. Make up your mind quick.

MOTHER COURAGE: Go on, roast it. It's last year's.

THE COOK: Last night's. That animal was still alive and kicking, I saw him myself.

MOTHER COURAGE: Alive and stinking, you mean.

THE COOK: I'll cook him five hours if need be. I'll just see if he's still tough. *He cuts into it.*

MOTHER COURAGE: Put plenty of pepper on it so his lordship the general don't smell the pong.

The general, a chaplain and Eilif enter the tent.

THE GENERAL *slapping Eilif on the shoulder*: Now then, Eilif my son, into your general's tent with you and sit thou at my right hand. For you accomplished a deed of heroism, like a pious cavalier; and doing what you did for God, and in a war of religion at that, is something I commend in you most highly, you shall have a gold bracelet as soon as we've taken this town. Here we are, come to save their souls for them, and what do those insolent dung-encrusted yokels go and do? Drive their beef away from us. They stuff it into those priests of theirs all right, back and front, but you taught 'em manners, ha! So here's a pot of red wine for you, the two of us'll knock it back at one gulp. *They do so.* Piss all for the chaplain, the old bigot. And now, what would you like for dinner, my darling?

EILIF: A bit of meat, why not?

THE GENERAL: Cook! Meat!

THE COOK: And then he goes and brings guests when there's nowt there.

Mother Courage silences him so she can listen.

EILIF: Hungry job cutting down peasants.

MOTHER COURAGE: Jesus Christ, it's my Eilif.

THE COOK: Your what?

MOTHER COURAGE: My eldest boy. It's two years since I lost sight of him, they pinched him from me on the road, must think well of him if the general's asking him to dinner, and what kind of a dinner can you offer? Nowt. You heard what the visitor wishes to eat: meat. Take my tip, you settle for the capon, it'll be a florin.

THE GENERAL *has sat down with Eilif, and bellows*: Food, Lamb, you foul cook, or I'll have your hide.

THE COOK: Give it over, dammit, this is blackmail.

MOTHER COURAGE: Didn't someone say it was a miserable bird?

THE COOK: Miserable; give it over, and a criminal price, fifty hellers.

MOTHER COURAGE: A florin, I said. For my eldest boy, the general's guest, no expense is too great for me.

THE COOK *gives her the money*: You might at least pluck it while I see to the fire.

MOTHER COURAGE *sits down to pluck the fowl*: He won't half be surprised to see me. He's my dashing clever son. Then I got a stupid one too, he's honest though. The girl's nowt. One good thing, she don't talk.

THE GENERAL: Drink up, my son, this is my best Falernian; only got a barrel or two left, but that's nothing to pay for a sign that's there's still true faith to be found in my army. As for that shepherd of souls he can just look on, because all he does is preach, without the least idea how it's to be carried out. And now, my son Eilif, tell us more about the neat way you smashed those yokels and captured the twenty oxen. Let's hope they get here soon.

EILIF: A day or two at most.

MOTHER COURAGE: Thoughtful of our Eilif not to bring the oxen in till tomorrow, else you lot wouldn't have looked twice at my capon.

EILIF: Well, it was like this, see. I'd heard peasants had been driving the oxen they'd hidden, out of the forest into one particular wood, on the sly and mostly by night. That's where people from the town were s'posed to come and pick them up. So I holds off and lets them drive their oxen together, reckoning they'd be better than me at finding 'em.

I had my blokes slavering after the meat, cut their emergency rations even further for a couple of days till their mouths was watering at the least sound of any word beginning with 'me-', like 'measles' say.

THE GENERAL: Very clever of you.

EILIF: Possibly. The rest was a piece of cake. Except that the peasants had cudgels and outnumbered us three to one and made a murderous attack on us. Four of 'em shoved me into a thicket, knocked my sword from my hand and bawled out 'Surrender!' What's the answer, I wondered; they're going to make mincemeat of me.

THE GENERAL: What did you do?

EILIF: I laughed.

THE GENERAL: You did what?

EILIF: Laughed. So we got talking. I put it on a business footing from the start, told them 'Twenty florins a head's too much. I'll give you fifteen'. As if I was meaning to pay. That threw them, and they began scratching their heads. In a flash I'd picked up my sword and was hacking 'em to pieces. Necessity's the mother of invention, eh, sir?

THE GENERAL: What is your view, pastor of souls?

THE CHAPLAIN: That phrase is not strictly speaking in the Bible, but when Our Lord turned the five loaves into five hundred there was no war on and he could tell people to love their neighbours as they'd had enough to eat. Today it's another story.

THE GENERAL laughs: Quite another story. You can have a swig after all for that, you old Pharisee. To Eilif: Hacked 'em to pieces, did you, so my gallant lads can get a proper bite to eat? What do the Scriptures say? 'Whatsoever thou doest for the least of my brethren, thou doest for me'. And what did you do for them? Got them a good square meal of beef, because they're not accustomed to mouldy bread, the old way was to fix a cold meal of rolls and wine in your helmet before you went out to fight for God.

EILIF: Aye, in a flash I'd picked up my sword and was hacking them to pieces.

THE GENERAL: You've the makings of a young Caesar. You ought to see the King.

EILIF: I have from a distance. He kind of glows. I'd like to model myself on him.

THE GENERAL: You've got something in common already. I appreciate soldiers like you, Eilif, men of courage. Somebody like that I treat as I would my own son. *He leads him over to the map.* Have a look at the situation, Eilif; it's a long haul still.

MOTHER COURAGE *who has been listening and now angrily plucks the fowl*: That must be a rotten general.

THE COOK: He's ravenous all right, but why rotten?

MOTHER COURAGE: Because he's got to have men of courage, that's why. If he knew how to plan a proper campaign what would he be needing men of courage for? Ordinary ones would do. It's always the same; whenever there's a load of special virtues around it means something stinks.

THE COOK: I thought it meant things is all right.

MOTHER COURAGE: No, that they stink. Look, s'pose some general or king is bone stupid and leads his men up shit creek, then those men've got to be fearless, there's another virtue for you. S'pose he's stingy and hires too few soldiers, then they got to be a crowd of Hercules's. And s'pose he's slapdash and don't give a bugger, then they got to be clever as monkeys else their number's up. Same way they got to show exceptional loyalty each time he gives them impossible jobs. Nowt but virtues no proper country and no decent king or general would ever need. In decent countries folk don't have to have virtues, the whole lot can be perfectly ordinary, average intelligence, and for all I know cowards.

THE GENERAL: I'll wager your father was a soldier.

EILIF: A great soldier, I been told. My mother warned me about it. There's a song I know.

THE GENERAL: Sing it to us. *Roars:* When's that dinner coming?

EILIF: It's called The Song of the Girl and the Soldier.

He sings it, dancing a war dance with his sabre:

> The guns blaze away, and the bay'nit'll slay
> And the water can't hardly be colder.
> What's the answer to ice? Keep off's my advice!
> That's what the girl told the soldier.
> Next thing the soldier, wiv' a round up the spout
> Hears the band playing and gives a great shout:
> Why, it's marching what makes you a soldier!
> So it's down to the south and then northwards once more:
> See him catching that bay'nit in his naked paw!
> That's what his comrades done told her.

> Oh, do not despise the advice of the wise
> Learn wisdom from those that are older
> And don't try for things that are out of your reach –
> That's what the girl told the soldier.
> Next thing the soldier, his bay'nit in place
> Wades into the river and laughs in her face
> Though the water comes up to his shoulder.
> When the shingle roof glints in the light o' the moon
> We'll be wiv' you again, not a moment too soon!
> That's what his comrades done told her.

MOTHER COURAGE *takes up the song in the kitchen, beating on a pot with her spoon*:

> You'll go out like a light! And the sun'll take flight
> For your courage just makes us feel colder.
> Oh, that vanishing light! May God see that it's right! –
> That's what the girl told the soldier.

EILIF: What's that?

MOTHER COURAGE *continues singing*:

> Next thing the soldier, his bay'nit in place
> Was caught by the current and went down without trace
> And the water couldn't hardly be colder.
> The the shingle roof froze in the light o' the moon
> As both soldier and ice drifted down to their doom –
> And d'you know what his comrades done told her?

> He went out like a light. And the sunshine took flight
> For his courage just made 'em feel colder.
> Oh, do not despise the advice of the wise!
> That's what the girl told the soldier.

THE GENERAL: The things they get up to in my kitchen these days.

EILIF *has gone into the kitchen. He flings his arms round his mother*: Fancy seeing you again, ma! Where's the others?

MOTHER COURAGE *in his arms*: Snug as a bug in a rug. They made Swiss Cheese paymaster of the Second Finnish; any road he'll stay out of fighting that way, I couldn't keep him out altogether.

EILIF: How's the old feet?

MOTHER COURAGE: Bit tricky getting me shoes on of a morning.

THE GENERAL *has joined them*: So you're his mother, I hope you've got plenty more sons for me like this one.

EILIF: Ain't it my lucky day? You sitting out there in the kitchen, ma, hearing your son commended . . .

MOTHER COURAGE: You bet I heard. *Slaps his face.*

EILIF *holding his cheek*: What's that for? Taking the oxen?

MOTHER COURAGE: No. Not surrendering when those four went for you and wanted to make mincemeat of you. Didn't I say you should look after yourself? You Finnish devil!

The general and the chaplain stand in the doorway laughing.

3

Three years later Mother Courage is taken prisoner along with elements of a Finnish regiment. She manages to save her daughter, likewise her covered cart, but her honest son is killed

Military camp.

Afternoon. A flagpole with the regimental flag. From her cart, festooned now with all kinds of goods, Mother Courage has stretched a washing line to a large cannon, across which she and Kattrin are folding the washing. She is bargaining at the same time with an armourer over a sack of shot. Swiss Cheese, now wearing a paymaster's uniform, is looking on.

A comely person, Yvette Pottier, is sewing a gaily coloured hat, a glass of brandy before her. She is in her stockinged feet, having laid aside her red high-heeled boots.

THE ARMOURER: I'll let you have that shot for a couple of florins. It's cheap at the price, I got to have the money because the colonel's been boozing with his officers since two days back, and the drink's run out.

MOTHER COURAGE: That's troops' munitions. They catch me with that, I'm for court-martial. You crooks flog the shot, and troops got nowt to fire at enemy.

THE ARMOURER: Have a heart, can't you; you scratch my back and I'll scratch yours.

MOTHER COURAGE: I'm not taking army property. Not at that price.

THE ARMOURER: You can sell it on the q.t. tonight to the Fourth Regiment's armourer for five florins, eight even, if you let him have a receipt for twelve. He's right out of ammunition.

MOTHER COURAGE: Why not you do it?

THE ARMOURER: I don't trust him, he's a pal of mine.

MOTHER COURAGE *takes the sack*: Gimme. *To Kattrin*: Take it away and pay him a florin and a half. *The armourer protests.* I said a florin and a half. *Kattrin drags the sack upstage, the armourer following her. Mother Courage addresses Swiss Cheese*: Here's your woollies, now look after them, it's October and autumn may set in any time. I ain't saying it's got to, cause I've learned nowt's got to come when you think it will, not even seasons of the year. But your regimental accounts got to add up right, come what may. Do they add up right?

SWISS CHEESE: Yes, mother.

MOTHER COURAGE: Don't you forget they made you paymaster cause you was honest, not dashing like your brother, and above all so stupid I bet you ain't even thought of clearing off with it, no not you. That's a big consolation to me. And don't lose those woollies.

SWISS CHEESE: No, mother, I'll put them under my mattress. *Begins to go.*

THE ARMOURER: I'll go along with you, paymaster.

MOTHER COURAGE: And don't you start learning him none of your tricks.

The armourer leaves with Swiss Cheese without any farewell gesture.

YVETTE *waving to him*: No reason not to say goodbye, armourer.

MOTHER COURAGE *to Yvette*: I don't like to see them together. He's wrong company for our Swiss Cheese. Oh well, war's off to a good start. Easily take four, five years before all countries are in. A bit of foresight, don't do nothing silly, and business'll flourish. Don't you know you ain't s'posed to drink before midday with your complaint?

YVETTE: Complaint, who says so, it's a libel.

MOTHER COURAGE: They all say so.

YVETTE: Because they're all telling lies, Mother Courage, and me at my wits' end cause they're all avoiding me like something the cat brought in thanks to those lies, what the hell am I remodelling my hat for? *She throws it away.* That's why I drink before midday. Never used to, gives you crows' feet, but now what the hell? All the Second Finnish know me. Ought to have stayed at home when my first fellow did me wrong. No good our sort being proud. Eat shit, that's what you got to do, or down you go.

MOTHER COURAGE: Now don't you start up again about that Pieter of yours and how it all happened, in front of my innocent daughter too.

YVETTE: She's the one should hear it, put her off love.

MOTHER COURAGE: Nobody can put 'em off that.

YVETTE: Then I'll go on, get it off my chest. It all starts with yours truly growing up in lovely Flanders, else I'd never of seen him and wouldn't be stuck here now in Poland, cause he was an army cook, fair-haired, a Dutchman but thin for once. Kattrin, watch out for the thin ones, only in those days I didn't know that, or that he'd got a girl already, or that they all called him Puffing Piet cause he never took his pipe out of his mouth when he was on the job, it meant that little to him. *She sings the Song of Fraternisation:*

> When I was only sixteen
> The foe came into our land.
> He laid aside his sabre
> And with a smile he took my hand.
> After the May parade
> The May light starts to fade.
> The regiment dressed by the right
> The drums were beaten, that's the drill.
> The foe took us behind the hill
> And fraternised all night.

There were so many foes then
But mine worked in the mess.
I loathed him in the daytime.
At night I loved him none the less.
After the May parade
The May light starts to fade.
The regiment dressed by the right
The drums were beaten, that's the drill.
The foe took us behind the hill
And fraternised all night.

The love which came upon me
Was wished on me by fate.
My friends could never grasp why
I found it hard to share their hate.
The fields were wet with dew
When sorrow first I knew.
The regiment dressed by the right
The drums were beaten, that's the drill.
And then the foe, my lover still
Went marching out of sight.

I followed him, fool that I was, but I never found him,
and that was five years back. *She walks unsteadily behind the
cart.*

MOTHER COURAGE: You left your hat here.

YVETTE: Anyone wants it can have it.

MOTHER COURAGE: Let that be a lesson, Kattrin. Don't
you start anything with them soldiers. Love makes the
world go round, I'm warning you. Even with fellows not in
the army it's no bed of roses. He says he'd like to kiss the
ground your feet walk on – reminds me, did you wash them
yesterday? – and after that you're his skivvy. Be thankful
you're dumb, then you can't contradict yourself and won't
be wanting to bite your tongue off for speaking the truth;

it's a godsend, being dumb is. And here comes the general's cook, now what's he after?

Enter the cook and the chaplain.

THE CHAPLAIN: I have a message for you from your son Eilif, and the cook has come along because you made such a profound impression on him.

THE COOK: I just came along to get a bit of air.

MOTHER COURAGE: That you can always do here if you behave yourself, and if you don't I can deal with you. What does he want? I got no spare cash.

THE CHAPLAIN: Actually I had a message for his brother the paymaster.

MOTHER COURAGE: He ain't here now nor anywhere else neither. He ain't his brother's paymaster. He's not to lead him into temptation nor be clever at his expense. *Giving him money from the purse slung round her:* Give him this, it's a sin, he's banking on mother's love and ought to be ashamed of himself.

THE COOK: Not for long, he'll have to be moving off with the regiment, might be to his death. Give him a bit extra, you'll be sorry later. You women are tough, then later on you're sorry. A little glass of brandy wouldn't have been a problem, but it wasn't offered and, who knows, a bloke may lie beneath the green sod and none of you people will ever be able to dig him up again.

THE CHAPLAIN: Don't give way to your feelings, cook. To fall in battle is a blessing, not an inconvenience, and why? It is a war of faith. None of your common wars but a special one, fought for the faith and therefore pleasing to God.

THE COOK: Very true. It's a war all right in one sense, what with requisitioning, murder and looting and the odd bit of rape thrown in, but different from all the other wars because it's a war of faith; stands to reason. But it's thirsty work at that, you must admit.

THE CHAPLAIN *to Mother Courage, indicating the Cook*: I tried to stop him, but he says he's taken a shine to you, you figure in his dreams.

THE COOK *lighting a stumpy pipe*: Just want a glass of brandy from a fair hand, what harm in that? Only I'm groggy already cause the chaplain here's been telling such jokes all the way along you bet I'm still blushing.

MOTHER COURAGE: Him a clergyman too. I'd best give the pair of you a drink or you'll start making me immoral suggestions cause you've nowt else to do.

THE CHAPLAIN: Behold a temptation, said the court preacher, and fell. *Turning back to look at Kattrin as he leaves:* And who is this entrancing young person?

MOTHER COURAGE: That ain't an entrancing but a decent young person. *The chaplain and the cook go behind the cart with Mother Courage. Kattrin looks after them, then walks away from her washing towards the hat. She picks it up and sits down, pulling the red boots towards her. Mother Courage can be heard in the background talking politics with the chaplain and the cook.*

MOTHER COURAGE: Those Poles here in Poland had no business sticking their noses in. Right, our king moved in on them, horse and foot, but did they keep the peace? no, went and stuck their noses into their own affairs, they did, and fell on king just as he was quietly clearing off. They committed a breach of peace, that's what, so blood's on their own head.

THE CHAPLAIN: All our king minded about was freedom. The emperor had made slaves of them all, Poles and Germans alike, and the king had to liberate them.

THE COOK: Just what I say, your brandy's first rate, I weren't mistaken in your face, but talk of the king, it cost the king dear trying to give freedom to Germany, what with giving Sweden the salt tax, what cost the poor folk a bit, so I've heard, on top of which he had to have the Germans locked up and drawn and quartered cause they wanted to carry on slaving for the emperor. Course the king took a serious view when anybody didn't want to be free. He set out by just trying to protect Poland against bad people, particularly the emperor, then it started to become a habit till he ended up protecting the whole of Germany. They didn't half kick. So the poor old king's had nowt but trouble for all his kindness and expenses, and that's something he had to make up for by taxes of course, which caused bad blood, not that he'd let a little matter like that depress him. One thing he had on his side, God's word, that was a help. Because otherwise folk would of been saying he done it all for himself and to make a bit on the side. So he's always had a good conscience, which was the main point.

MOTHER COURAGE: Anyone can see you're no Swede or you wouldn't be talking that way about the Hero King.

THE CHAPLAIN: After all he provides the bread you eat.

THE COOK: I don't eat it, I bake it.

MOTHER COURAGE: They'll never beat him, and why, his men got faith in him. *Seriously:* To go by what the big shots say, they're waging war for almighty God and in the name of everything that's good and lovely. But look closer, they ain't so silly, they're waging it for what they can get. Else little folk like me wouldn't be in it at all.

THE COOK: That's the way it is.

THE CHAPLAIN: As a Dutchman you'd do better to glance at the flag above your head before venting your opinions here in Poland.

MOTHER COURAGE: All good Lutherans here. Prosit!

Kattrin has put on Yvette's hat and begun strutting around in imitation of her way of walking.

Suddenly there is a noise of cannon fire and shooting. Drums. Mother Courage, the Cook and the Chaplain rush out from behind the cart, the two last-named still carrying their glasses. The armourer and another soldier run up to the cannon and try to push it away.

MOTHER COURAGE: What's happening? Wait till I've taken my washing down, you louts! *She tries to rescue her washing.*

THE ARMOURER: The Catholics! Broken through. Don't know if we'll get out of here. *To the soldier:* Get that gun shifted! *Runs on.*

THE COOK: God, I must find the general. Courage, I'll drop by in a day or two for another talk.

MOTHER COURAGE: Wait, you forgot your pipe.

THE COOK *in the distance:* Keep it for me. I'll be needing it.

MOTHER COURAGE: Would happen just as we're making a bit of money.

THE CHAPLAIN: Ah well, I'll be going too. Indeed, if the enemy is so close as that it might be dangerous. Bléssed are the peacemakers is the motto in wartime. If only I had a cloak to cover me.

MOTHER COURAGE: I ain't lending no cloaks, not on your life. I been had too often.

THE CHAPLAIN: But my faith makes it particularly dangerous for me.

MOTHER COURAGE *gets him a cloak:* Goes against my conscience, this does. Now you run along.

THE CHAPLAIN: Thank you, dear lady, that's very generous of you, but I think it might be wiser for me to remain seated here; it could arouse suspicion and bring the enemy down on me if I were seen to run.

MOTHER COURAGE *to the soldier:* Leave it, you fool, who's going to pay you for that? I'll look after it for you, you're risking your neck.

THE SOLDIER *running away:* You can tell 'em I tried.

MOTHER COURAGE: Cross my heart. *Sees her daughter with the hat.* What you doing with that strumpet's hat? Take that lid off, you gone crazy? And the enemy arriving any minute! *Pulls the hat off Kattrin's head.* Want 'em to pick you up and make a prostitute of you? And she's gone and put those boots on, whore of Babylon! Off with those boots! *Tries to tug them off her.* Jesus Christ, chaplain, gimme a hand, get those boots off her, I'll be right back. *Runs to the cart.*

YVETTE *arrives, powdering her face*: Fancy that, the Catholics are coming. Where's my hat? Who's been kicking it around? I can't go about looking like this if the Catholics are coming. What'll they think of me? No mirror either. *To the chaplain:* How do I look? Too much powder?

THE CHAPLAIN: Exactly right.

YVETTE: And where are them red boots? *Fails to find them as Kattrin hides her feet under her skirt.* I left them here all right. Now I'll have to get to me tent barefoot. It's an outrage. *Exit.*

Swiss Cheese runs in carrying in a small box.

MOTHER COURAGE *arrives with her hands full of ashes. To Kattrin*: Here some ashes. *To Swiss Cheese:* What's that you're carrying?

SWISS CHEESE: Regimental cash box.

MOTHER COURAGE: Chuck it away. No more paymastering for you.

SWISS CHEESE: I'm responsible. *He goes to the rear.*

MOTHER COURAGE *to the chaplain*: Take your clerical togs off, padre, or they'll spot you under that cloak. *She rubs Kattrin's face with ash.* Keep still, will you? There you are, a bit of muck and you'll be safe. What a disaster. Sentries were drunk. Hide your light under a bushel, it says. Take a soldier, specially a Catholic one, add a clean face, and there's your instant whore. For weeks they get nowt to eat, then soon as they manage to get it by looting they're falling on anything in skirts. That ought to do. Let's have a look. Not bad. Looks like you been grubbing in muckheap. Stop trembling. Nothing'll happen to you like that. *To Swiss Cheese:* Where d'you leave cash box?

SWISS CHEESE: Thought I'd put it in cart.

MOTHER COURAGE *horrified*: What, my cart? Sheer criminal

idiocy. Only take me eyes off you one instant. Hang us all three, they will.

SWISS CHEESE: I'll put it somewhere else then, or clear out with it.

MOTHER COURAGE: You sit on it, it's too late now.

CHAPLAIN *who is changing his clothes downstage:* For heaven's sake, the flag!

MOTHER COURAGE *hauls down the regimental flag:* Bozhe moi! I'd given up noticing it were there. Twenty-five years I've had it.

The thunder of cannon intensifies.

A morning three days later. The cannon has gone. Mother Courage, Kattrin, the Chaplain and Swiss Cheese are sitting gloomily over a meal.

SWISS CHEESE: That's three days I been sitting around with nowt to do, and sergeant's always been kind to me but any moment now he'll start asking where's Swiss Cheese with the pay box?

MOTHER COURAGE: You thank your stars they ain't after you.

THE CHAPLAIN: What can I say? I can't even hold a service here, it might make trouble for me. Whosoever hath a full heart, his tongue runneth over, it says, but heaven help me if mine starts running over.

MOTHER COURAGE: That's how it goes. Here they sit, one with his faith and the other with his cash box. Dunno which is more dangerous.

THE CHAPLAIN: We are all of us in God's hands.

MOTHER COURAGE: Oh, I don't think it's as bad as that yet, though I must say I can't sleep nights. If it weren't for you, Swiss Cheese, things'd be easier. I think I got meself cleared. I told 'em I didn't hold with Antichrist, the Swedish one with horns on, and I'd observed left horn was a bit unserviceable. Half way through their interrogation I asked

where I could get church candles not too dear. I knows the
lingo cause Swiss Cheese's dad were Catholic, often used to
make jokes about it, he did. They didn't believe me all that
much, but they ain't got no regimental canteen lady. So
they're winking an eye. Could turn out for the best, you
know. We're prisoners, but same like fleas on dog.

THE CHAPLAIN: That's good milk. But we'll need to cut
down our Swedish appetites a bit. After all, we've been
defeated.

MOTHER COURAGE: Who's been defeated? Look, victory
and defeat ain't bound to be same for the big shots up top
as for them below, not by no means. Can be times the
bottom lot find a defeat really pays them. Honour's lost,
nowt else. I remember once up in Livonia our general took
such a beating from enemy I got a horse off our baggage
train in the confusion, pulled me cart seven months, he did,
before we won and they checked up. As a rule you can say
victory and defeat both come expensive to us ordinary folk.
Best thing for us is when politics get bogged down solid.
To Swiss Cheese: Eat up.

SWISS CHEESE: Got no appetite for it. What's sergeant to do
when pay day comes round?

MOTHER COURAGE: They don't have pay days on a retreat.

SWISS CHEESE: It's their right, though. They needn't retreat
if they don't get paid. Needn't stir a foot.

MOTHER COURAGE: Swiss Cheese, you're that conscientious
it makes me quite nervous. I brought you up to be honest,
you not being clever, but you got to know where to stop.
Chaplain and me, we're off now to buy Catholic flag and
some meat. Dunno anyone so good at sniffing meat, like
sleepwalking it is, straight to target. I'd say he can pick out
a good piece by the way his mouth starts watering. Well,
thank goodness they're letting me go on trading. You don't
ask tradespeople their faith but their prices. And Lutheran
trousers keep cold out too.

THE CHAPLAIN: What did the mendicant say when he heard the Lutherans were going to turn everything in town and country topsy-turvy? 'They'll always need beggars'. *Mother Courage disappears into the cart.* So she's still worried about the cash box. So far they've taken us all for granted as part of the cart, but how long for?

SWISS CHEESE: I can get rid of it.

THE CHAPLAIN: That's almost more dangerous. Suppose you're seen. They have spies. Yesterday a fellow popped up out of the ditch in front of me just as I was relieving myself first thing. I was so scared I only just suppressed an ejaculatory prayer. That would have given me away all right. I think what they'd like best is to go sniffing people's excrement to see if they're Protestants. The spy was a little runt with a patch over one eye.

MOTHER COURAGE *clambering out of the cart with a basket*: What have I found, you shameless creature? *She holds up the red boots in triumph.* Yvette's red high-heeled boots! Coolly went and pinched them, she did. Cause you put it in her head she was an enchanting young person. *She lays them in the basket.* I'm giving them back. Stealing Yvette's boots! She's wrecking herself for money. That's understandable. But you'd do it for nothing, for pleasure. What did I tell you: you're to wait till it's peace. No soldiers for you. You're not to start exhibiting yourself till it's peacetime.

THE CHAPLAIN: I don't find she exhibits herself.

MOTHER COURAGE: Too much for my liking. Let her be like a stone in Dalecarlia, where there's nowt else, so folk say 'Can't see that cripple', that's how I'd lief have her. Then nowt'll happen to her. *To Swiss Cheese:* You leave that box where it is, d'you hear? And keep an eye on your sister, she needs it. The pair of you'll have me in grave yet. Sooner be minding a bagful of fleas.

She leaves with the Chaplain. Kattrin clears away the dishes.

SWISS CHEESE: Won't be able to sit out in the sun in shirtsleeves much longer. *Kattrin points at a tree.* Aye, leaves turning yellow. *Kattrin asks by gestures if he wants a drink.* Don't want no drink. I'm thinking. *Pause.* Said she can't sleep. Best if I got rid of that box, found a good place for it. All right, let's have a glass. *Kattrin goes behind the cart.* I'll stuff it down the rat-hole by the river for the time being. Probably pick it up tonight before first light and take it to Regiment. How far can they have retreated in three days? Bet sergeant's surprised. I'm agreeably disappointed in you, Swiss Cheese, he'll say. I make you responsible for the cash, and you go and bring it back.

As Kattrin emerges from behind the cart with a full glass in her hand, two men confront her. One is a sergeant, the other doffs his hat to her. He has a patch over one eye.

THE MAN WITH THE PATCH: God be with you, mistress. Have you seen anyone round here from Second Finnish Regimental Headquarters?

Kattrin, badly frightened, runs downstage, spilling the brandy. The two men look at one another, then withdraw on seeing Swiss Cheese sitting there.

SWISS CHEESE *interrupted in his thoughts*: You spilt half of it. What are those faces for? Jabbed yourself in eye? I don't get it. And I'll have to be off, I've thought it over, it's the only way. *He gets up. She does everything possible to make him realise the danger. He only shrugs her off.* Wish I knew what you're trying to say. Sure you mean well, poor creature, just can't get words out. What's it matter your spilling my brandy, I'll drink plenty more glasses yet, what's one more or less? *He gets the box from the cart and takes it under his tunic.* Be back in a moment. Don't hold me up now, or I'll be angry. I know you mean well. Too bad you can't speak.

As she tries to hold him back he kisses her and tears himself away. Exit. She is desperate, running hither and thither uttering little noises. The Chaplain and Mother Courage return. Kattrin rushes to her mother.

MOTHER COURAGE: What's all this? Pull yourself together, love. They done something to you? Where's Swiss Cheese? Tell it me step by step, Kattrin. Mother understands you. What, so that bastard did take the box? I'll wrap it round his ears, the little hypocrite. Take your time and don't gabble, use your hands, I don't like it when you howl like a dog, what'll his reverence say? Makes him uncomfortable. What, a one-eyed man came along?

THE CHAPLAIN: That one-eyed man is a spy. Have they arrested Swiss Cheese? *Kattrin shakes her head, shrugs her shoulders.* We're done for.

MOTHER COURAGE *fishes in her basket and brings out a Catholic flag, which the Chaplain fixes to the mast*: Better hoist new flag.

THE CHAPLAIN *bitterly*: All good Catholics here.

Voices are heard from the rear. The two men bring in Swiss Cheese.

SWISS CHEESE: Let me go, I got nowt. Don't twist my shoulder, I'm innocent.

SERGEANT: Here's where he came from. You know each other.

MOTHER COURAGE: Us? How?

SWISS CHEESE: I don't know her. Got no idea who she is, had nowt to do with them. I bought me dinner here, ten hellers it cost. You might have seen me sitting here, it was too salty.

SERGEANT: Who are you people, eh?

MOTHER COURAGE: We're law-abiding folk. That's right, he bought a dinner. Said it was too salty.

SERGEANT: Trying to pretend you don't know each other, that it?

MOTHER COURAGE: Why should I know him? Can't know everyone. I don't go asking 'em what they're called and are they a heretic; if he pays he ain't a heretic. You a heretic?

SWISS CHEESE: Go on.

THE CHAPLAIN: He sat there very properly, never opening his mouth except when eating. Then he had to.

SERGEANT: And who are you?

MOTHER COURAGE: He's just my potboy. Now I expect you gentlemen are thirsty, I'll get you a glass of brandy, you must be hot and tired with running.

SERGEANT: No brandy on duty. *To Swiss Cheese:* You were carrying something. Must have hidden it by the river. Was a bulge in your tunic when you left here.

MOTHER COURAGE: You sure it was him?

SWISS CHEESE: You must be thinking of someone else. I saw someone bounding off with a bulge in his tunic. I'm the wrong man.

MOTHER COURAGE: I'd say it was a misunderstanding too, such things happen. I'm a good judge of people, I'm Courage, you heard of me, everyone knows me, and I tell you that's an honest face he has.

SERGEANT: We're on the track of the Second Finnish Regiment's cash box. We got the description of the fellow responsible for it. Been trailing him two days. It's you.

SWISS CHEESE: It's not me.

SERGEANT: And you better cough it up, or you're a goner, you know. Where is it?

MOTHER COURAGE *urgently*: Of course he'd give it over rather than be a goner. Right out he'd say: I got it, here it is, you're too strong. He ain't all that stupid. Speak up, stupid idiot, here's the sergeant giving you a chance.

SWISS CHEESE: S'pose I ain't got it.

SERGEANT: Then come along. We'll get it out of you. *They lead him off.*

MOTHER COURAGE *calls after them*: He'd tell you. He's not that stupid. And don't you twist his shoulder! *Runs after them.*

Evening of the same day. The Chaplain and dumb Kattrin are cleaning glasses and polishing knives.

THE CHAPLAIN: Cases like that, where somebody gets caught, are not unknown in religious history. It reminds me of the Passion of Our Lord and Saviour. There's an old song about that. *He sings the Song of the Hours:*

> In the first hour Jesus mild
> Who had prayed since even
> Was betrayed and led before
> Pontius the heathen.

> Pilate found him innocent
> Free from fault and error
> Therefore, having washed his hands
> Sent him to King Herod.

> In the third hour he was scourged
> Stripped and clad in scarlet
> And a plaited crown of thorns
> Set upon his forehead.

> On the Son of Man they spat
> Mocked him and made merry.
> Then the cross of death was brought
> Given him to carry.

> At the sixth hour with two thieves
> To the cross they nailed him
> And the people and the thieves
> Mocked him and reviled him.

> This is Jesus King of Jews
> Cried they in derision
> Till the sun withdrew its light
> From that awful vision.

At the ninth hour Jesus wailed
Why hast thou me forsaken?
Soldiers brought him vinegar
Which he left untaken.

Then he yielded up the ghost
And the earth was shaken.
Rended was the temple's veil
And the saints were wakened.

Soldiers broke the two thieves' legs
As the night descended
Thrust a spear in Jesus' side
When his life had ended.

Still they mocked, as from his wound
Flowed the blood and water
And blasphemed the Son of Man
With their cruel laughter.*

MOTHER COURAGE *entering excitedly*: It's touch and go. They say sergeant's open to reason though. Only we mustn't let on it's Swiss Cheese else they'll say we helped him. It's a matter of money, that's all. But where's money to come from? Hasn't Yvette been round? I ran into her, she's got her hooks on some colonel, maybe he'd buy her a canteen business.

THE CHAPLAIN: Do you really wish to sell?

MOTHER COURAGE: Where's money for sergeant to come from?

THE CHAPLAIN: What'll you live on, then?

MOTHER COURAGE: That's just it.

Yvette Pottier arrives with an extremely ancient colonel.

YVETTE *embracing Mother Courage*: My dear Courage, fancy

* Song translated by Ralph Manheim

seeing you so soon. *Whispers:* He's not unwilling. *Aloud:* This is my good friend who advises me in business matters. I happened to hear you wanted to sell your cart on account of circumstances. I'll think it over.

MOTHER COURAGE: Pledge it, not sell, just not too much hurry, tain't every day you find a cart like this in wartime.

YVETTE *disappointed:* Oh, pledge. I though it was for sale. I'm not so sure I'm interested. *To the colonel:* How do you feel about it?

THE COLONEL: Just as you feel, pet.

MOTHER COURAGE: I'm only pledging it.

YVETTE: I thought you'd got to have the money.

MOTHER COURAGE *firmly:* I got to have it, but sooner run myself ragged looking for a bidder than sell outright. And why? The cart's our livelihood. It's a chance for you, Yvette; who knows when you'll get another like it and have a special friend to advise you, am I right?

YVETTE: Yes, my friend thinks I should clinch it, but I'm not sure. If it's only a pledge . . . so you agree we ought to buy outright?

THE COLONEL: I agree, pet.

MOTHER COURAGE: Best look and see if you can find anything for sale then; maybe you will if you don't rush it, take your friend along with you, say a week or fortnight, might find something suits you.

YVETTE: Then let's go looking. I adore going around looking for things, I adore going around with you, Poldi, it's such fun, isn't it? No matter if it takes a fortnight. How soon would you pay the money back if you got it?

MOTHER COURAGE: I'd pay back in two weeks, maybe one.

YVETTE: I can't make up my mind, Poldi chéri, you advise me. *Takes the colonel aside:* She's got to sell, I know, no problem there. And there's that ensign, you know, the fair-haired one, he'd be glad to lend me the money. He's crazy about me, says there's someone I remind him of. What do you advise?

THE COLONEL: You steer clear of him. He's no good. He's only making use of you. I said I'd buy you something, didn't I, pussykins?

YVETTE: I oughtn't to let you. Of course if you think the ensign might try to take advantage ... Poldi, I'll accept it from you.

THE COLONEL: That's how I feel too.

YVETTE: Is that your advice?

THE COLONEL: That is my advice.

YVETTE *to Courage once more*: My friend's advice would be to accept. Make me out a receipt saying the cart's mine once two weeks are up, with all its contents, we'll check it now, I'll bring the two hundred florins later. *To the colonel:* You go back to the camp, I'll follow, I got to check it all and see there's nothing missing from my cart. *She kisses him. He leaves. She climbs up on the cart.* Not all that many boots, are there?

MOTHER COURAGE: Yvette, it's no time for checking your cart, s'posing it is yours. You promised you'd talk to sergeant about Swiss Cheese, there ain't a minute to lose, they say in an hour he'll be courtmartialled.

YVETTE: Just let me count the shirts.

MOTHER COURAGE *pulling her down by the skirt*: You bloody vampire. Swiss Cheese's life's at stake. And not a word about who's making the offer, for God's sake, pretend it's your friend, else we're all done for cause we looked after him.

YVETTE: I fixed to meet that one-eyed fellow in the copse, he should be there by now.

THE CHAPLAIN: It doesn't have to be the whole two hundred either, I'd go up to a hundred and fifty, that may be enough.

MOTHER COURAGE: Since when has it been your money? You kindly keep out of this. You'll get your hotpot all right, don't worry. Hurry up and don't haggle, it's life or death. *Pushes Yvette off.*

THE CHAPLAIN: Far be it from me to interfere, but what are we going to live on? You're saddled with a daughter who can't earn her keep.

MOTHER COURAGE: I'm counting on regimental cash box, Mr Clever. They'll allow it as his expenses.

THE CHAPLAIN: But will she get the message right?

MOTHER COURAGE: It's her interest I should spend her two hundred so she gets the cart. She's set on that, God knows how long that colonel of hers'll last. Kattrin, polish the knives, there's the pumice. And you, stop hanging round like Jesus on Mount of Olives, get moving, wash them glasses, we'll have fifty or more of cavalry in tonight and I don't want to hear a lot of 'I'm not accustomed to having to run about, oh my poor feet, we never ran in church'. Thank the Lord they're corruptible. After all, they ain't wolves, just humans out for money. Corruption in humans is same as compassion in God. Corruption's our only hope. Long as we have it there'll be lenient sentences and even an innocent man'll have a chance of being let off.

YVETTE *comes in panting*: They'll do it for two hundred. But it's got to be quick. Soon be out of their hands. Best thing is I go right away to my colonel with the one-eyed man. He's admitted he had the box, they put the thumbscrews on him. But he chucked it in the river soon as he saw they were on his track. The box is a write-off. I'll go and get the money from my colonel, shall I?

MOTHER COURAGE: Box is a write-off? How'm I to pay back two hundred then?

YVETTE: Oh, you thought you'd get it from the box, did you? And I was to be Joe Soap I suppose? Better not count on that. You'll have to pay up if you want Swiss Cheese back, or would you sooner I dropped the whole thing so's you can keep your cart?

MOTHER COURAGE: That's something I didn't allow for. Don't worry, you'll get your cart, I've said goodbye to it, had it seventeen years, I have. I just need a moment to think, it's bit sudden, what'm I to do, two hundred's too much for me, pity you didn't beat 'em down. Must keep a bit back, else any Tom, Dick and Harry'll be able to shove me in ditch. Go and tell them I'll pay hundred and twenty florins, else it's all off, either way I'm losing me cart.

YVETTE: They won't do it. That one-eyed man's impatient already, keeps looking over his shoulder, he's so worked up. Hadn't I best pay them the whole two hundred?

MOTHER COURAGE in despair: I can't pay that. Thirty years I been working. She's twenty-five already, and no husband. I got her to think of too. Don't push me, I know what I'm doing. Say a hundred and twenty, or it's off.

YVETTE: It's up to you. Rushes off.

Without looking at either the Chaplain or her daughter, Mother Courage sits down to help Kattrin polish knives.

MOTHER COURAGE: Don't smash them glasses, they ain't ours now. Watch what you're doing, you'll cut yourself. Swiss Cheese'll be back, I'll pay two hundred if it comes to the pinch. You'll get your brother, love. For eighty florins we could fill a pack with goods and start again. Plenty of folk has to make do.

THE CHAPLAIN: The Lord will provide, it says.

MOTHER COURAGE: See they're properly dry. She cleans knives in silence. Kattrin suddenly runs behind the cart, sobbing.

YVETTE comes running in: They won't do it. I told you so. The one-eyed man wanted to leave right away, said there was no point. He says he's just waiting for the drum-roll; that means sentence has been pronounced. I offered a hundred and fifty. He didn't even blink. I had to convince him to stay there so's I could have another word with you.

MOTHER COURAGE: Tell him I'll pay the two hundred. Hurry! *Yvette runs off. They sit in silence. The Chaplain has stopped polishing the glasses.* I reckon I bargained too long. *In the distance drumming is heard. The Chaplain gets up and goes to the rear. Mother Courage remains seated. It grows dark. The drumming stops. It grows light once more. Mother Courage is sitting exactly as before.*

YVETTE *arrives, very pale*: Well, you got what you asked for, with your haggling and trying to keep your cart. Eleven bullets they gave him, that's all. You don't deserve I should bother any more about you. But I did hear they don't believe the box really is in the river. They've an idea it's here and anyhow that you're connected with him. They're going to bring him here, see if you gives yourself away when you sees him. Thought I'd better warn you so's you don't recognise him, else you'll all be for it. They're right on my heels, best tell you quick. Shall I keep Kattrin away? *Mother Courage shakes her head.* Does she know? She mayn't have heard the drumming or know what it meant.

MOTHER COURAGE: She knows. Get her.

Yvette fetches Kattrin, who goes to her mother and stands beside her. Mother Courage takes her hand. Two lansequenets come carrying a stretcher with something lying on it covered by a sheet. The sergeant marches beside them. They set down the stretcher.

SERGEANT: Here's somebody we dunno the name of. It's got to be listed, though, so everything's shipshape. He had a meal here. Have a look, see if you know him. *He removes the sheet.* Know him? *Mother Courage shakes her head.* What, never see him before he had that meal here? *Mother Courage shakes her head.* Pick him up. Chuck him in the pit. He's got nobody knows him. *They carry him away.*

4

Mother Courage sings the Song of the Grand Capitulation

Outside an officer's tent.

Mother Courage is waiting. A clerk looks out of the tent.

THE CLERK: I know you. You had a paymaster from the Lutherans with you, what was in hiding. I'd not complain if I were you.

MOTHER COURAGE: But I got a complaint to make. I'm innocent, would look as how I'd a bad conscience if I let this pass. Slashed everything in me cart to pieces with their sabres, they did, then wanted I should pay five taler fine for nowt, I tell you, nowt.

CLERK: Take my tip, better shut up. We're short of canteens, so we let you go on trading, specially if you got a bad conscience and pay a fine now and then.

MOTHER COURAGE: I got a complaint.

CLERK: Have it your own way. Then you must wait till the captain's free. *Withdraws inside the tent.*

YOUNG SOLDIER *enters aggressively*: Bouque la Madonne! Where's that bleeding pig of a captain what's took my reward money to swig with his tarts? I'll do him.

OLDER SOLDIER *running after him*: Shut up. They'll put you in irons.

YOUNG SOLDIER: Out of there, you thief! I'll slice you into pork chops, I will. Pocketing my prize money after I'd swum the river, only one in the whole squadron, and now I can't even buy meself a beer. I'm not standing for that. Come on out there so I can cut you up!

OLDER SOLDIER: Blessed Mother of God, he's asking for trouble.

MOTHER COURAGE: Is it some reward he weren't paid?

YOUNG SOLDIER: Lemme go, I'll slash you too while I'm at it.

OLDER SOLDIER: He rescued the colonel's horse and got no reward for it. He's young yet, still wet behind the ears.

MOTHER COURAGE: Let him go, he ain't a dog you got to chain up. Wanting your reward is good sound sense. Why be a hero otherwise?

YOUNG SOLDIER: So's he can sit in there and booze. You're shit-scared, the lot of you. I done something special and I want my reward.

MOTHER COURAGE: Don't you shout at me, young fellow. Got me own worries, I have; any road you should spare your voice, be needing it when captain comes, else there he'll be and you too hoarse to make a sound, which'll make it hard for him to clap you in irons till you turn blue. People what shouts like that can't keep it up ever; half an hour, and they have to be rocked to sleep, they're so tired.

YOUNG SOLDIER: I ain't tired and to hell with sleep. I'm hungry. They make our bread from acorns and hemp-seed, and they even skimp on that. He's whoring away my reward and I'm hungry. I'll do him.

MOTHER COURAGE: Oh I see, you're hungry. Last year that general of yours ordered you all off roads and across fields so corn should be trampled flat; I could've got ten florins for a pair of boots s'pose I'd had boots and s'pose anyone'd been able to pay ten florins. Thought he'd be well away from that area this year, he did, but here he is, still there, and hunger is great. I see what you're angry about.

YOUNG SOLDIER: I won't have it, don't talk to me, it ain't fair and I'm not standing for that.

MOTHER COURAGE: And you're right; but how long? How long you not standing for unfairness? One hour, two hours? Didn't ask yourself that, did you, but it's the whole point, and why, once you're in irons it's too bad if you suddenly finds you can put up with unfairness after all.

YOUNG SOLDIER: What am I listening to you for, I'd like to know? Bouque la Madonne, where's that captain?

MOTHER COURAGE: You been listening to me because you knows it's like what I say, your anger has gone up in smoke already, it was just a short one and you needed a long one, but where you going to get it from?

YOUNG SOLDIER: Are you trying to tell me asking for my reward is wrong?

MOTHER COURAGE: Not a bit. I'm just telling you your anger ain't long enough, it's good for nowt, pity. If you'd a long one I'd be trying to prod you on. Cut him up, the swine, would be my advice to you in that case; but how about if you don't cut him up cause you feels your tail going between your legs? Then I'd look silly and captain'd take it out on me.

OLDER SOLDIER: You're perfectly right, he's just a bit crazy.

YOUNG SOLDIER: Very well, let's see if I don't cut him up. *Draws his sword.* When he arrives I'm going to cut him up.

CLERK *looks out*: The captain'll be here in one minute. Sit down.

The Young Soldier sits down.

MOTHER COURAGE: He's sitting now. See, what did I say? You're sitting now. Ah, how well they know us, no one need tell 'em how to go about it. Sit down! and, bingo, we're sitting. And sitting and sedition don't mix. Don't try to stand up, you won't stand the way you was standing before. I shouldn't worry about what I think; I'm no better, not one moment. Bought up all our fighting spirit, they have. Eh? S'pose I kick back, might be bad for business. Let me tell you a thing or two about the Grand Capitulation. *She sings the Song of the Grand Capitulation:*

Back when I was young, I was brought to realise
What a very special person I must be
(Not just any old cottager's daughter, what with my looks
    and my talents and my urge towards Higher Things)
And insisted that my soup should have no hairs in it.
No one makes a sucker out of me!
(All or nothing, only the best is good enough, each man for
    himself, nobody's telling *me* what to do.)
Then I heard a tit
Chirp: Wait a bit!
    And you'll be marching with the band
    In step, responding to command
    And striking up your little dance:
    Now we advance.
    And now: parade, form square!
    Then men swear God's there –
    Not the faintest chance!

In no time at all anyone who looked could see
That I'd learned to take my medicine with good grace.
(Two kids on my hands and look at the price of bread, and
    things they expect of you!)
When they finally came to feel that they were through with
    me
They'd got me grovelling on my face.
(Takes all sorts to make a world, you scratch my back and
    I'll scratch yours, no good banging your head against a
    brick wall.)
Then I heard that tit
Chirp: Wait a bit!
    And you'll be marching with the band
    In step, responding to command
    And striking up your little dance:
    Now they advance.
    And now: parade, form square!

Then men swear God's there –
Not the faintest chance!

I've known people tried to storm the summits:
There's no star too bright or seems too far away.
(Dogged does it, where there's a will there's a way, by hook
  or by crook.)
As each peak disclosed fresh peaks to come, it's
Strange how much a plain straw hat could weigh.
(You have to cut your coat according to your cloth.)
Then I hear the tit
Chirp: Wait a bit!
    And they'll be marching with the band
    In step, responding to command
    And striking up their little dance:
    Now they advance
    And now: parade, form square!
    Then men swear God's there –
    Not the faintest chance!

MOTHER COURAGE *to the young soldier*: That's why I reckon
you should stay there with your sword drawn if you're
truly set on it and your anger's big enough, because you got
grounds, I agree, but if your anger's a short one best leave
right away.

YOUNG SOLDIER: Oh stuff it. *He staggers off with the older
soldier following.*

CLERK *sticks his head out*: Captain's here now. You can make
your complaint.

MOTHER COURAGE: I changed me mind. I ain't complaining. *Exit.*

5

Two years have gone by. The war is spreading
to new areas. Ceaselessly on the move, Courage's
little cart crosses Poland, Moravia, Bavaria, Italy
then Bavaria again. 1631. Tilly's victory at
Magdeburg costs Mother Courage four officers'
shirts

Mother Courage's cart has stopped in a badly shot-up village.

*Thin military music in the distance. Two soldiers at the bar being
served by Kattrin and Mother Courage. One of them has a lady's fur
coat over his shoulders.*

MOTHER COURAGE: Can't pay, that it? No money, no
schnapps. They give us victory parades, but catch them
giving men their pay.
SOLDIER: I want my schnapps. I missed the looting. That
double-crossing general only allowed an hour's looting in
the town. He ain't an inhuman monster, he said. Town
must of paid him.
THE CHAPLAIN *stumbles in*: There are people still lying in
that yard. The peasant's family. Somebody give me a hand.
I need linen.
*The second soldier goes off with him. Kattrin becomes very excited
and tries to make her mother produce linen.*
MOTHER COURAGE: I got none. All my bandages was sold
to regiment. I ain't tearing up my officer's shirts for that
lot.
CHAPLAIN *calling back*: I need linen, I tell you.
MOTHER COURAGE *blocking Kattrin's way into the cart by*

sitting on the step: I'm giving nowt. They'll never pay, and why, nowt to pay with.

CHAPLAIN *bending over a woman he has carried in*: Why d'you stay around during the gunfire?

PEASANT WOMAN *feebly*: Farm.

MOTHER COURAGE: Catch them abandoning anything. But now I'm s'posed to foot the bill. I won't do it.

FIRST SOLDIER: Those are Protestants. What they have to be Protestants for?

MOTHER COURAGE: They ain't bothering about faith. They lost their farm.

SECOND SOLDIER: They're no Protestants. They're Catholics like us.

FIRST SOLDIER: No way of sorting 'em out in a bombardment.

A PEASANT *brought in by the chaplain*: My arm's gone.

THE CHAPLAIN: Where's that linen?

MOTHER COURAGE: I can't give nowt. What with expenses, taxes, loan interest and bribes. *Making guttural noises, Kattrin raises a plank and threatens her mother with it.* You gone plain crazy? Put that plank away or I'll paste you one, you cow. I'm giving nowt, don't want to, got to think of meself. *The Chaplain lifts her off the steps and sets her on the ground, then starts pulling out shirts and tearing them into strips.* My officers' shirts! Half a florin apiece! I'm ruined. *From the house comes the cry of a child in pain.*

THE PEASANT: The baby's in there still. *Kattrin dashes in.*

THE CHAPLAIN *to the woman*: Don't move. They'll get it out.

MOTHER COURAGE: Stop her, roof may fall in.

THE CHAPLAIN: I'm not going back in there.

MOTHER COURAGE *torn both ways*: Don't waste my precious linen.

Kattrin brings a baby out of the ruins.

MOTHER COURAGE: How nice, found another baby to cart around? Give it to its ma this instant, unless you'd have me fighting for hours to get it off you, like last time, d'you hear? *To the second soldier:* Don't stand there gawping, you go back and tell them cut out that music, we can see it's a victory with our own eyes. All your victories mean to me is losses.

THE CHAPLAIN *tying a bandage:* Blood's coming through. *Kattrin is rocking the baby and making lullaby noises.*

MOTHER COURAGE: Look at her, happy as a queen in all this misery; give it back at once, its mother's coming round. *She catches the first soldier, who has been attacking the drinks and is trying to make off with one of the bottles.* Psia krew! Thought you'd score another victory, you animal? Now pay.

FIRST SOLDIER: I got nowt.

MOTHER COURAGE *pulling the fur coat off his back:* Then leave that coat, it's stolen any road.

THE CHAPLAIN: There's still someone under there.

6

Outside the Bavarian town of Ingolstadt Courage participates in the funeral of the late Imperial commander Tilly. Discussions are held about war heroes and the war's duration. The Chaplain complains that his talents are lying fallow, and dumb Kattrin gets the red boots. The year is 1632

Inside a canteen tent.

It has a bar towards the rear. Rain. Sound of drums and Funeral music. The Chaplain and the regimental clerk are playing a board game. Mother Courage and her daughter are stocktaking.

THE CHAPLAIN: Now the funeral procession will be moving off.

MOTHER COURAGE: Too bad about commander in chief – twenty-two pairs those socks – he fell by accident, they say. Mist over fields, that was the trouble. General had just been haranguing a regiment saying they must fight to last man and last round, he was riding back when mist made him lose direction so he was up front and a bullet got him in midst of battle – only four hurricane lamps left. *A whistle from the rear. She goes to the bar.* You scrimshankers, dodging your commander in chief's funeral, scandal I call it. *Pours drinks.*

THE CLERK: They should never of paid troops out before the funeral. Instead of going now they're all getting pissed.

THE CHAPLAIN *to the clerk*: Aren't you supposed to go to the funeral?

THE CLERK: Dodged it cause of the rain.

MOTHER COURAGE: It's different with you, your uniform might get wet. I heard they wanted to toll bells for funeral as usual, except it turned out all churches had been blown to smithereens by his orders, so poor old commander in chief won't be hearing no bells as they let the coffin down. They're going to let off three salvoes instead to cheer things up – seventeen belts.

SHOUTS *from the bar*: Hey, Missis, a brandy!

MOTHER COURAGE: Let's see your money. No, I ain't having you in my tent with your disgusting boots. You can drink outside, rain or no rain. *To the clerk:* I'm only letting in sergeants and up. Commander in chief had been having his worries, they say. S'posed to have been trouble with Second Regiment cause he stopped their pay, said it was a war of faith and they should do it for free. *Funeral march. All look to the rear.*

THE CHAPLAIN: Now they'll be filing past the noble corpse.

MOTHER COURAGE: Can't help feeling sorry for those

generals and emperors, there they are maybe thinking they're doing something extra special what folk'll talk about in years to come, and earning a public monument, like conquering the world for instance, that's a fine ambition for a general, how's he to know any better? I mean, he plagues hisself to death, then it all breaks down on account of ordinary folk what just wants their beer and bit of a chat, nowt higher. Finest plans get bolloxed up by the pettiness of them as should be carrying them out, because emperors can't do nowt themselves, they just counts on soldiers and people to back 'em up whatever happens, am I right?

THE CHAPLAIN *laughs*: Courage, you're right, aside from the soldiers. They do their best. Give me that lot outside there, for instance, drinking their brandy in the rain, and I'd guarantee to make you one war after another for a hundred years if need be, and I'm no trained general.

MOTHER COURAGE: You don't think war might end, then?

THE CHAPLAIN: What, because the commander in chief's gone? Don't be childish. They're two a penny, no shortage of heroes.

MOTHER COURAGE: Ee, I'm not asking for fun of it, but because I'm thinking whether to stock up, prices are low now, but if war's going to end it's money down the drain.

THE CHAPLAIN: I realise it's a serious question. There've always been people going round saying 'the war can't go on for ever'. I tell you there's nothing to stop it going on for ever. Of course there can be a bit of a breathing space. The war may need to get its second wind, it may even have an accident so to speak. There's no guarantee against that; nothing's perfect on this earth of ours. A perfect war, the sort you might say couldn't be improved on, that's something we shall probably never see. It can suddenly come to a standstill for some quite unforeseen reason, you can't allow for everything. A slight case of negligence, and it's bogged down up to the axles. And then it's a matter of hauling the war out of the mud again. But emperor and kings and popes will come to its rescue. So on the whole it has nothing serious to worry about, and will live to a ripe old age.

A SOLDIER *sings at the bar*:

A schnapps, landlord, you're late!
A soldier cannot wait
To do his emperor's orders.

Make it a double, this is a holiday.

MOTHER COURAGE: S'pose I went by what you say . . .

THE CHAPLAIN: Think it out for yourself. What's to compete with the war?

THE SOLDIER *at the rear*:

Your breast, my girl, you're late!
A soldier cannot wait
To ride across the borders.

THE CLERK *unexpectedly*: And what about peace? I'm from Bohemia and I'd like to go home some day.

THE CHAPLAIN: Would you indeed? Ah, peace. Where is the hole once the cheese has been eaten?

THE SOLDIER *at the rear*:

Lead trumps, my friend, you're late!
A soldier cannot wait.
His emperor needs him badly.

Your blessing, priest, you're late!
A soldier cannot wait.
Must lay his life down gladly.

THE CLERK: In the long run life's impossible if there's no peace.

THE CHAPLAIN: I'd say there's peace in war too; it has its peaceful moments. Because war satisfies all requirements, peaceable ones included, they're catered for, and it would simply fizzle out if they weren't. In war you can do a crap like in the depths of peacetime, then between one battle and the next you can have a beer, then even when you're moving up you can lay your head on your arms and have a bit of shuteye in the ditch, it's entirely possible. During a charge you can't play cards maybe, but nor can you in the depths of peacetime when you're ploughing, and after a victory there are various openings. You may get a leg blown off, then you start by making a lot of fuss as though it were serious, but afterwards you calm down or get given a schnapps, and you end up hopping around and the war's no worse off than before. And what's to stop you being fruitful and multiplying in the middle of all the butchery, behind a barn or something, in the long run you can't be held back from it, and then the war will have your progeny and can use them to carry on with. No, the war will always find an outlet, mark my words. Why should it ever stop?

Kattrin has ceased working and is staring at the Chaplain.

MOTHER COURAGE: I'll buy fresh stock then. If you say so. *Kattrin suddenly flings a basket full of bottles to the ground and runs off.* Kattrin! *Laughs.* Damn me if she weren't waiting for peace. I promised her she'd get a husband soon as peace came. *Hurries after her.*

THE CLERK *standing up*: I won. You been talking too much. Pay up.

MOTHER COURAGE *returning with Kattrin*: Don't be silly, war'll go on a bit longer, and we'll make a bit more money, and peacetime'll be all the nicer for it. Now you go into town, that's ten minutes' walk at most, fetch things from Golden Lion, the expensive ones, we can fetch rest in cart later, it's all arranged, regimental clerk here will go with you. Nearly everybody's attending commander in chief's funeral, nowt can happen to you. Careful now, don't let them steal nowt, think of your dowry.

Kattrin puts a cloth over her head and leaves with the clerk.

THE CHAPLAIN: Is that all right to let her go with the clerk?

MOTHER COURAGE: She's not that pretty they'd want to ruin her.

THE CHAPLAIN: I admire the way you run your business and always win through. I see why they called you Courage.

MOTHER COURAGE: Poor folk got to have courage. Why, they're lost. Simply getting up in morning takes some doing in their situation. Or ploughing a field, and in a war at that. Mere fact they bring kids into world shows they got courage, cause there's no hope for them. They have to hang one another and slaughter one another, so just looking each other in face must call for courage. Being able to put up with emperor and pope shows supernatural courage, cause those two cost 'em their lives. *She sits down, takes a little pipe from her purse and smokes.* You might chop us a bit of kindling.

THE CHAPLAIN *reluctantly removing his coat and preparing to chop up sticks*: I happen to be a pastor of souls, not a wood-cutter.

MOTHER COURAGE: I got no soul, you see. Need firewood, though.

THE CHAPLAIN: Where's that stumpy pipe from?

MOTHER COURAGE: Just a pipe.

THE CHAPLAIN: What d'you mean, 'just', it's a quite particular pipe, that.

MOTHER COURAGE: Aha?

THE CHAPLAIN: That stumpy pipe belongs to the Oxenstierna Regiment's cook.

MOTHER COURAGE: If you know that already why ask, Mr Clever?

THE CHAPLAIN: Because I didn't know if you were aware what you're smoking. You might just have been rummaging around in your things, come across some old pipe or other, and used it out of sheer absence of mind.

MOTHER COURAGE: And why not?

THE CHAPLAIN: Because you didn't. You're smoking that deliberately.

MOTHER COURAGE: And why shouldn't I?

THE CHAPLAIN: Courage, I'm warning you. It's my duty. Probably you'll never clap eyes on the gentleman again, and that's no loss but your good fortune. He didn't make at all a reliable impression on me. Quite the opposite.

MOTHER COURAGE: Really? Nice fellow that.

THE CHAPLAIN: So he's what you would call a nice fellow? I wouldn't. Far be it from me to bear him the least ill-will, but nice is not what I would call him. More like one of those Don Juans, a slippery one. Have a look at that pipe if you don't believe me. You must admit it tells you a good deal about his character.

MOTHER COURAGE: Nowt that I can see. Worn out, I'd call it.

THE CHAPLAIN: Practically bitten through, you mean. A man of wrath. That is the pipe of an unscrupulous man of wrath; you must see that if you have any discrimination left.

MOTHER COURAGE: Don't chop my chopping block in two.

THE CHAPLAIN: I told you I'm not a woodcutter by trade. I studied to be a pastor of souls. My talent and abilities are being abused in this place, by manual labour. My God-given endowments are denied expression. It's a sin. You have never heard me preach. One sermon of mine can put a regiment in such a frame of mind it'll treat the enemy like a flock of sheep. Life to them is a smelly old foot-cloth which they fling away in a vision of final victory. God has given me the gift of speech. I can preach so you'll lose all sense of sight and hearing.

MOTHER COURAGE: I don't wish to lose my sense of sight and hearing. Where'd that leave me?

THE CHAPLAIN: Courage, I have often thought that your

dry way of talking conceals more that just a warm heart.
You too are human and need warmth.

MOTHER COURAGE: Best way for us to get this tent warm is
have plenty of firewood.

THE CHAPLAIN: Don't change the subject. Seriously,
Courage, I sometimes ask myself what it would be like if
our relationship were to become somewhat closer. I mean,
given that the whirlwind of war has so strangely whirled us
together.

MOTHER COURAGE: I'd say it was close enough. I cook
meals for you and you run around and chop firewood for
instance.

THE CHAPLAIN *coming closer*: You know what I mean by
closer; it's not a relationship founded on meals and wood-
chopping and other such base necessities. Let your head
speak, harden thyself not.

MOTHER COURAGE: Don't you come at me with that axe.
That'd be too close a relationship.

THE CHAPLAIN: You shouldn't make a joke of it. I'm a
serious person and I've thought about what I'm saying.

MOTHER COURAGE: Be sensible, padre. I like you. I don't
want to row you. All I'm after is get myself and children
through all this with my cart. I don't see it as mine, and
I ain't in the mood for private affairs. Right now I'm taking
a gamble, buying stores just when commander in chief's
fallen and all the talk's of peace. Where d'you reckon you'd
turn if I'm ruined? Don't know, do you? You chop us some
kindling wood, then we can keep warm at night, that's
quite something these times. What's this? *She gets up. Enter
Kattrin, out of breath, with a wound above her eye. She is carrying
a variety of stuff: parcels, leather goods, a drum and so on.*

MOTHER COURAGE: What happened, someone assault you?
On way back? She was assaulted on her way back. Bet it
was that trooper was getting drunk here. I shouldn't have
let you go, love. Drop that stuff. Not too bad, just a flesh

wound you got. I'll bandage it and in a week it'll be all right. Worse than wild beasts, they are. *She ties up the wound.*

THE CHAPLAIN: It's not them I blame. They never went raping back home. The fault lies with those that start wars, it brings humanity's lowest instincts to the surface.

MOTHER COURAGE: Calm down. Didn't clerk come back with you? That's because you're respectable, they don't bother. Wound ain't a deep one, won't leave no mark. There you are, all bandaged up. You'll get something, love, keep calm. Something I put aside for you, wait till you see. *She delves into a sack and brings out Yvette's red high-heeled boots.* Made you open your eyes, eh? Something you always wanted. They're yours. Put 'em on quick, before I change me mind. Won't leave no mark, and what if it does? Ones I'm really sorry for's the ones they fancy. Drag them around till they're worn out, they do. Those they don't care for they leaves alive. I seen girls before now had pretty faces, then in no time looking fit to frighten a hyaena. Can't even go behind a bush without risking trouble, horrible life they lead. Same like with trees, straight well-shaped ones get chopped down to make beams for houses and crooked ones live happily ever after. So it's a stroke of luck for you really. Them boots'll be all right, I greased them before putting them away.

Kattrin leaves the boots where they are and crawls into the cart.

THE CHAPLAIN: Let's hope she's not disfigured.

MOTHER COURAGE: She'll have a scar. No use her waiting for peacetime now.

THE CHAPLAIN: She didn't let them steal the things.

MOTHER COURAGE: Maybe I shouldn't have dinned that into her so. Wish I knew what went on in that head of hers. Just once she stayed out all night, once in all those years. Afterwards she went around like before, except she worked harder. Couldn't get her to tell what had happened. Worried

me quite a while, that did. *She collects the articles brought by Kattrin, and sorts them angrily.* That's war for you. Nice way to get a living!
Sound of cannon fire.

THE CHAPLAIN: Now they'll be burying the commander in chief. This is a historic moment.

MOTHER COURAGE: What I call a historic moment is them bashing my daughter over the eye. She's half wrecked already, won't get no husband now, and her so crazy about kids; any road she's only dumb from war, soldier stuffed something in her mouth when she was little. As for Swiss Cheese I'll never see him again, and where Eilif is God alone knows. War be damned.

7

Mother Courage at the peak of her business career

High road.

The Chaplain, Mother Courage and Kattrin are pulling the cart, which is hung with new wares. Mother Courage is wearing a necklace of silver coins.

MOTHER COURAGE: I won't have you folk spoiling my war for me. I'm told it kills off the weak, but they're write-off in peacetime too. And war gives its people a better deal.
She sings:

> And if you feel your forces fading
> You won't be there to share the fruits.

But what is war but private trading
That deals in blood instead of boots?

And what's the use of settling down? Them as does are
first to go. *Sings:*

Some people think to live by looting
The goods some others haven't got.
You think it's just a line they're shooting
Until you hear they have been shot.

And some I saw dig six feet under
In haste to lie down and pass out.
Now they're at rest perhaps they wonder
Just what was all their haste about.

They pull it further.

8

The same year sees the death of the Swedish
king Gustavus Adolphus at the battle of Lützen.
Peace threatens to ruin Mother Courage's business. Courage's dashing son performs one heroic
deed too many and comes to a sticky end

Camp.

*A summer morning. In front of the cart stand an old woman and her
son. The son carries a large sack of bedding.*

MOTHER COURAGE'S VOICE *from inside the cart*: Does it
need to be this ungodly hour?

THE YOUNG MAN: We walked twenty miles in the night and got to be back today.

MOTHER COURAGE'S VOICE: What am I to do with bedding? Folk've got no houses.

THE YOUNG MAN: Best have a look first.

THE OLD WOMAN: This place is no good either. Come on.

THE YOUNG MAN: What, and have them sell the roof over our head for taxes? She might pay three florins if you throw in the bracelet. *Bells start ringing.* Listen, mother.

VOICES *from the rear*: Peace! Swedish king's been killed.

MOTHER COURAGE *sticks her head out of the cart. She has not yet done her hair*: What's that bell-ringing about in mid-week?

THE CHAPLAIN *crawling out from under the cart*: What are they shouting? Peace?

MOTHER COURAGE: Don't tell me peace has broken out just after I laid in new stock.

THE CHAPLAIN *calling to the rear*: That true? Peace?

VOICES: Three weeks ago, they say, only no one told us.

THE CHAPLAIN *to Courage*: What else would they be ringing the bells for?

VOICES: A whole lot of Lutherans have driven into town, they brought the news.

THE YOUNG MAN: Mother, it's peace. What's the matter? *The old woman has collapsed.*

MOTHER COURAGE *speaking into the cart*: Holy cow! Kattrin, peace! Put your black dress on, we're going to church. Least we can do for Swiss Cheese. Is it true, though?

THE YOUNG MAN: The people here say so. They've made peace. Can you get up? *The old woman stands up dumbfounded.* I'll get the saddlery going again, I promise. It'll all work out. Father will get his bedding back. Can you walk? *To the Chaplain:* She came over queer. It's the news. She never thought there'd be peace again. Father always said so. We're going straight home. *They go off.*

MOTHER COURAGE'S VOICE: Give her a schnapps.

THE CHAPLAIN: They've already gone.

MOTHER COURAGE'S VOICE: What's up in camp?

THE CHAPLAIN: They're assembling. I'll go on over. Shouldn't I put on my clerical garb?

MOTHER COURAGE'S VOICE: Best check up before parading yourself as heretic. I'm glad about peace, never mind if I'm ruined. Any road I'll have got two of me children through the war. Be seeing Eilif again now.

THE CHAPLAIN: And who's that walking down the lines? Bless me, the army commander's cook.

THE COOK *somewhat bedraggled and carrying a bundle*: What do I behold? The padre!

THE CHAPLAIN: Courage, we've got company.

Mother Courage clambers out.

THE COOK: I promised I'd drop over for a little talk soon as I had the time. I've not forgotten your brandy, Mrs Fierling.

MOTHER COURAGE: Good grief, the general's cook! After all these years! Where's my eldest boy Eilif?

THE COOK: Hasn't he got here? He left before me, he was on his way to see you too.

THE CHAPLAIN: I shall don my clerical garb, just a moment. *Goes off behind the cart.*

MOTHER COURAGE: Then he may be here any minute. *Calls into the cart:* Kattrin, Eilif's on his way. Get cook a glass of brandy, Kattrin! *Kattrin does not appear.* Drag your hair down over it, that's all right. Mr Lamb's no stranger. *Fetches the brandy herself.* She don't like to come out, peace means nowt to her. Took too long coming, it did. They gave her a crack over one eye, you barely notice it now but she thinks folks are staring at her.

THE COOK: Ah yes. War. *He and Mother Courage sit down.*

MOTHER COURAGE: Cooky, you caught me at bad moment. I'm ruined.

THE COOK: What? That's hard.

MOTHER COURAGE: Peace'll wring my neck. I went and took Chaplain's advice, laid in fresh stocks only t'other day. And now they're going to demobilise and I'll be left sitting on me wares.

THE COOK: What d'you want to go and listen to padre for? If I hadn't been in such a hurry that time, the Catholics arriving so quickly and all, I'd warned you against that man. All piss and wind, he is. So he's the authority around here, eh?

MOTHER COURAGE: He's been doing washing-up for me and helping pull.

THE COOK: Him pull! I bet he told you some of those jokes of his too, I know him, got a very unhealthy view of women, he has, all my good influence on him went for nowt. He ain't steady.

MOTHER COURAGE: You steady then?

THE COOK: Whatever else I ain't, I'm steady. Mud in your eye!

MOTHER COURAGE: Steady, that's nowt. I only had one steady fellow, thank God. Hardest I ever had to work in me life; he flogged the kids' blankets soon as autumn came, and he called me mouth-organ an unchristian instrument. Ask me, you ain't saying much for yourself admitting you're steady.

THE COOK: Still tough as nails, I see; but that's what I like about you.

MOTHER COURAGE: Now don't tell me you been dreaming of me nails.

THE COOK: Well, well, here we are, along with armistice bells and your brandy like what nobody else ever serves, it's famous, that is.

MOTHER COURAGE: I don't give two pins for your armistice bells just now. Can't see 'em handing out all the back pay what's owing, so where does that leave me with my famous brandy? Had your pay yet?

THE COOK *hesitantly*: Not exactly. That's why we all shoved
off. If that's how it is, I thought, I'll go and visit friends.
So here I am sitting with you.

MOTHER COURAGE: Other words you got nowt.

THE COOK: High time they stopped that bloody clanging.
Wouldn't mind getting into some sort of trade. I'm fed up
being cook to that lot. I'm s'posed to rustle them up meals
out of tree roots and old bootsoles, then they fling the hot
soup in my face. Cook these days is a dog's life. Sooner do
war service, only of course it's peacetime now. *He sees the
chaplain reappearing in his old garments.* More about that later.

THE CHAPLAIN: It's still all right, only had a few moths
in it.

THE COOK: Can't see why you bother. You won't get your
old job back, who are you to inspire now to earn his pay
honourably and lay down his life? What's more I got a
bone to pick with you, cause you advised this lady to buy a
lot of unnecessary goods saying war would go on for ever.

THE CHAPLAIN *heatedly*: I'd like to know what concern that
is of yours.

THE COOK: Because it's unscrupulous, that sort of thing is.
How dare you meddle in other folks' business arrangements
with your unwanted advice?

THE CHAPLAIN: Who's meddling? *To Courage:* I never knew
this gentleman was such an intimate you had to account to
him for everything.

MOTHER COURAGE: Keep your hair on, cook's only giving
his personal opinion and you can't deny your war was a
flop.

THE CHAPLAIN: You should not blaspheme against peace,
Courage. You are a hyaena of the battlefield.

MOTHER COURAGE: I'm what?

THE COOK: If you're going to insult this lady you'll have to
settle with me.

THE CHAPLAIN: It's not you I'm talking to. Your intentions are only too transparent. *To Courage:* But when I see you picking up peace betwixt your finger and your thumb like some dirty old snot-rag, then my humanity feels outraged; for then I see that you don't want peace but war, because you profit from it; in which case you shouldn't forget the ancient saying that whosoever sups with the devil needs a long spoon.

MOTHER COURAGE: I got no use for war, and war ain't got much use for me. But I'm not being called no hyaena, you and me's through.

THE CHAPLAIN: Then why grumble about peace when everybody's breathing sighs of relief? Because of some old junk in your cart?

MOTHER COURAGE: My goods ain't old junk but what I lives by, and you too up to now.

THE CHAPLAIN: Off war, in other words. Aha.

THE COOK *to the chaplain*: You're old enough to know it's always a mistake offering advice. *To Courage:* Way things are, your best bet's to get rid of certain goods quick as you can before prices hit rock-bottom. Dress yourself and get moving, not a moment to lose.

MOTHER COURAGE: That ain't bad advice. I'll do that, I guess.

THE CHAPLAIN: Because cooky says it.

MOTHER COURAGE: Why couldn't you say it? He's right, I'd best go off to market. *Goes inside the cart.*

THE COOK: That's one to me, padre. You got no presence of mind. What you should of said was: what, me offer advice, all I done was discuss politics. Better not take me on. Cock-fighting don't suit that get-up.

THE CHAPLAIN: If you don't stop your gob I'll murder you, get-up or no get-up.

THE COOK *pulling off his boots and unwrapping his foot-cloths*: Pity the war made such a godless shit of you, else you'd easily get another parsonage now it's peacetime. Cooks won't be needed, there's nowt to cook, but faith goes on just the same, nowt changed in that direction.

THE CHAPLAIN: Mr Lamb, I'm asking you not to elbow me out. Since I came down in the world I've become a better person. I couldn't preach to anyone now.

Enter Yvette Pottier in black, dressed up to the nines, carrying a cane. She is much older and fatter, and heavily powdered. She is followed by a manservant.

YVETTE: Hullo there, everybody. Is this Mother Courage's establishment?

THE CHAPLAIN: It is. And with whom have we the honour . . .?

YVETTE: With the Countess Starhemberg, my good man. Where's Courage?

THE CHAPLAIN *calls into the cart*: The Countess Starhemberg wishes to speak to you.

MOTHER COURAGE'S VOICE: Just coming.

YVETTE: It's Yvette.

MOTHER COURAGE'S VOICE: Oh, Yvette!

YVETTE: Come to see how you are. *Sees the cook turn round aghast*: Pieter!

THE COOK: Yvette!

YVETTE: Well I never! How d'you come to be here?

THE COOK: Got a lift.

THE CHAPLAIN: You know each other then? Intimately?

YVETTE: I should think so. *She looks the cook over.* Fat.

THE COOK: Not all that skinny yourself.

YVETTE: All the same I'm glad to see you, you shit. Gives me a chance to say what I think of you.

THE CHAPLAIN: You say it, in full; but don't start till Courage is out here.

MOTHER COURAGE *coming out with all kinds of goods*: Yvette! *They embrace.* But what are you in mourning for?

YVETTE: Suits me, don't it? My husband the colonel died a few years back.

MOTHER COURAGE: That old fellow what nearly bought
the cart?

YVETTE: His elder brother.

MOTHER COURAGE: Then you're sitting pretty. Nice to
find somebody what's made it in this war.

YVETTE: Up and down and up again, that's the way it went.

MOTHER COURAGE: I'm not hearing a word against
colonels, they make a mint of money.

THE CHAPLAIN: I would put my boots back on if I were
you. *To Yvette:* You promised you would say what you
think of the gentleman.

THE COOK: Don't kick up a stink here, Yvette.

MOTHER COURAGE: Yvette, this is a friend of mine.

YVETTE: That's old Puffing Piet.

THE COOK: Let's drop the nicknames. I'm called Lamb.

MOTHER COURAGE *laughs*: Puffing Piet! Him as made all
the women crazy! Here, I been looking after your pipe for
you.

THE CHAPLAIN: Smoking it, too.

YVETTE: What luck I can warn you against him. Worst of
the lot, he was, rampaging along the whole Flanders coast-
line. Got more girls in trouble than he has fingers.

THE COOK: That's all a long while ago. Tain't true anyhow.

YVETTE: Stand up when a lady brings you into the conversation! How I loved this man! All the time he had a little
dark girl with bandy legs, got her in trouble too of course.

THE COOK: Got you into high society more like, far as I can
see.

YVETTE: Shut your trap, you pathetic remnant! Better watch
out for him, though; fellows like that are still dangerous
even when on their last legs.

MOTHER COURAGE *to Yvette*: Come along, got to get rid of
my stuff afore prices start dropping. You might be able to
put a word in for me at regiment, with your connections.
Calls into the cart: Kattrin, church is off, I'm going to

market instead. When Eilif turns up, one of you give him a drink. *Exit with Yvette.*

YVETTE *as she leaves*: Fancy a creature like that ever making me leave the straight and narrow path. Thank my lucky stars I managed to reach the top all the same. But I've cooked your goose, Puffing Piet, and that's something that'll be credited to me one day in the world to come.

THE CHAPLAIN: I would like to take as a text for our little talk 'The mills of God grind slowly'. Weren't you complaining about my jokes?

THE COOK: Dead out of luck, I am. It's like this, you see: I thought I might get a hot meal. Here am I starving, and now they'll be talking about me and she'll get quite a wrong picture. I think I'll clear out before she's back.

THE CHAPLAIN: I think so too.

THE COOK: Padre, I'm fed up already with this bloody peace. Human race has to go through fire and sword cause it's sinful from the cradle up. I wish I could be roasting a fat capon once again for the general, wherever he's got to, in mustard sauce with a carrot or two.

THE CHAPLAIN: Red cabbage. Red cabbage for a capon.

THE COOK: You're right, but carrots was what he had to have.

THE CHAPLAIN: No sense of what's fitting.

THE COOK: Not that it stopped you guzzling your share.

THE CHAPLAIN: With misgivings.

THE COOK: Anyway you must admit those were the days.

THE CHAPLAIN: I might admit it if pressed.

THE COOK: Now you've called her a hyaena your days here are finished. What you staring at?

THE CHAPLAIN: Eilif! *Eilif arrives, followed by soldiers with pikes. His hands are fettered. His face is chalky-white.* What's wrong?

EILIF: Where's mother?

THE CHAPLAIN: Gone into town.

EILIF: I heard she was around. They've allowed me to come and see her.

THE COOK *to the soldiers*: What you doing with him?

A SOLDIER: Something not nice.

THE CHAPLAIN: What's he been up to?

THE SOLDIER: Broke into a peasant's place. The wife's dead.

THE CHAPLAIN: How could you do a thing like that?

EILIF: It's what I did last time, ain't it?

THE COOK: Aye, but it's peace now.

EILIF: Shut up. All right if I sit down till she comes?

THE SOLDIER: We've no time.

THE CHAPLAIN: In wartime they recommended him for that, sat him at the general's right hand. Dashing, it was, in those days. Any chance of a word with the provost-marshal?

THE SOLDIER: Wouldn't do no good. Taking some peasant's cattle, what's dashing about that?

THE COOK: Dumb, I call it.

EILIF: If I'd been dumb you'd of starved, clever bugger.

THE COOK: But as you were clever you're going to be shot.

THE CHAPLAIN: We'd better fetch Kattrin out anyhow.

EILIF: Sooner have a glass of schnapps, could do with that.

THE SOLDIER: No time, come along.

THE CHAPLAIN: And what shall we tell your mother?

EILIF: Tell her it wasn't any different, tell her it was the same thing. Or tell her nowt. *The soldiers propel him away.*

THE CHAPLAIN: I'll accompany you on your grievous journey.

EILIF: Don't need any bloody parsons.

THE CHAPLAIN: Wait and see. *Follows him.*

THE COOK *calls after them*: I'll have to tell her, she'll want to see him.

THE CHAPLAIN: I wouldn't tell her anything. At most that

he was here and will come again, maybe tomorrow. By then I'll be back and can break it to her. *Hurries off.*

The cook looks after him, shaking his head, then walks restlessly around. Finally he comes up to the cart.

THE COOK: Hoy! Don't you want to come out? I can understand you hiding away from peace. Like to do the same myself. Remember me, I'm general's cook? I was wondering if you'd a bit of something to eat while I wait for your mum. I don't half feel like a bit of pork, or bread even, just to fill the time. *Peers inside.* Head under blanket. *Sound of gunfire off.*

MOTHER COURAGE *runs in, out of breath and with all her goods still:* Cooky, peacetime's over. War's been on again three days now. Heard news before selling me stuff, thank God. They're having a shooting match with Lutherans in town. We must get cart away at once. Kattrin, pack up! What you in the dumps for? What's wrong?

THE COOK: Nowt.

MOTHER COURAGE: Something is. I see it way you look.

THE COOK: Cause war's starting up again, I s'pose. Looks as if it'll be tomorrow night before I get next hot food inside me.

MOTHER COURAGE: You're lying, cooky.

THE COOK: Eilif was here. Had to leave almost at once, though.

MOTHER COURAGE: Was he now? Then we'll be seeing him on march. I'm joining our side this time. How's he look?

THE COOK: Same as usual.

MOTHER COURAGE: Oh, he'll never change. Take more than war to steal him from me. Clever, he is. You going to help me get packed? *Begins to pack up.* What's his news? Still in general's good books? Say anything about his deeds of valour?

THE COOK *glumly:* Repeated one of them, I'm told.

MOTHER COURAGE: Tell it me later, we got to move off. *Kattrin appears.* Kattrin, peacetime's finished now. We're moving on. *To the cook:* How about you?

THE COOK: Have to join up again.

MOTHER COURAGE: Why don't you . . . Where's padre?

THE COOK: Went into town with Eilif.

MOTHER COURAGE: Then you come along with us a way. Need somebody to help me.

THE COOK: That business with Yvette, you know. . .

MOTHER COURAGE: Done you no harm in my eyes. Opposite. Where there's smoke there's fire, they say. You coming along?

THE COOK: I won't say no.

MOTHER COURAGE: The Twelfth moved off already. Take the shaft. Here's a bit of bread. We must get round behind to Lutherans. Might even be seeing Eilif tonight. He's my favourite one. Short peace, wasn't it? Now we're off again.

She sings as the cook and Kattrin harness themselves up:

From Ulm to Metz, from Metz to Munich
Courage will see the war gets fed.
The war will show a well-filled tunic
Given its daily shot of lead.
But lead alone can hardly nourish
It must have soldiers to subsist.
It's you it needs to make it flourish.
The war's still hungry. So enlist!

9

It is the seventeenth year of the great war of faith. Germany has lost more than half her inhabitants. Those who survive the bloodbath are killed off by terrible epidemics. Once fertile areas are ravaged by famine, wolves roam the burnt-out towns. In autumn 1634 we find Courage in the Fichtelgebirge, off the main axis of the Swedish armies. The winter this year is early and harsh. Business is bad, so that there is nothing to do but beg. The cook gets a letter from Utrecht and is sent packing

Outside a semi-dilapidated parsonage.

Grey morning in early winter. Gusts of wind. Mother Courage and the cook in shabby sheepskins, drawing the cart.

THE COOK: It's all dark, nobody up yet.

MOTHER COURAGE: Except it's parson's house. Have to crawl out of bed to ring bells. Then he'll have hot soup.

THE COOK: What from when whole village is burnt, we seen it.

MOTHER COURAGE: It's lived in, though, dog was barking.

THE COOK: S'pose parson's got, he'll give nowt.

MOTHER COURAGE: Maybe if we sing. . . .

THE COOK: I've had enough. *Abruptly:* Got a letter from Utrecht saying mother died of cholera and inn's mine. Here's letter if you don't believe me. No business of yours the way aunty goes on about my mode of existence, but have a look.

MOTHER COURAGE *reads the letter*: Lamb, I'm tired too of always being on the go. I feel like butcher's dog, dragging meat round customers and getting nowt off it. I got nowt left to sell, and folk got nowt left to buy nowt with. Saxony a fellow in rags tried landing me a stack of old books for two eggs, Württemberg they wanted to swap their plough for a titchy bag of salt. What's to plough for? Nowt growing no more, just brambles. In Pomerania villages are s'posed to have started in eating the younger kids, and nuns have been caught sticking folk up.

THE COOK: World's dying out.

MOTHER COURAGE: Sometimes I sees meself driving through hell with me cart selling brimstone, or across heaven with packed lunches for hungry souls. Give me my kids what's left, let's find some place they ain't shooting, and I'd like a few more years undisturbed.

THE COOK: You and me could get that inn going, Courage, think it over. Made up me mind in the night, I did: back to Utrecht with or without you, and starting today.

MOTHER COURAGE: Have to talk to Kattrin. That's a bit quick for me; I'm against making decisions all freezing cold and nowt inside you. Kattrin! *Kattrin climbs out of the cart*. Kattrin, got something to tell you. Cook and I want to go to Utrecht. He's been left an inn there. That'd be a settled place for you, let you meet a few people. Lots of 'em respect somebody mature, looks ain't everything. I'd like it too. I get on with cook. Say one thing for him, got a head for business. We'd have our meals for sure, not bad, eh? And your own bed too; like that, wouldn't you? Road's no life really. God knows how you might finish up. Lousy already, you are. Have to make up our minds, see, we could move with the Swedes, up north, they're somewhere up that way. *She points to the left.* Reckon that's fixed, Kattrin.

THE COOK: Anna, I got something private to say to you.

MOTHER COURAGE: Get back in cart, Kattrin.

Kattrin climbs back.

THE COOK: I had to interrupt, cause you don't understand, far as I can see. I didn't think there was need to say it, sticks out a mile. But if it don't, then let me tell you straight, no question of taking her along, not on your life. You get me, eh.

Kattrin sticks her head out of the cart behind them and listens.

MOTHER COURAGE: You mean I'm to leave Kattrin back here?

THE COOK: Use your imagination. Inn's got no room. It ain't one of the sort got three bar parlours. Put our backs in it we two'll get a living, but not three, no chance of that. She can keep cart.

MOTHER COURAGE: Thought she might find husband in Utrecht.

THE COOK: Go on, make me laugh. Find a husband, how? Dumb and that scar on top of it. And at her age?

MOTHER COURAGE: Don't talk so loud.

THE COOK: Loud or soft, no getting over facts. And that's another reason why I can't have her in the inn. Customers don't want to be looking at that all the time. Can't blame them.

MOTHER COURAGE: Shut your big mouth. I said not so loud.

THE COOK: Light's on in parson's house. We can try singing.

MOTHER COURAGE: Cooky, how's she to pull the cart on her own? War scares her. She'll never stand it. The dreams she must have... I hear her nights groaning. Mostly after a battle. What's she seeing in those dreams, I'd like to know. She's got a soft heart. Lately I found she'd got another hedgehog tucked away what we'd run over.

THE COOK: Inn's too small. *Calls out:* Ladies and gentlemen, domestic staff and other residents! We are now going to give you a song concerning Solomon, Julius Caesar and other famous personages what had bad luck. So's you can see we're respectable folk, which makes it difficult to carry on, particularly in winter.

They sing:

You saw sagacious Solomon
You know what came of him.
To him complexities seemed plain.
He cursed the hour that gave birth to him
And saw that everything was vain.
How great and wise was Solomon!
The world however didn't wait
But soon observed what followed on.
It's wisdom that had brought him to this state –
How fortunate the man with none!

Yes, the virtues are dangerous stuff in this world, as this fine song proves, better not to have them and have a pleasant life and breakfast instead, hot soup for instance. Look at me: I haven't any but I'd like some. I'm a serving soldier but what good did my courage do me in all them battles, nowt, here I am starving and better have been shit-scared and stayed at home. For why?

You saw courageous Caesar next
You know what he became.
They deified him in his life
Then had him murdered just the same.
And as they raised the fatal knife
How loud he cried: You too, my son!
The world however didn't wait
But soon observed what followed on.
It's courage that had brought him to that state.
How fortunate the man with none!

Sotto voce: Don't even look out. *Aloud:* Ladies and gentlemen, domestic staff and other inmates! All right, you may
say, gallantry never cooked a man's dinner, what about
trying honesty? You can eat all you want then, or anyhow
not stay sober. How about it?

> You heard of honest Socrates
> The man who never lied:
> They weren't so grateful as you'd think
> Instead the rulers fixed to have him tried
> And handed him the poisoned drink.
> How honest was the people's noble son!
> The world however didn't wait
> But soon observed what followed on.
> It's honesty that brought him to that state.
> How fortunate the man with none!

Ah yes, they say, be unselfish and share what you've got,
but how about if you got nowt? It's all very well to say
the do-gooders have a hard time, but you still got to have
something. Aye, unselfishness is a rare virtue, cause it just
don't pay.

> Saint Martin couldn't bear to see
> His fellows in distress.
> He met a poor man in the snow
> And shared his cloak with him, we know.
> Both of them therefore froze to death.
> His place in Heaven was surely won!
> The world however didn't wait
> But soon observed what followed on.
> Unselfishness had brought him to that state.
> How fortunate the man with none!

That's how it is with us. We're respectable folk, stick
together, don't steal, don't murder, don't burn places

down. And all the time you might say we're sinking lower and lower, and it's true what the song says, and soup is few and far between, and if we weren't like this but thieves and murderers I dare say we'd be eating our fill. For virtues aren't their own reward, only wickednesses are, that's how the world goes and it didn't ought to.

> Here you can see respectable folk
> Keeping to God's own laws.
> So far he hasn't taken heed.
> You who sit safe and warm indoors
> Help to relieve our bitter need!
> How virtuously we had begun!
> The world however didn't wait
> But soon observed what followed on.
> It's fear of God that brought us to that state.
> How fortunate the man with none!

VOICE *from above*: Hey, you there! Come on up! There's hot soup if you want.

MOTHER COURAGE: Lamb, me stomach won't stand nowt. 'Tain't that it ain't sensible, what you say, but is that your last word? We got on all right.

THE COOK: Last word. Think it over.

MOTHER COURAGE: I've nowt to think. I'm not leaving her here.

THE COOK: That's proper senseless, nothing I can do about it though. I'm not a brute, just the inn's a small one. So now we better get on up, or there'll be nowt here either and wasted time singing in the cold.

MOTHER COURAGE: I'll get Kattrin.

THE COOK: Better bring a bit back for her. Scare them if they sees three of us coming. *Exeunt both.*

Kattrin climbs out of the cart with a bundle. She looks around to see if the other two have gone. Then she takes an old pair of trousers of the cook's and a skirt of her mother's, and lays them side by side on one of the wheels, so that they are easily seen. She has finished and is picking up her bundle to go, when Mother Courage comes back from the house.

MOTHER COURAGE *with a plate of soup*: Kattrin! Will you stop there? Kattrin! Where you off to with that bundle? Has devil himself taken you over? *She examines the bundle.* She's packed her things. You been listening? I told him nowt doing, Utrecht, his rotten inn, what'd we be up to there? You and me, inn's no place for us. Still plenty to be got out of war. *She sees the trousers and the skirt.* You're plain stupid. S'pose I'd seen that, and you gone away? *She holds Kattrin back as she tries to break away.* Don't you start thinking it's on your account I given him the push. It was cart, that's it. Catch me leaving my cart I'm used to, it ain't you, it's for cart. We'll go off in t'other direction, and we'll throw cook's stuff out so he finds it, silly man. *She climbs in and throws out a few other articles in the direction of the trousers.* There, he's out of our business now, and I ain't having nobody else in, ever. You and me'll carry on now. This winter will pass, same as all the others. Get hitched up, it looks like snow.

They both harness themselves to the cart, then wheel it round and drag it off. When the cook arrives he looks blankly at his kit.

10

During the whole of 1635 Mother Courage and her daughter Kattrin travel over the highroads of central Germany, in the wake of the increasingly bedraggled armies

High road.

Mother Courage and Kattrin are pulling the cart. They pass a peasant's house inside which there is a voice singing.

THE VOICE:
    The roses in our arbour
    Delight us with their show:
    They have such lovely flowers
    Repaying all our labour
    After the summer showers.
    Happy are those with gardens now:
    They have such lovely flowers.

    When winter winds are freezing
    As through the woods they blow
    Our home is warm and pleasing.
    We fixed the thatch above it
    With straw and moss we wove it.
    Happy are those with shelter now
    When winter winds are freezing.

Mother Courage and Kattrin pause to listen, then continue pulling.

11

January 1636. The emperor's troops are threatening the Protestant town of Halle. The stone begins to speak. Mother Courage loses her daughter and trudges on alone. The war is a long way from being over

The cart is standing, much the worse for wear, alongside a peasant's house with a huge thatched roof, backing on a wall of rock. It is night.

An ensign and three soldiers in heavy armour step out of the wood.

THE ENSIGN: I want no noise now. Anyone shouts, shove your pike into him.

FIRST SOLDIER: Have to knock them up, though, if we're to find a guide.

THE ENSIGN: Knocking sounds natural. Could be a cow bumping the stable wall.
  The soldiers knock on the door of the house. The peasant's wife opens it. They stop her mouth. Two soldiers go in.

MAN'S VOICE *within*: What is it?
  The soldiers bring out the peasant and his son.

THE ENSIGN *pointing at the cart, where Kattrin's head has appeared*: There's another one. *A soldier drags her out.* Anyone else live here beside you lot?

THE PEASANTS: This is our son. And she's dumb. Her mother's gone into town to buy stuff. For their business, cause so many people's getting out and selling things cheap. They're just passing through. Canteen folk.

THE ENSIGN: I'm warning you, keep quiet, or if there's the least noise you get a pike across your nut. Now I want someone to come with us and show us the path to the town. *Points to the young peasant.* Here, you.

THE YOUNG PEASANT: I don't know no path.

SECOND SOLDIER *grinning*: He don't know no path.

THE YOUNG PEASANT: I ain't helping Catholics.

THE ENSIGN *to the second soldier*: Stick your pike in his ribs.

THE YOUNG PEASANT *forced to his knees, with the pike threatening him*: I won't do it, not to save my life.

FIRST SOLDIER: I know what'll change his mind. *Goes towards the stable.* Two cows and an ox. Listen, you: if you're not reasonable I'll chop up your cattle.

THE YOUNG PEASANT: No, not that!

THE PEASANT'S WIFE *weeps*: Please spare our cattle, captain, it'd be starving us to death.

THE ENSIGN: They're dead if he goes on being obstinate.

FIRST SOLDIER: I'm taking the ox first.

THE YOUNG PEASANT *to his father*: Have I got to? *The wife nods.* Right.

THE PEASANT'S WIFE: And thank you kindly, captain, for sparing us, for ever and ever, Amen.

The peasant stops his wife from further expressions of gratitude.

FIRST SOLDIER: I knew the ox was what they minded about most, was I right?

Guided by the young peasant, the ensign and his men continue on their way.

THE PEASANT: What are they up to, I'd like to know. Nowt good.

THE PEASANT'S WIFE: Perhaps they're just scouting. What you doing?

THE PEASANT *putting a ladder against the roof and climbing up it*: Seeing if they're on their own. *From the top:* Something moving in the wood. Can see something down by the quarry. And there are men in armour in the clearing. And a gun. That's at least a regiment. God's mercy on the town and everyone in it!

THE PEASANT'S WIFE: Any lights in the town?

THE PEASANT: No. They'll all be asleep. *Climbs down*. If those people get in they'll butcher the lot.

THE PEASANT'S WIFE: Sentries're bound to spot them first.

THE PEASANT: Sentry in the tower up the hill must have been killed, or he'd have blown his bugle.

THE PEASANT'S WIFE: If only there were more of us.

THE PEASANT: Just you and me and that cripple.

THE PEASANT'S WIFE: Nowt we can do, you'd say....

THE PEASANT: Nowt.

THE PEASANT'S WIFE: Can't possibly run down there in the blackness.

THE PEASANT: Whole hillside's crawling with 'em. We could give a signal.

THE PEASANT'S WIFE: What, and have them butcher us too?

THE PEASANT: You're right, nowt we can do.

THE PEASANT'S WIFE *to Kattrin*: Pray, poor creature, pray! Nowt we can do to stop bloodshed. You can't talk, maybe, but at least you can pray. He'll hear you if no one else can. I'll help you. *All kneel, Kattrin behind the two peasants.* Our Father, which art in Heaven, hear Thou our prayer, let not the town be destroyed with all what's in it sound asleep and suspecting nowt. Arouse Thou them that they may get up and go to the walls and see how the enemy approacheth with pikes and guns in the blackness across fields below the slope. *Turning to Kattrin:* Guard Thou our mother and ensure that the watchman sleepeth not but wakes up, or it will be too late. Succour our brother-in-law also, he is inside there with his four children, spare Thou them, they are innocent and know nowt. *To Kattrin, who gives a groan:* One of them's not two yet, the eldest's seven. *Kattrin stands up distractedly.* Our Father, hear us, for only Thou canst help; we look to be doomed, for why, we are weak and have no pike and nowt and can risk nowt and are in Thy hand along with our cattle and all the farm, and same with the town, it too is in Thy hand and the enemy is before the walls in great strength.

Unobserved, Kattrin has slipped away to the cart and taken from it something which she hides beneath her apron; then she climbs up the ladder on to the stable roof.

THE PEASANT'S WIFE: Forget not the children, what are in danger, the littlest ones especially, the old folk what can't move, and every living creature.

THE PEASANT: And forgive us our trespasses as we forgive them that trespass against us. Amen.

Sitting on the roof, Kattrin begins to beat the drum which she has pulled out from under her apron.

THE PEASANT'S WIFE: Jesus Christ, what's she doing?

THE PEASANT: She's out of her mind.

THE PEASANT'S WIFE: Quick, get her down.

The peasant hurries to the ladder, but Kattrin pulls it up on to the roof.

THE PEASANT'S WIFE: She'll do us in.

THE PEASANT: Stop drumming at once, you cripple!

THE PEASANT'S WIFE: Bringing the Catholics down on us!

THE PEASANT *looking for stones to throw*: I'll stone you.

THE PEASANT'S WIFE: Where's your feelings? Where's your heart? We're done for if they come down on us. Slit our throats, they will. *Kattrin stares into the distance towards the town and carries on drumming.*

THE PEASANT'S WIFE *to her husband*: I told you we shouldn't have allowed those vagabonds on to farm. What do they care if our last cows are taken?

THE ENSIGN *runs in with his soldiers and the young peasant*: I'll cut you to ribbons, all of you!

THE PEASANT'S WIFE: Please, sir, it's not our fault, we couldn't help it. It was her sneaked up there. A foreigner.

THE ENSIGN: Where's the ladder?

THE PEASANT: There.

THE ENSIGN *calls up*: I order you, throw that drum down.
Kattrin goes on drumming.

THE ENSIGN: You're all in this together. It'll be the end of
you.

THE PEASANT: They been cutting pine trees in that wood.
How about if we got one of the trunks and poked her
off. . . .

FIRST SOLDIER *to the ensign*: Permission to make a suggestion, sir! *He whispers something in the ensign's ear.* Listen,
we got a suggestion could help you. Get down off there
and come into town with us right away. Show us which
your mother is and we'll see she ain't harmed.
Kattrin goes on drumming.

THE ENSIGN *pushes him roughly aside*: She doesn't trust you;
with a mug like yours it's not surprising. *Calls up:* Suppose
I gave you my word? I can give my word of honour as an
officer.
Kattrin drums harder.

THE ENSIGN: Is nothing sacred to her?

THE YOUNG PEASANT: There's more than her mother involved, sir.

FIRST SOLDIER: This can't go on much longer. They're
bound to hear in the town.

THE ENSIGN: We'll have somehow to make a noise that's
louder than her drumming. What can we make a noise
with?

FIRST SOLDIER: Thought we weren't s'posed to make no
noise.

THE ENSIGN: A harmless one, you fool. A peaceful one.

THE PEASANT: I could chop wood with my axe.

THE ENSIGN: Good: you chop. *The peasant fetches his axe and
attacks a tree-trunk.* Chop harder! Harder! You're chopping
for your life. *Kattrin has been listening, drumming less loudly
the while. She now looks wildly round, and goes on drumming.*

THE ENSIGN: Not loud enough. *To the first soldier:* You chop too.

THE PEASANT: Only got the one axe. *Stops chopping.*

THE ENSIGN: We'll have to set the farm on fire. Smoke her out, that's it.

THE PEASANT: It wouldn't help, captain. If the townspeople see a fire here they'll know what's up.

Kattrin has again been listening as she drums. At this point she laughs.

THE ENSIGN: Look at her laughing at us. I'm not having that. I'll shoot her down, and damn the consequences. Fetch the harquebus.

Three soldiers hurry off. Kattrin goes on drumming.

THE PEASANT'S WIFE: I got it, captain. That's their cart. If we smash it up she'll stop. Cart's all they got.

THE ENSIGN *to the young peasant:* Smash it up. *Calls up:* We're going to smash up your cart if you don't stop drumming. *The young peasant gives the cart a few feeble blows.*

THE PEASANT'S WIFE: Stop it, you animal!

Desperately looking towards the cart, Kattrin emits pitiful noises. But she goes on drumming.

THE ENSIGN: Where are those clodhoppers with the harquebus?

FIRST SOLDIER: Can't have heard nowt in town yet, else we'd be hearing their guns.

THE ENSIGN *calls up:* They can't hear you at all. And now we're going to shoot you down. For the last time: throw down that drum!

THE YOUNG PEASANT *suddenly flings away his plank:* Go on drumming! Or they'll all be killed! Go on, go on. . . .

The soldier knocks him down and beats him with his pike. Kattrin starts to cry, but she goes on drumming.

THE PEASANT'S WIFE: Don't strike his back! For God's sake, you're beating him to death!

The soldiers hurry in with the arquebus.

SECOND SOLDIER: Colonel's frothing at the mouth, sir. We're all for court-martial.

THE ENSIGN: Set it up! Set it up! *Calls up while the gun is being erected:* For the very last time: stop drumming! *Kattrin, in tears, drums as loud as she can.* Fire! *The soldiers fire. Kattrin is hit, gives a few more drumbeats and then slowly crumples.*

THE ENSIGN: That's the end of that.

But Kattrin's last drumbeats are taken up by the town's cannon. In the distance can be heard a confused noise of tocsins and gunfire.

FIRST SOLDIER: She's made it.

12

Before first light. Sound of the fifes and drums of troops marching off into the distance

In front of the cart Mother Courage is squatting by her daughter. The peasant family are standing near her.

THE PEASANTS *with hostility:* You must go, missis. There's only one more regiment behind that one. You can't go on your own.

MOTHER COURAGE: I think she's going to sleep. *She sings:*

Lullaby baby
What's that in the hay?
Neighbours' kids grizzle
But my kids are gay.
Neighbours' are in tatters
And you're dressed in lawn
Cut down from the raiment an

Angel has worn.
Neighbours' kids go hungry
And you shall eat cake
Suppose it's too crumbly
You've only to speak.
Lullaby baby
What's that in the hay?
The one lies in Poland
The other – who can say?

Better if you'd not told her nowt about your brother-in-law's kids.

THE PEASANT: If you'd not gone into town to get your cut it might never of happened.

MOTHER COURAGE: Now she's asleep.

THE PEASANT'S WIFE: She ain't asleep. Can't you see she's passed over?

THE PEASANT: And it's high time you got away yourself. There are wolves around and, what's worse, marauders.

MOTHER COURAGE: Aye.

She goes and gets a tarpaulin to cover the dead girl with.

THE PEASANT'S WIFE: Ain't you got nobody else? What you could go to?

MOTHER COURAGE: Aye, one left. Eilif.

THE PEASANT *as Mother Courage covers the dead girl*: Best look for him, then. We'll mind her, see she gets proper burial. Don't you worry about that.

MOTHER COURAGE: Here's money for expenses.

She counts out coins into the peasant's hands.

The peasant and his son shake hands with her and carry Kattrin away.

THE PEASANT'S WIFE *as she leaves*: I'd hurry.

MOTHER COURAGE *harnessing herself to the cart*: Hope I can pull cart all right by meself. Be all right, nowt much inside it. Got to get back in business again.

Another regiment with its fifes and drums marches past in the background.

MOTHER COURAGE *tugging the cart*: Take me along!

Singing is heard from offstage:

> With all its luck and all its danger
> The war is dragging on a bit
> Another hundred years or longer
> The common man won't benefit.
> Filthy his food, no soap to shave him
> The regiment steals half his pay.
> But still a miracle may save him:
> Tomorrow is another day!
> > The new year's come. The watchmen shout.
> > The thaw sets in. The dead remain.
> > Wherever life has not died out
> > It staggers to its feet again.

The Good Person of Szechwan

A parable play

COLLABORATORS: R. Berlau and M. Steffin

MUSIC: Paul Dessau

TRANSLATOR: John Willett

Written in 1938-41. First produced in the Zürich Schauspielhaus
on 4 February 1943

CHARACTERS

*Wang, a water-seller: Shen Teh-Shui Ta: Yang Sun, an un-
employed airman: Mrs Yang, his mother: Mrs Shin, a widow:
the family of eight: Lin To, a carpenter: Mrs Mi Tzu, a property
owner: the policeman: the carpet-dealer and his wife: the young
prostitute: Shu Fu, the barber: the priest: the unemployed man:
the waiter: passers-by of the Prologue.*

PROLOGUE

A Street in the Capital of Szechwan

It is evening. Wang, the water-seller, introduces himself to the audience.

WANG: I am a water-seller in the capital of Szechwan province. My job is tedious. When water is short I have to go far for it. And when it is plentiful I earn nothing. But utter poverty is the rule in our province. All agree that only the gods can help us. To my inexpressible joy a widely-travelled cattle dealer has told me that some of the highest gods are already on their way, and that Szechwan may see them too. They say that the heavens are deeply disturbed by the many complaints that have been going up. For the last three days I have waited at this entrance to the city, especially towards evening, so that I may be the first to greet them. There will hardly be a chance for me later; they will be surrounded by important people and there will be far too many demands on them. But shall I be able to recognise them? They may not arrive in a group. Perhaps they will come singly, so as not to attract attention. It cannot be those men – *he studies some workmen passing by* – they are coming away from work. Their shoulders are bent by the burdens they have to carry. That fellow is no god either, he has inky fingers. At most he may be some kind of clerk in a cement works. I would not take those gentlemen – *two gentlemen walk past* – for gods even: they have the brutal faces of men who beat people, and the gods find that unnecessary. But look at these three! They seem very different. They are well nourished, show no evidence of any kind of employment, and have dust on their shoes, so they must have travelled far. It is them! Yours to command, Illustrious Ones!

He flings himself to the ground.

THE FIRST GOD, *pleased*: Have you been expecting us?

WANG *gives them a drink*: For a long while. But only I knew that you were coming.

THE FIRST GOD: We must find a lodging for tonight. Do you know of one?

WANG: One? Lots! The city is at your service, O Illustrious Ones. Where do you wish to stay?

The gods exchange significant looks.

THE FIRST GOD: Try the first house, my son. Take the very first one first.

WANG: I only fear that I may attract the enmity of the powerful, if I give one of them the preference.

THE FIRST GOD: Then take it as an order: try the first one.

WANG: That's Mr Fo opposite. One moment.

He runs to a house and hammers on the door. It opens, but one can see him being turned away. He comes hesitantly back.

WANG: How stupid. Mr Fo happens to be out just now, and his servants dare not take the responsibility, as he is very strict. Won't he be angry when he finds who has been turned away!

THE GODS, *smiling*: Indeed.

WANG: Another moment then! The house next door is the widow Su's. She will be beside herself with joy.

He runs there, but is apparently turned away once more.

I shall have to ask across the road. She says she has only one very small room, and it's in no fit state. I will go straight to Mr Cheng's.

THE SECOND GOD: But a small room is all we need. Tell her that we are coming.

WANG: Even if it has not been cleaned? Suppose it is crawling with spiders?

THE SECOND GOD: No matter. The more spiders, the fewer flies.

THE THIRD GOD, *in an amiable way*: Try Mr Cheng or anybody else you like, my son. I admit I find spiders a little unattractive.

Wang knocks at another door and is admitted.

A VOICE FROM THE HOUSE: Get away with your gods! We've got enough troubles of our own.

WANG, *returning to the gods*: Mr Cheng is extremely sorry, he has his whole house full of relatives and dare not appear before you, Illustrious Ones. Between ourselves, I think there are evil men among them whom he would prefer you not to see. He is much too frightened of your judgment. That must be it.

THE THIRD GOD: Are we all that frightening?

WANG: Only to evil people, isn't it? We all know that Kwan province has suffered from floods for years.

THE SECOND GOD: Oh? And why is that?

WANG: Because they are not god-fearing people, I suppose.

THE SECOND GOD: Rubbish. Because they didn't look after the dam properly.

THE FIRST GOD: Sh! *To Wang*: Any other prospects, my son?

WANG: How can you ask? I have only to go to the next house, and I can have my pick. They are all falling over each other to entertain you. An unlucky combination of circumstances, you understand. Half a minute.

He walks away hesitantly and stands in the street unable to make up his mind.

THE SECOND GOD: What did I tell you?

THE THIRD GOD: It may just be circumstances.

THE SECOND GOD: Circumstances in Shun, circumstances in Kwan, and now circumstances in Szechwan. There are no god-fearing people left: that is the naked truth which you will not recognize. Our mission is hopeless, and you had better admit it.

THE FIRST GOD: We may still come across good people at any moment. We cannot expect to have things all our own way.

THE THIRD GOD: The resolution says: the world can go on as it is if we find enough good people, able to lead a decent human existence. The water-seller himself is such a person, if I am not deceived.

He goes up to Wang, who is still standing uncertain.

THE SECOND GOD: He is always deceived. When the water man let us drink out of his measure I saw something. Look.

He shows it to the first god.

THE FIRST GOD: It has got a false bottom.
THE SECOND GOD: A swindler.
THE FIRST GOD: Very well, we strike him out. But what does it matter if one man is corrupted? We shall soon find plenty who fulfil the conditions. We must find someone. For two thousand years we have been hearing the same complaint, that the world cannot go on as it is. No one can stay on earth and remain good. We must at last be able to show some people who are in a position to keep our commandments.
THE THIRD GOD, *to Wang*: Is it too difficult for you to find us a place?
WANG: Such guests as you? What are you thinking of? It is my fault that you were not taken in immediately; I am a bad guide.
THE THIRD GOD: Not that, certainly.

He turns back to the others.

WANG: They have begun to realise. *He accosts a gentleman*: Honoured sir, forgive me for addressing you, but three of the highest gods, whose impending advent has been the talk of all Szechwan for years, have now really arrived and are looking for a place to spend the night. Don't walk away. Look for yourself. One glance will convince you. For heaven's sake do something about it. It's the chance of a lifetime! Invite the gods to visit your home before someone else snaps them up; they are sure to accept.

The gentleman has walked on. Wang turns to another.

You, sir, you heard what it's about. Have you any room? It needn't be palatial. The intention is what matters.

THE GENTLEMAN: How am I to tell what sort of gods yours are? Heaven knows who I might be letting into my house.

He goes into a tobacconist's. Wang runs back to the three.

WANG: I have found somebody who is sure to take you.

He sees his measure on the ground, looks embarrassedly at the gods, picks it up and runs back again.

THE FIRST GOD: That does not sound encouraging.

WANG, *as the man steps out of the shop*: What about the accommodation?

THE GENTLEMAN: How do you know I'm not living in rooms myself?

THE FIRST GOD: He will find nothing. We had better write Szechwan off too.

WANG: It's three of the chief gods. Truly. Their images in the temples are just like them. If you get your invitation in now they might perhaps accept.

THE GENTLEMAN *laughs*: I suppose they're a lot of prize swindlers you're trying to foist off on someone.

Off.

WANG, *shouting after him*: You swivel-eyed chiseller! Have you no reverence? You'll all roast in brimstone for your lack of interest. The gods crap on the lot of you. And you'll be sorry for it. You shall pay for it unto the fourth generation. You have disgraced the whole province. *Pause.* That leaves us with Shen Teh the prostitute; she can't refuse.

He calls 'Shen Teh!' Shen Teh looks out of the window above.

They've arrived, and I can't find them a room. Could you possibly have them for one night?

SHEN TEH: Not much hope, Wang. I am expecting someone. But how is it that you can't find a room for them?

WANG: I can't explain now. Szechwan is nothing but one big muck-heap.

SHEN TEH: I should have to hide when he arrives. Then he might
    go away. He was supposed to be taking me out.

WANG: Can we come up in the meantime?

SHEN TEH: If you don't talk too loudly. Do I have to be careful
    what I say?

WANG: Very. They mustn't find out how you earn your living.
    We had better wait downstairs. But you won't be going off
    with him, will you?

SHEN TEH: I've had no luck lately, and if I can't find the rent by
    tomorrow they'll throw me out.

WANG: You shouldn't think of money at a moment like this.

SHEN TEH: I don't know: I'm afraid that a rumbling stomach is
    no respecter of persons. But very well, I will take them in.

She is seen to put out her light.

THE FIRST GOD: It looks hopeless to me.

They go up to Wang.

WANG, *startled to see them standing behind him*: You are fixed up
    for the night.

He wipes the sweat off his face.

THE GODS: Really? Then let us go.

WANG: There is no great hurry. Take your time. The room is
    not quite ready.

THE THIRD GOD: Very good, we will sit here and wait.

WANG: But isn't there too much traffic here? Let's cross the
    road.

THE SECOND GOD: We like looking at people. That is exactly
    what we came for.

WANG: It's a windy spot.

THE THIRD GOD: Does this seem all right to you?

They sit on a doorstep. Wang sits on the ground somewhat to one side.

WANG, *with a rush*: You are lodging with a girl who lives on her
    own. She is the best person in Szechwan.

THE THIRD GOD: That is gratifying.

WANG, *to the audience*: When I picked up my mug just then they
gave me a peculiar look. Do you think they noticed anything?
I daren't look them in the face any longer.

THE THIRD GOD: You seem exhausted.

WANG: A little. I have been running.

THE FIRST GOD: Do people here find life very hard?

WANG: Good people do.

THE FIRST GOD, *seriously*: Do you?

WANG: I know what you mean. I am not good. But I too find
life hard.

*Meanwhile a gentleman has appeared in front of Shen Teh's house
and whistled a number of times. Each time Wang gives a nervous
jerk.*

THE THIRD GOD, *in an undertone to Wang*: It looks as if he has
given up.

WANG, *confused*: It does.

*He jumps up and runs into the open, leaving his carrying-pole behind.
But the following has occurred: the man waiting has gone off and
Shen Teh, after opening the door quietly and calling 'Wang!' in a
low voice, has gone down the street in search of Wang. When Wang
in turn calls 'Shen Teh!' in a low voice he gets no reply.*

WANG: She has let me down. She has gone off to get the money
for the rent, and I have no place for the Illustrious Ones.
They are waiting there, exhausted. I cannot go back yet again
and tell them: no good, sorry. My own sleeping place under
the culvert is out of the question. And I am sure the gods
would not care to lodge with a man whose dirty business they
have seen through. I would not go back for anything in the
world. But my carrying-pole is still there. What shall I do?
I dare not fetch it. I shall leave the capital and find somewhere where I can hide from their eyes, for I failed to do
anything to help those I honour.

*He hurries away. As soon as he has gone, Shen Teh returns, searches
for him on the opposite side and sees the gods.*

SHEN TEH: Are you the Illustrious Ones? My name is Shen Teh.
I should be happy if you consented to make do with my small
room.

THE THIRD GOD: But where has the water-seller disappeared to?

SHEN TEH: I must have missed him.

THE FIRST GOD: He probably thought you were not coming,
and then felt too scared to come back to us.

THE THIRD GOD *picks up the carrying-pole*: We will ask you to
look after it. He needs it.

*They enter the house led by Shen Teh. It grows dus², then light
again. In the half-light of the dawn the gods again leave the door,
led by Shen Teh guiding them with a lantern. They take their leave.*

THE FIRST GOD: Dear Shen Teh, we are grateful for your hospitality. We shall not forget that it was you who took us in.
Will you give the water-seller his pole back? And tell him
that we are grateful to him too for having shown us a good
person.

SHEN TEH: I am not good. I have an admission to make: when
Wang asked me if I could shelter you I had hesitations.

THE FIRST GOD: Hesitations do not count if you overcome them.
Know that you gave us more than a lodging. There are many,
including even certain of us gods, who have begun to doubt
whether such a thing as a good person still exists. To check
up was the main object of our journey. We are now happy
to continue it, for we have succeeded in finding one. Farewell.

SHEN TEH: Wait, Illustrious Ones. I am by no means sure that
I am good. I should certainly like to be, but how am I to pay
the rent? Let me admit: I sell myself in order to live, and
even so I cannot manage, for there are so many forced to do
this. I would take on anything, but who would not? Of course
I should like to obey the commandments: to honour my
parents and respect the truth. Not to covet my neighbour's
house would be a joy to me, and to love, honour and cherish
a husband would be very pleasant. Nor do I wish to exploit
other men or to rob the defenceless. But how can it be done?

Even by breaking one or two of the commandments I can
barely manage.

THE FIRST GOD: All these, Shen Teh, are but the doubts of a
good person.

THE THIRD GOD: Goodbye, Shen Teh. And give our warmest
greetings to the water-seller. He was a good friend to us.

THE SECOND GOD: I fear we did but little good to him.

THE THIRD GOD: The best of luck.

THE FIRST GOD: Above all, be good, Shen Teh. Goodbye.

They turn to go. They begin to wave goodbye.

SHEN TEH, *nervously*: But I am not certain of myself, Illustrious
Ones. How can I be good when everything is so expensive?

THE SECOND GOD: Alas, that is beyond our powers. We cannot
meddle in the sphere of economics.

THE THIRD GOD: Wait! Just a minute. If she were better provided she might stand more chance.

THE SECOND GOD: We cannot give her anything. We could not
answer for it up there.

THE FIRST GOD: Why not?

They put their heads together and confer animatedly.

THE FIRST GOD, *awkwardly, to Shen Teh*: We understand that
you have no money for the rent. We are not poor people, so
it is natural that we should pay for our lodging. Here you are.
He gives her money. But please let nobody know that we paid.
It might be misinterpreted.

THE SECOND GOD: Only too easily.

THE THIRD GOD: No, it is permissible. We can quite well pay
for our lodging. There was nothing against it in the resolution. So fare you well.

The gods exeunt rapidly.

I

A small Tobacconist's

The shop is not yet properly installed, and not yet open.

SHEN TEH, *to the audience*: It is now three days since the gods left. They told me they wanted to pay for their lodging. And when I looked at what they had given me I saw that it was more than a thousand silver dollars. I have used the money to buy a tobacconist's business. I moved in here yesterday, and now I hope to be able to do a great deal of good. Look at Mrs Shin, for instance, the old owner of the shop. Yesterday she came to ask for rice for her children. And today I again see her bringing her pot across the square.

Enter Mrs Shin. The women bow to one another.

SHEN TEH: Good evening, Mrs Shin.

MRS SHIN: Good evening, Miss Shen Teh. What do you think of your new home?

SHEN TEH: I like it. How did the children spend the night?

MRS SHIN: Oh, in someone's house, if you can call that shack a house. The baby's started coughing.

SHEN TEH: That's bad.

MRS SHIN: You don't know what's bad. You've got it good. But you'll find plenty to learn in a dump like this. The whole district's a slum.

SHEN TEH: That is right what you told me, though? That the cement workers call in here at midday?

MRS SHIN: But not a customer otherwise, not even the locals.

SHEN TEH: You didn't tell me that when you sold me the business.

MRS SHIN: That's right: throw it in my face. First you take the roof away over the children's heads, and then it's nothing but dump and slum. It's more than I can bear.

She weeps.

SHEN TEH, *quickly*: I'll get your rice.

MRS SHIN: I was going to ask you if you could lend me some money.

SHEN TEH, *as she pours rice into her bowl*: I can't do that. I haven't sold anything yet.

MRS SHIN: But I need it. What am I to live on? You've taken everything I've got. Now you're cutting my throat. I'll leave my children on your door-step, you bloodsucker!

She snatches the pot from her hands.

SHEN TEH: Don't be so bad-tempered. You'll spill your rice.

Enter an elderly couple and a shabbily dressed man.

THE WOMAN: Ah, Shen Teh, my dear, we heard you were doing so nicely now. Why, you've set up in business! Just fancy, we're without a home. Our tobacconist's shop has folded up. We wondered if we mightn't spend a night with you. You know my nephew? He can't abide being separated from us.

THE NEPHEW, *looking round*: Smashing shop.

MRS SHIN: Who's this lot?

SHEN TEH: When I arrived here from the country they were my first landlords. *To the audience*: When my small funds ran out they threw me on the street. They are probably frightened that I will say no. They are poor.

> They have no shelter.
> They have no friends.
> They need someone.
> How can they be refused?

Addressing the woman in a friendly voice: Welcome to you, I will gladly give you lodging. But all I have is a tiny room at the back of the shop.

THE MAN: That'll do us. Don't you worry. *While Shen Teh fetches them tea*: We'd better move in behind here, so as not to be in your way. I suppose you picked on a tobacconist's to remind you of your first home? We'll be able to give you one or two tips. That's another reason for coming to you.

MRS SHIN, *sardonically*: Let's hope one or two customers come too.

THE WOMAN: Is that meant for us?

THE MAN: Sh. Here's a customer already.

Enter a tattered man.

THE UNEMPLOYED MAN: Excuse me, miss, I'm out of a job.

Mrs Shin laughs.

SHEN TEH: What can I do for you?

THE UNEMPLOYED MAN: They say you're opening up tomorrow.
   I thought people sometimes find things in bad condition
   when they unpack them. Can you spare a fag?

THE WOMAN: What cheek, begging for tobacco. 'Tisn't as if it
   had been bread.

THE UNEMPLOYED MAN: Bread's expensive. A few puffs at a
   fag and I'm a new man. I'm so done in.

SHEN TEH *gives him cigarettes*: That's very important, being a
   new man. I shall open up with you, you'll bring me luck.

*The unemployed man hastily lights a cigarette, inhales and goes off
coughing.*

THE WOMAN: Was that wise, my dear?

MRS SHIN: If that's how you open up you'll be closing down
   before three days are out.

THE MAN: I bet he had money on him all right.

SHEN TEH: But he said he hadn't anything.

THE NEPHEW: How do you know he wasn't having you on?

SHEN TEH, *worked up*: How do I know he was having me on?

THE WOMAN, *shaking her head*: She can't say no. You're too
   good, Shen Teh. If you want to hang on to your shop you'd
   better be able to refuse sometimes.

THE MAN: Say it isn't yours. Say it belongs to a relation and he
   insists on strict accounts. Why not try it?

MRS SHIN: Anyone would who didn't always want to play Lady
   Bountiful.

SHEN TEH *laughs*: Grumble away. The room won't be available
   and the rice goes back in the sack.

THE WOMAN, *shocked*: Is the rice yours too?

SHEN TEH, *to the audience*:

> They are bad.
> They are no man's friend.
> They grudge even a bowl of rice.
> They need it all themselves.
> How can they be blamed?

Enter a little man.

MRS SHIN *sees him and leaves hurriedly*: I'll look in tomorrow then. *Off.*

THE LITTLE MAN *starts after her*: Hey, Mrs Shin! Just the person I want.

THE WOMAN: Does she come regularly? Has she got some claim on you?

SHEN TEH: No claim, but she's hungry: and that's more important.

THE LITTLE MAN: She knows why she's running away. Are you the new proprietress? I see you're stocking up your shelves. But they aren't yours, let me tell you. Unless you pay for them. That old ragamuffin who was squatting here didn't pay. *To the others*: I'm the carpenter, see?

SHEN TEH: But I thought that was part of the fittings I paid for.

THE CARPENTER: Crooks. A pack of crooks. You and this Mrs Shin are thick as thieves. I want my 100 silver dollars, or my name's not Lin To.

SHEN TEH: How can I pay? I've got no money left.

THE CARPENTER: Then I'll have you sold up! On the spot. Pay on the spot or you'll be sold up.

THE MAN *prompts Shen Teh*: Your cousin ...

SHEN TEH: Can't you make it next month?

THE CARPENTER, *shouting*: No.

SHEN TEH: Don't be too hard, Mr Lin To. I can't satisfy all demands at once. *To the audience*:

> A slight connivance, and one's powers are doubled.
> Look how the cart-horse stops before a tuft of grass:
> Wink one eye for an instant and the horse pulls better.
> Show but a little patience in June and the tree

> By August is sagging with peaches. How
> But for patience could we live together?
> A brief postponement
> Brings the most distant goal within reach.

To the carpenter: Please be patient, just a little, Mr Lin To.

THE CARPENTER: And who is going to be patient with me and my family? *He pulls some of the shelving away from the wall, as if to take it down.* You pay, else I take the shelves with me.

THE WOMAN: My dear Shen Teh, why don't you refer the whole thing to your cousin? *To the carpenter*: Put your claim in writing, and Miss Shen Teh's cousin will pay.

THE CARPENTER: We all know those cousins.

THE NEPHEW: Don't stand there laughing like an idiot. He's a personal friend of mine.

THE MAN: He's sharp as a knife.

THE CARPENTER: All right, he'll get my bill.

He tips the shelving over, sits down on it and writes out his bill.

THE WOMAN: He'll have the clothes off your back for his rotten old planks if you don't stop him. My advice is never admit a claim, right or wrong, or you'll be smothered in claims, right or wrong. Throw a bit of meat in your dustbin, and every mongrel in the place will be at each other's throats in your back yard. What are solicitors for?

SHEN TEH: He has done some work and can't go away with nothing. He has a family too. It's dreadful that I can't pay him. What will the gods say?

THE MAN: You did your bit when you took us in, that's more than enough.

Enter a limping man and a pregnant woman.

THE LIMPING MAN, *to the couple*: So there you are. A credit to the family, I don't think. Going and leaving us waiting at the corner.

THE WOMAN, *embarrassed*: This is my brother Wung and my sister-in-law. *To the two*: Stop nagging and sit quietly out of the way, and don't bother our old friend Miss Shen Teh. *To Shen Teh*: We ought to take them both in, I think, what

with my sister-in-law being four months gone. Or are you
against it?

SHEN TEH: You are welcome.

THE WOMAN: Thank her. The cups are over there. *To Shen
Teh*: They would never have known where to go. Just as
well you've got this shop.

SHEN TEH, *laughing to the audience as she brings tea*: Yes, just as
well I have got it.

Enter Mrs Mi Tzu, the proprietress, with a document in her hand.

MRS MI TZU: Miss Shen Teh, I am Mrs Mi Tzu, the proprietress
of this building. I hope we will get on together. Here is the
agreement for the lease. *While Shen Teh studies the agreement*: An auspicious moment, do you not think, gentlemen,
when a small business is opened? *She looks round her.* A few
gaps on the shelves still, but it will do. I suppose you can
provide me with one or two references?

SHEN TEH: Is that necessary?

MRS MI TZU: You see, I have really no idea who you are.

THE MAN: Can we vouch for Miss Shen Teh, maybe? We've
known her ever since she first came to town, and we'd cut
off our right hands for her.

MRS MI TZU: And who are you?

THE MAN: I am Ma Fu, tobacconist.

MRS MI TZU: Where's your shop?

THE MAN: I haven't got a shop at the moment. It's like this:
I've just sold it.

MRS MI TZU: Aha. *To Shen Teh*: And is there no one else who
can give me any information about you?

THE WOMAN, *prompting*: Cousin . . . your cousin . . .

MRS MI TZU: But you must have someone who can tell me what
kind of tenant I'm getting in my house. This is a respectable
house, my dear. I can't sign any agreement with you otherwise.

SHEN TEH, *slowly, with lowered eyes*: I have got a cousin.

MRS MI TZU: Oh, so you've got a cousin? Round here? We
could go straight over now. What is he?

SHEN TEH: He doesn't live here; he's in another town.

THE WOMAN: In Shung, weren't you saying?

SHEN TEH: Mr Shui Ta. In Shung.

THE MAN: But of course I know him. Tall, skinny.

THE NEPHEW, *to the carpenter*: You've had to do with Miss Shen Teh's cousin too, chum. Over the shelving.

THE CARPENTER, *grumpily*: I'm just making out his bill. There you are. *He hands it over*. I'll be back first thing in the morning. *Exit*.

THE NEPHEW, *calling after him, for the proprietress's benefit*: Don't you worry. Her cousin will pay.

MRS MI TZU, *with a keen look at Shen Teh*: Well, I shall also be glad to meet him. Good evening, madam. *Exit*.

THE WOMAN, *after an interval*: It's bound to come out now. You can bet she'll know all about you by the morning.

THE SISTER-IN-LAW, *quietly to the nephew*: This set-up won't last long!

Enter an old man, guided by a boy.

THE BOY, *calling back*: Here they are.

THE WOMAN: Hello, grandpa. *To Shen Teh*: The dear old man. He must have been worrying about us. And the youngster, look how he's grown. He eats like an ostrich. Who else have you got with you?

THE MAN, *looking out*: Only your niece. *To Shen Teh*: A young relation up from the country. I hope we aren't too many for you. We weren't such a big family when you used to live with us, were we? Ah yes, we grew and grew. The worse it got, the more of us there seemed to be. And the more of us there were the worse it got. But we'd better lock up or we'll have no peace.

She shuts the door and all sit down.

THE WOMAN: The great thing is, we mustn't get in your way in the shop. It's up to you to keep the home fires burning. We planned it like this: the kids'll be out during the day, and only grandpa and my sister-in-law will stay, and perhaps me. The others will just be looking in once or twice during the

daytime, see? Light that lamp, boys, and make yourselves
at home.

THE NEPHEW, *facetiously*: I hope that cousin doesn't blow in
tonight, tough old Mr Shui Ta! *The sister-in-law laughs.*

THE BROTHER, *reaching for a cigarette*: One more or less won't
matter.

THE MAN: You bet.

*They all help themselves to something to smoke. The brother hands
round a jug of wine.*

THE NEPHEW: Drinks on old cousin!

THE GRANDFATHER, *solemnly to Shen Teh*: Hullo!

*Shen Teh is confused by this delayed greeting, and bows. In one hand
she holds the carpenter's bill, in the other the agreement for the lease.*

THE WOMAN: Can't you people sing something to entertain our
hostess?

THE NEPHEW: Grandpa can kick off.

They sing:

SONG OF THE SMOKE

THE GRANDFATHER:

Once I believed intelligence would aid me
I was an optimist when I was younger
Now that I'm old I see it hasn't paid me:
How can intelligence compete with hunger?
           And so I said: drop it!
           Like smoke twisting grey
           Into ever colder coldness you'll
           Blow away.

THE MAN:

I saw the conscientious man get nowhere
And so I tried the crooked path instead
But crookedness makes our sort travel slower.
There seems to be no way to get ahead.
           Likewise I say: drop it!
           Like smoke twisting grey
           Into ever colder coldness you'll
           Blow away.

THE NIECE:
> The old, they say, find little fun in hoping.
> Time's what they need, and time begins to press.
> But for the young, they say, the gates are open.
> They open, so they say, on nothingness.
>> And I too say: drop it!
>> Like smoke twisting grey
>> Into ever colder coldness you'll
>> Blow away.

THE NEPHEW: Where did that wine come from?

THE SISTER-IN-LAW: He pawned the sack of tobacco.

THE MAN: What? That tobacco was all we had left. We didn't touch it even to get a bed. You dirty bastard!

THE BROTHER: Call me a bastard just because my wife's half frozen? And who's been drinking it? Give me that jug.

They struggle. The shelves collapse.

SHEN TEH *touches them*: O look out for the shop, don't smash everything! It's a gift of the gods. Take whatever's there if you want, but don't smash it!

THE WOMAN, *sceptically*: It's a smaller shop than I thought. A pity we went and told Aunty and the others. If they turn up too there won't be much room.

THE SISTER-IN-LAW: Our hostess is getting a bit frosty too.

There are voices outside, and a knocking on the door.

CRIES: Open up! It's us!

THE WOMAN: Is that you, Aunty? How are we going to manage now?

SHEN TEH: My beautiful shop! Oh, such hopes! No sooner opened, than it is no more. *To the audience*:
> The dinghy which might save us
> Is straightway sucked into the depths:
> Too many of the drowning
> Snatch greedily at it.

CRIES *from outside*: Open up!

INTERLUDE
Under a Bridge

The water-seller is crouching by the stream.

WANG, *looking round*: All quiet. That makes four days I have been hiding. They won't find me, I've got my eyes open. I took the same direction as them on purpose. The second day they crossed the bridge; I heard their footsteps overhead. By now they must be a long way off; I have nothing more to fear.

He has leant back and gone to sleep. Music. The slope becomes transparent, and the gods appear.

WANG, *holding his arm in front of his face, as though he were about to be struck*: Don't say anything! I know! I failed to find anybody who would take you into his house! Now I have told you! Now go your way!

THE FIRST GOD: No, you did find somebody. As you left they came up. They took us in for the night; they watched over our sleep; and they lighted our way next morning when we left them. You had told us that she was a good person, and she was good.

WANG: So it was Shen Teh who lodged you?

THE THIRD GOD: Of course.

WANG: And I ran away, I had so little faith! Just because I thought she couldn't come. Because she had been down on her luck she couldn't come.

THE GODS:
O feeble one!
Well-meaning but feeble man!
Where hardship is, he thinks there is no goodness.
Where danger lies, he thinks there is no courage.
O feebleness, that believes no good whatever!
O hasty judgement! O premature despair!

WANG: I am deeply ashamed, Illustrious Ones.

THE FIRST GOD: And now, O water-seller, be so good as to return quickly to the city and look to dear Shen Teh, so that you can keep us posted about her. She is doing well now. She is said to have acquired the money to set up a small shop, so she can freely follow the impulses of her gentle heart. Show some interest in her goodness, for no one can be good for long if goodness is not demanded of him. We for our part wish to travel further and continue our search, and discover still more people like our good person in Szechwan, so that we can put a stop to the rumour which says that the good have found our earth impossible to live on.

They vanish.

2

The Tobacconist's

Sleeping bodies everywhere. The lamp is still burning. A knock.

THE WOMAN *raises herself, drunk with sleep*: Shen Teh! Somebody knocking! Where has the girl got to?

THE NEPHEW: Getting breakfast, I expect. It's on her cousin.

The woman laughs and slouches to the door. Enter a young gentleman, the carpenter behind him.

THE YOUNG GENTLEMAN: I am her cousin.

THE WOMAN, *falling from the clouds*: What did you say you were?

THE YOUNG GENTLEMAN: My name is Shui Ta.

THE FAMILY, *shaking one another awake*: Her cousin! But it was all a joke, she's got no cousin! But here's someone who says he's her cousin! Don't tell me, and at this hour of the day!

THE NEPHEW: If you're our hostess's cousin, mister, get us some breakfast right away, will you?

SHUI TA, *turning out the lamp*: The first customers will be arriving any moment. Please be quick and get dressed so that I can open up my shop.

THE MAN: Your shop? I fancy this shop belongs to our friend Shen Teh? *Shui Ta shakes his head.* What, do you mean to say it's not her shop at all?

THE SISTER-IN-LAW: So she's been having us on. Where's she slunk off to?

SHUI TA: She has been detained. She wishes me to tell you that now I am here she can no longer do anything for you.

THE WOMAN, *shaken*: And we thought she was such a good person.

THE NEPHEW: Don't you believe him! Go and look for her!

THE MAN: Right, we will. *He organises them*: You and you and you and you, go and comb the place for her. Grandpa and us will stay here and hold the fort. The boy can go and find us something to eat. *To the boy*: See that baker's at the corner. Nip over and stuff your shirt full.

THE SISTER-IN-LAW: And don't forget some of those little round cakes.

THE MAN: But mind the baker doesn't catch you. And keep clear of the policeman!

The boy nods and goes off. The others get fully dressed.

SHUI TA: Won't cake-stealing damage the reputation of the shop which has given you refuge?

THE NEPHEW: Don't mind him, we'll soon find her. She'll tell him what's what.

Exeunt nephew, brother, sister-in-law and niece.

THE SISTER-IN-LAW, *as she goes*: Leave us a bit of breakfast.

SHUI TA, *calmly*: You won't find her. My cousin naturally regrets being unable to make unbounded concessions to the laws of hospitality. But I fear you are too numerous. This is a tobacconist's, and it is Miss Shen Teh's livelihood.

THE MAN: Our Shen Teh could never bring herself to say such things.

SHUI TA: You may be right. *To the carpenter*: The unfortunate fact is that the poverty in this city is too much for any individual to correct. Alas, nothing has changed in the eleven centuries since a poet wrote:

That so many of the poor should suffer from cold what can we do to prevent?

To bring warmth to a single body is not much use.
I wish I had a big rug ten thousand feet long,
Which at one time could cover up every inch of the City.*

He starts clearing up the shop.

THE CARPENTER: I see you are trying to straighten out your cousin's affairs. There is a small bill to be settled for the shelves; she has admitted it before witnesses. 100 silver dollars.

SHUI TA, *drawing the bill out of his pocket, not unkindly*: Wouldn't you say that 100 silver dollars was rather much?

THE CARPENTER: No. I can't do it for less. I've a wife and family to look after.

SHUI TA, *hard*: How many children?

THE CARPENTER: Four.

SHUI TA: Then my offer is 20 silver dollars.

THE CARPENTER *laughs*: Are you crazy? These shelves are walnut.

SHUI TA: Then take them away.

THE CARPENTER: What do you mean?

SHUI TA: I can't afford it. I suggest you take your walnut shelves away.

THE WOMAN: One up to you. *She in turn laughs.*

THE CARPENTER, *uncertainly*: I would like Miss Shen Teh to be fetched. She seems to be a decent person, unlike you.

SHUI TA: Obviously. She is ruined.

THE CARPENTER *resolutely seizes some shelving and takes it to the door*: You can stack your goods on the floor then. It doesn't matter to me.

SHUI TA, *to the man*: Give him a hand.

THE MAN *takes some more shelving and takes it to the door with a grin*: Here we go. Chuck the lot out!

THE CARPENTER: You bastard. Do you want my family to starve?

SHUI TA: Let me repeat my offer: you can have 20 silver dollars, to save me stacking my goods on the floor.

* "The Big Rug," from *170 Chinese Poems* by Arthur Waley.

THE CARPENTER: 100.

Shui Ta looks indifferently out of the window. The man sets about removing the shelves.

THE CARPENTER: Anyway, don't smash them into the doorpost, you fool! *In confusion*: But they're made to fit. They won't go anywhere else. The boards had to be cut to size, sir.

SHUI TA: Exactly. That's why I can't offer you more than 20 silver dollars. Because the boards were cut to size.

The woman squeals with delight.

THE CARPENTER *suddenly decides he has had enough*: I can't go on. Keep the shelves and pay me what you like.

SHUI TA: 20 silver dollars.

He lays two big coins on the table. The carpenter takes them.

THE MAN, *bringing back the shelves*: Good enough for a lot of cut-up boards!

THE CARPENTER: About good enough to get drunk on! *Exit.*

THE MAN: Good riddance!

THE WOMAN, *wiping away tears of laughter*: 'But they're walnut!' – 'Take them away!' – '100 silver dollars, I've got four children!' – 'Then I'll pay 20!' – 'But they've been cut to fit!' – 'Exactly, 20 silver dollars!' That's the way to deal with his sort!

SHUI TA: Yes. *Seriously*: Leave here at once.

THE MAN: What, us?

SHUI TA: Yes, you. You are thieves and parasites. Leave at once, waste no time in arguing, and you can still save your skins.

THE MAN: It is better not to take any notice of him. No arguing on an empty stomach. I wonder where the nipper is?

SHUI TA: Yes, where is he? I told you I will not have him here with stolen cakes. *Suddenly shouting*: For the second time. Get out!

They remain seated.

SHUI TA, *calm once more*: All right then.

He walks to the door and bows deeply to someone outside. A police-man looms up in the doorway.

SHUI TA: I take it I am addressing the police representative for this district?

THE POLICEMAN: You are, Mr . . .

SHUI TA: Shui Ta. *They exchange smiles.* Pleasant weather today!

THE POLICEMAN: A trifle warm, perhaps.

SHUI TA: Perhaps a trifle warm.

THE MAN, *softly to his wife*: If he goes on gassing till the kid gets back we'll be done for.

He tries to make Shui Ta a surreptitious sign.

SHUI TA, *without noticing*: It all depends whether one is contem-plating the weather from a cool establishment like this or from the dusty street.

THE POLICEMAN: It certainly does.

THE WOMAN: Don't worry. He'll keep away when he sees the copper standing in the door.

SHUI TA: But do come in. It really is cooler here. My cousin and I have opened a shop. Let me tell you that we consider it highly important to be on good terms with the authorities.

THE POLICEMAN *enters*: That is very kind of you, sir. Why yes, it really is cooler in here.

THE MAN, *softly*: He's asked him in just so the kid won't see him.

SHUI TA: Some guests. Distant acquaintances of my cousin's, apparently. They have a journey to make. *Bows are exchanged.* We were just saying goodbye.

THE MAN, *hoarsely*: All right then, we'll be going.

SHUI TA: I will tell my cousin that you thanked her for her hospitality, but could not wait for her return.

Noises from the street and cries of 'Stop thief!'

THE POLICEMAN: What's that about?

The boy appears in the door. Cakes and rolls are tumbling out of his shirt. The woman motions him desperately to get out. He turns and tries to go off.

THE POLICEMAN: You stay here. *He catches hold of him.* Where d'you get those cakes from?

THE BOY: Over there.

THE POLICEMAN: Aha. Stolen, eh?

THE WOMAN: We knew nothing about it. It was the boy's own idea. Little wretch.

THE POLICEMAN: Mr Shui Ta, can you throw any light on this?

Shui Ta remains silent.

THE POLICEMAN: Right. You all come along to the station with me.

SHUI TA: I am exceedingly sorry that anything like this should happen in my shop.

THE WOMAN: He watched the boy go off!

SHUI TA: I can assure you, officer, that I should hardly have invited you in if I had been wanting to conceal a robbery.

THE POLICEMAN: I quite see. You realise I'm only doing my duty, Mr Shui Ta, in taking these persons in custody. *Shui Ta bows.* Get moving, you! *He pushes them out.*

THE GRANDFATHER, *peacefully from the doorway*: Hullo.

Exeunt all except Shui Ta. Enter Mrs Mi Tzu.

MRS MI TZU: So you are the cousin I've heard about? How do the police come to be escorting people away from my building? What does your cousin mean by starting a boarding-house here? That's what comes of taking in people who a moment ago were in cheap digs, begging for crusts from the baker on the corner. I know all about it, you see.

SHUI TA: I do see. People have been speaking against my cousin. They have blamed her for being hungry! She has a bad name for living in poverty. Her reputation is the worst possible: she was down and out!

MRS MI TZU: She was a common or garden . . .

SHUI TA: Pauper; let's say the nasty word aloud.

MRS MI TZU: Oh, don't try and play on my feelings. I am speaking of her way of life, not her income. I have no doubt there was an income from somewhere, or she would hardly have started this shop. No doubt one or two elderly gentlemen

looked after that. How does one get hold of a shop? This is a
respectable house, sir. The tenants here aren't paying to live
under the same roof as that sort of person: no, sir. *Pause*
I am not inhuman, but I have got my obligations.

SHUI TA, *coldly*: Mrs Mi Tzu, I'm a busy man. Just tell me
what it will cost to live in this highly respectable house.

MRS MI TZU: Well, you are a cold fish, I'll give you that!

SHUI TA *takes the form of agreement out of the drawer*: It is a
very high rent. I take it from this agreement that it is to be
paid monthly?

MRS MI TZU, *quickly*: Not for your cousin's sort.

SHUI TA: What does that mean?

MRS MI TZU: That means that people like your cousin have to
pay six months' rent in advance: 200 silver dollars.

SHUI TA: 200 silver dollars! That is plain murder! Where am I
to find that much? I cannot count on a big turnover here.
My one hope is the girls who sew sacks in the cement works
who are supposed to smoke a lot because they find the work
so exhausting. But they are badly paid.

MRS MI TZU: You should have thought of that sooner.

SHUI TA: Mrs Mi Tzu, please have a heart! I realise that my
cousin made the unforgiveable mistake of giving shelter to
some unfortunates. But she will learn. I shall see that she
learns. Against that, where could you find a better tenant than
one who knows the gutter because he came from there? He'll
work his fingers to the bone to pay his rent punctually, he'll
do anything, go without anything, sell anything, stick at
nothing, and at the same time be as quiet as a mouse, gentle
as a fly, submit to you utterly rather than return there. A
tenant like that is worth his weight in gold.

MRS MI TZU: 200 silver dollars in advance, or she goes back on
the street, where she came from.

Enter the policeman.

THE POLICEMAN: Don't let me disturb you, Mr Shui Ta!

MRS MI TZU: The police really seem remarkably interested in
this shop.

THE POLICEMAN: Mrs Mi Tzu, I hope you haven't got a wrong impression. Mr Shui Ta did us a service, and I have come in the name of the police to thank him.

MRS MI TZU: Well, that's no affair of mine. Mr Shui Ta, I trust my proposition will be agreeable to your cousin. I like to be on good terms with my tenants. Good morning, gentlemen.

Exit.

SHUI TA: Good morning, Mrs Mi Tzu.

THE POLICEMAN: Have you been having trouble with Mrs Mi Tzu?

SHUI TA: She is demanding the rent in advance, as she doesn't think my cousin is respectable.

THE POLICEMAN: And can't you raise the money? *Shui Ta remains silent.* But Mr Shui Ta, surely someone like you ought to be able to get credit.

SHUI TA: I dare say. But how is someone like Shen Teh to get credit?

THE POLICEMAN: Are you not staying here then?

SHUI TA: No. And I shall not be able to come again. I could only give her a hand because I was passing through; I just saved her from the worst. Any minute she will be thrown back on her own resources. I am worried as to what will happen.

THE POLICEMAN: Mr Shui Ta, I am sorry to hear that you are having trouble over the rent. I must admit that we began by viewing this shop with mixed feelings, but your decisive action just now showed us the sort of man you are. Speaking for the authorities, we soon find out who we can rely on as a friend of law and order.

SHUI TA, *bitterly*: To save this little shop, officer, which my cousin regards as a gift of the gods, I am prepared to go to the utmost limits of the law. But toughness and duplicity will serve only against one's inferiors, for those limits have been cleverly defined. I am in the position of a man who has just got the rats out of his cellar, when along come the floods. *After a short pause*: Do you smoke?

THE POLICEMAN, *putting two cigars in his pocket*: Our station would be sorry to see you go, Mr Shui Ta. But you've got to understand Mrs Mi Tzu's point of view. Shen Teh, let's face it, lived by selling herself to men. You may ask, what else was she to do? For instance, how was she to pay her rent? But the fact remains: it is not respectable. Why not? A: you can't earn your living by love, or it becomes immoral earnings. B: respectability means, not with the man who can pay, but with the man one loves. C: it mustn't be for a handful of rice but for love. All right, you may say: what's the good of being so clever over spilt milk? What's she to do? When she has to find six months' rent? Mr Shui Ta, I must admit I don't know. *He thinks hard.* Mr Shui Ta, I have got it! All you need do is to find a husband for her.

Enter a little old woman.

THE OLD WOMAN: I want a good cheap cigar for my husband. Tomorrow is our fortieth wedding anniversary, you see, and we are having a little celebration.

SHUI TA, *politely*: Forty years, and still something to celebrate!

THE OLD WOMAN: As far as our means allow! That's our carpet shop over the way. I hope we are going to be good neighbours, it's important in these hard times.

SHUI TA *spreads various boxes before her*: Two very familiar words, I'm afraid.

THE POLICEMAN: Mr Shui Ta, what we need is capital. So I suggest a marriage.

SHUI TA, *excusing himself to the old woman*: I have been allowing myself to tell the officer some of my private troubles.

THE POLICEMAN: We've got to find six months' rent. Right, we marry a bit of money.

SHUI TA: That will not be easy.

THE POLICEMAN: Why not? She's a good match. She owns a small and promising business. *To the old woman*: What do you think?

THE OLD WOMAN, *doubtfully*: Well ...

THE POLICEMAN: An advertisement in the personal column.

THE OLD WOMAN, *reluctant*: If the young lady agrees ...

THE POLICEMAN: Why shouldn't she agree? I'll draft it out for
you. One good turn deserves another. Don't think the authorities have no sympathy for the small and struggling shop-
keeper. You play along with us, and in return we draft your
matrimonial advertisements! Hahaha!

*He hastens to pull out his notebook, licks his pencil stump and starts
writing.*

SHUI TA, *slowly*: It's not a bad idea.

THE POLICEMAN: 'What respectable gentleman . . . small capital . . . widower considered . . . desires marriage . . . into progressive tobacconist's?' And then we'll add: 'With charming
attractive brunette.' How's that?

SHUI TA: You don't feel that's overstating it?

THE OLD WOMAN, *kindly*: Certainly not. I have seen her.

*The policeman tears the page out of his notebook and hands it to
Shui Ta.*

SHUI TA: With horror I begin to realise how much luck one
needs to avoid being crushed! What brilliant ideas! What
faithful friends! *To the policeman*: Thus for all my decisive-
ness I was at my wits' end over the rent. And then you came
along and helped me with good advice. I really begin to see
a way out.

3
Evening in a Public Park

*A young man in tattered clothes is watching an aeroplane, which is
evidently making a high sweep over the park. He takes a rope from
his pocket and looks round him for something. He is making for a
big willow-tree, when two prostitutes come up to him. One of them
is old, the other is the niece from the family of eight.*

THE YOUNG ONE: Evening, young fellow. Coming home with
me, dear?

SUN: It could be done, ladies, if you'll stand me a meal.

THE OLD ONE: Are you nuts? *To the young one*: Come on, love. He's just a waste of time. That's that out-of-work pilot.

THE YOUNG ONE: But there won't be a soul in the park now, it's going to rain.

THE OLD ONE: There's always a chance.

They walk on. Sun looks round him, pulls out his rope and throws it over a branch of a willow tree. But he is interrupted again. The two prostitutes return rapidly. They do not see him.

THE YOUNG ONE: It's going to pelt with rain.

Shen Teh is walking up.

THE OLD ONE: Hullo, here she is, the bitch! She got your lot into trouble all right!

THE YOUNG ONE: Not her. It was her cousin. She took us in, and in the end she offered to pay for the cakes. I haven't any bone to pick with her.

THE OLD ONE: I have. *Loudly*: Why, there's our fancy friend with all the money. She's got a shop, but she still wants to pinch our boys off us.

SHEN TEH: Don't jump down my throat! I'm going down to the teahouse by the lake.

THE YOUNG ONE: Is it true you're marrying a widower with three children?

SHEN TEH: Yes, I'm meeting him there.

SUN, *impatiently*: Do your cackling somewhere else, will you? Isn't there anywhere one can get a bit of peace?

THE OLD ONE: Shut up!

Exeunt the two prostitutes.

SUN *calls after them*: Scavengers! *To the audience*: Even in this remote spot they fish tirelessly for victims, even in the thickets, in the rain, they pursue their desperate hunt for custom.

SHEN TEH, *angry*: What call have you got to slang them? *She sees the rope.* Oh!

SUN: What are you gooping at?

SHEN TEH: What's that rope for?

SUN: Move on, sister, move on! I've got no money, nothing, not a copper. And if I had I'd buy a drink of water, not you.

It starts raining.

SHEN TEH: What's that rope for? You're not to do it!

SUN: Mind your own business! And get out of the way!

SHEN TEH: It's raining.

SUN: Don't you try sheltering under my tree.

SHEN TEH *remains motionless in the rain*: No.

SUN: Why not give up, sister, it's no use. You can't do business with me. Besides, you're too ugly, Bandy legs.

SHEN TEH: That's not true.

SUN: I don't want to see them! All right, come under the bloody tree, since it's raining!

She approaches slowly and sits down under the tree.

SHEN TEH: Why do you want to do that?

SUN: Would you like to know? Then I'll tell you, so as to be rid of you. *Pause.* Do you know what an airman is?

SHEN TEH: Yes, I once saw some airmen in a teahouse.

SUN: Oh no you didn't. One or two windy idiots in flying helmets, I expect: the sort who's got no ear for his engine and no feeling for his machine. Gets into a kite by bribing the hangar superintendent. Tell a type like that: now stall your crate at 2,000, down through the clouds, then catch her up with the flick of the stick, and he'll say: But that's not in the book. If you can't land your kite gently as lowering your bottom you're not an airman, you're an idiot. Me, I'm an airman. And yet I'm the biggest idiot of the lot, because I read all the manuals in flying school at Pekin. But just one page of one manual I happened to miss, the one where it says Airmen Not Wanted. And so I became an airman without an aircraft, a mail pilot without mail. What that means you wouldn't understand.

SHEN TEH: I think I do understand all the same.

SUN: No, I'm telling you you can't understand. And that means you can't understand.

SHEN TEH, *half laughing, half crying*: When we were children
we had a crane with a broken wing. He was very tame and
didn't mind our teasing him, and used to come strutting
after us and scream if we went too fast for him. But in the
autumn and the spring, when the great flocks of birds flew
over our village, he became very restless, and I could understand why.

SUN: Stop crying.

SHEN TEH: Yes.

SUN: It's bad for the complexion.

SHEN TEH: I'm stopping.

*She dries her tears on her sleeve. Leaning against the tree, but
without turning towards her, he reaches for her face.*

SUN: You don't even know how to wipe your face properly.

He wipes it for her with a handkerchief.

SUN: If you've got to sit there and stop me from hanging
myself you might at least say something.

SHEN TEH: I don't know what.

SUN: Why do you want to hack me down, sister, as a matter of
interest?

SHEN TEH: It frightens me. I'm sure you only felt like that
because the evening's so dreary. *To the audience*:
    In our country
    There should be no dreary evenings
    Or tall bridges over rivers
    Even the hour between night and morning
    And the whole winter season too, that is dangerous.
    For in face of misery
    Only a little is needed
    Before men start throwing
    Their unbearable life away.

SUN: Tell me about yourself.

SHEN TEH: What is there? I've got a small shop.

SUN, *ironically*: Oh, so you haven't got a flat, you've got a shop!

SHEN TEH, *firmly*: I've got a shop, but before that I was on the
streets.

SUN: And the shop, I take it, was a gift of the gods?

SHEN TEH: Yes.

SUN: One fine evening they stood before you and said: Here's some money for you.

SHEN TEH, *laughing quietly*: One morning.

SUN: You're not exactly entertaining.

SHEN TEH, *after a pause*: I can play the zither a bit, and do imitations. *In a deep voice she imitates a dignified gentleman*: 'How idiotic, I must have come without my wallet!' But then I got the shop. The first thing I did was give away my zither. From now on, I told myself, you can be a complete jellyfish and it won't matter.

How rich I am, I told myself.

I walk alone. I sleep alone.

For one whole year, I told myself

I'll have no dealings with a man.

SUN: But now you're going to marry one? The one in the tea-house by the lake.

Shen Teh says nothing.

SUN: As a matter of interest, what do you know of love?

SHEN TEH: Everything.

SUN: Nothing, sister. Or was it perhaps pleasant?

SHEN TEH: No.

Sun strokes her face, without turning towards her.

SUN: Is that pleasant?

SHEN TEH: Yes.

SUN: Easily satisfied, you are. God, what a town.

SHEN TEH: Haven't you got friends?

SUN: A whole lot, but none that like hearing that I'm still out of a job. They make a face as if someone were complaining that the sea's wet. Have you got a friend, if it comes to that?

SHEN TEH, *hesitantly*: A cousin.

SUN: Then don't you trust him an inch.

SHEN TEH: He was only here once. Now he has gone off and is never coming back. But why do you talk as if you'd given up hope? They say: to give up hope, is to give up kindness.

SUN: Just talk on! At least it's something to hear a human voice.

SHEN TEH, *eagerly*: There are still friendly people, for all our wretchedness. When I was little once I was carrying a bundle of sticks and fell. An old man helped me up and even gave me a penny. I have often thought of it. Those who have least to eat give most gladly. I suppose people just like showing what they are good at; and how can they do it better than by being friendly? Crossness is just a way of being inefficient. Whenever someone is singing a song or building a machine or planting rice it is really friendliness. You are friendly too.

SUN: It doesn't seem hard by your definition.

SHEN TEH: And that was a raindrop.

SUN: Where?

SHEN TEH: Between my eyes.

SUN: More to the left or more to the right?

SHEN TEH: More to the left.

SUN: Good. *After a moment, sleepily*: So you're through with men?

SHEN TEH, *smiling*: But my legs aren't bandy.

SUN: Perhaps not.

SHEN TEH: Definitely not.

SUN, *wearily leaning back against the tree*: But as I haven't eaten for two days or drunk for one, I couldn't love you, sister, even if I wanted.

SHEN TEH: It is good in the rain.

Wang, the water-seller appears. He sings.

WANG:

THE WATER-SELLER'S SONG IN THE RAIN

> I sell water. Who will taste it?
> – Who would want to in this weather?
> All my labour has been wasted
> Fetching these few pints together.
> I stand shouting Buy my Water!
> And nobody thinks it
> Worth stopping and buying
> Or greedily drinks it.

(Buy water, you devils!)

> O to stop the leaky heaven
> Hoard what stock I've got remaining:
> Recently I dreamt that seven
> Years went by without it raining.
> How they'd all shout Give me Water!
> How they'd fight for my good graces
> And I'd make their further treatment
> Go by how I liked their faces.

(Stay thirsty, you devils!)

> Wretched weeds, you're through with thirsting
> Heaven must have heard you praying.
> You can drink until you're bursting
> Never bother about paying.
> I'm left shouting Buy my Water!
> And nobody thinks it
> Worth stopping and buying
> Or greedily drinks it.

(Buy water, you devils!)

The rain has stopped. Shen Teh sees Wang and runs towards him.

SHEN TEH: Oh Wang, so you have come back. I have looked after your pole for you.

WANG: Thank you for taking care of it! How are you, Shen Teh?

SHEN TEH: Well. I have got to know a very brave and clever person. And I should like to buy a cup of your water.

WANG: Throw your head back and open your mouth, and you can have as much water as you want. The willow tree is still dripping.

SHEN TEH: But I want your water, Wang.

> Laboriously carried
> Exhausting to its bearer
> And hard to sell, because it is raining.
> And I need it for the man over yonder.
> He is an airman. An airman
> Is braver than other humans. With the clouds for
>   companions

> Daring enormous tempests
> He flies through the heavens and brings
> To friends in far countries
> The friendly post.

She pays and runs over to Sun with the cup.

SHEN TEH *calls back to Wang, laughing*: He has fallen asleep. Hopelessness and the rain and I have tired him out.

INTERLUDE

Wang's sleeping-place under a Culvert

The water-seller is asleep. Music. The culvert becomes transparent, and the gods appear to him as he dreams.

WANG, *beaming*: I have seen her, O Illustrious Ones! She has not changed.

THE FIRST GOD: That gives us pleasure.

WANG: She is in love! She showed me her friend. Truly things are going well for her.

THE FIRST GOD: That is good to hear. Let us hope that she will be strengthened in her pursuit of goodness.

WANG: Indeed yes! She is performing all the charitable deeds she can.

THE FIRST GOD: Charitable deeds? What sort? Tell us about them, dear Wang.

WANG: She has a friendly word for everyone.

THE FIRST GOD, *keenly*: What else?

WANG: It is rare that a man is allowed to leave her shop without something to smoke, just for lack of money.

THE FIRST GOD: That sounds satisfactory. Any more?

WANG: She has taken in a family of eight.

THE FIRST GOD, *triumphantly to the second*: Eight, indeed! *To Wang*: Have you anything else you can tell us?

WANG: Although it was raining she bought a cup of water from me.

THE FIRST GOD: Yes, minor charities of that sort. Of course.

WANG: But they eat into the money. A small business doesn't make all that much.

THE FIRST GOD: True, true! But a prudent gardener can work wonders with his little patch.

WANG: That is just what she does! Every morning she distributes rice; believe me, it must cost more than half her earnings!

THE FIRST GOD, *slightly disappointed*: I am not denying it. I am not displeased with her start.

WANG: Remember, times are not easy! She had to call in a cousin once, as her shop was getting into difficulties.

> Hardly was a shelter erected against the wind
> Than the ruffled birds of the whole wintry heaven
> Came tumbling flying and
> Squabbled for a place and the hungry fox gnawed through
> The flimsy wall and the one-legged wolf
> Knocked the little rice-bowl over.

In other words the business was too much for her to manage. But everyone agrees that she is a good girl. They have begun to call her 'The Angel of the Slums'. So much good goes out from her shop. Whatever Lin To the carpenter may say!

THE FIRST GOD: What's that? Does Lin To the carpenter speak ill of her?

WANG: Oh, he only says the shelving in the shop wasn't quite paid for.

THE SECOND GOD: What are you telling us? A carpenter not paid? In Shen Teh's shop? How could she permit that?

WANG: I suppose she didn't have the money.

THE SECOND GOD: No matter: one pays one's debts. One cannot afford even the appearance of irregularity. The letter of the law has first to be fulfilled; then its spirit.

WANG: But Illustrious Ones, it was only her cousin, not herself.

THE SECOND GOD: Then that cousin must never again enter her door.

WANG, *dejected*: I have understood, Illustrious One! But in Shen Teh's defence let me just say that her cousin is supposed to be a most reputable business man. Even the police respect him.

THE FIRST GOD: This cousin will not be condemned without a hearing either. I know nothing of business, I admit; perhaps we ought to find out what is thought usual in such matters. But business indeed! Is it so very necessary? Nowadays there is nothing but business. Were the Seven Good Kings in business? Did Kung the Just sell fish? What has business to do with an upright and honourable life?

THE SECOND GOD, *with a bad cold*: In any case it must not be allowed to occur again.

He turns to leave. The other two gods likewise turn.

THE THIRD GOD, *the last to leave, embarrassedly*: Forgive our rather sharp tone today! We are very tired, and we have slept too little. Oh, those nights! The well-off give us the best possible recommendations to the poor, but the poor have too few rooms.

THE GODS *grumble as they move off*: Broken reeds, even the best of them! Nothing conclusive! Pitiful, pitiful! All from the heart, of course, but it adds up to nothing! At least she ought to . . .

They can no longer be heard.

WANG *calls after them*: Do not be too hard on us, O Illustrious Ones! Do not ask for everything at once!

4

Square in front of Shen Teh's Shop

A barber's, a carpet shop and Shen Teh's tobacconist's shop. It is Monday. Outside Shen Teh's shop wait two survivors of the family of eight – the grandfather and the sister-in-law. Also the unemployed man and Mrs Shin.

THE SISTER-IN-LAW: She never came home last night!

MRS SHIN: Astonishing behaviour! We manage to get rid of this maniac of a cousin and there's nothing to stop her having a little rice to spare now and again, when off she goes for the night chasing around God knows where!

Loud voices are heard from the barber's. Wang staggers out followed by Mr Shu Fu, the stout barber, with a heavy pair of curling tongs in his hand.

MR SHU FU: I'll teach you to come bothering my customers with your stinking water! Take your mug and get out!

Wang reaches for the mug which Mr Shu Fu is holding out to him, and gets a blow on the hand with the curling tongs, so that he screams.

MR SHU FU: Take that! Let that be a lesson to you.

He puffs back to his shop.

THE UNEMPLOYED MAN *picks up the mug and hands it to Wang*: You can have him up for hitting you.

WANG: My hand's gone.

THE UNEMPLOYED MAN: Any bones broken?

WANG: I can't move it.

THE UNEMPLOYED MAN: Sit down and bathe it a bit.

MRS SHIN: The water won't cost you much, anyway.

THE SISTER-IN-LAW: Eight o'clock already, and one can't even lay hands on a bit of rag here. She has to go gallivanting off! A disgrace!

MRS SHIN, *darkly*: She's forgotten us, that's what!

Shen Teh comes down the street carrying a pot of rice.

SHEN TEH, *to the audience*: I had never seen the city at dawn.
These were the hours when I used to lie with my filthy
blanket over my head, terrified to wake up. Today I mixed
with the newsboys, with the men who were washing down
the streets, with the ox-carts bringing fresh vegetables in from
the fields. It was a long walk from Sun's neighbourhood to
here, but with every step I grew happier. I had always been
told that when one is in love one walks on air, but the
wonderful thing is that one walks on earth, on tarmac. I tell
you, at dawn the blocks of buildings are like rubbish heaps
with little lights glowing in them; the sky is pink but still
transparent, clear of dust. I tell you, you miss a great deal if
you are not in love and cannot see your city at that hour when
she rises from her couch like a sober old craftsman, filling his
lungs with fresh air and reaching for his tools, as the poets
have it. *To the group waiting*: Good morning! Here is your
rice! *She shares it out, then notices Wang*: Good morning,
Wang. I am light-headed today. All along the way I looked
at my reflection in the shop windows, and now I would like
to buy myself a shawl. *After a short hesitation*: I should so
like to look beautiful.

She turns quickly into the carpet shop.

MR SHU FU, *who is again standing in his doorway, to the audience*:
I am smitten today with the beauty of Miss Shen Teh, the
owner of the tobacconist's opposite, whom I have never
previously noticed. I have watched her for three minutes,
and I believe I am already in love. An infinitely charming
person! *To Wang*: Get to hell, you lout!

*He turns back into the barber's shop. Shen Teh and an extremely
old couple, the carpet-dealer and his wife, come out of the carpet-
shop. Shen Teh is carrying a shawl, the carpet-dealer a mirror.*

THE OLD WOMAN: It's very pretty and not at all dear; there's a
small hole at the bottom.

SHEN TEH, *trying the shawl on the old woman's arm*: I like the
green one too.

THE OLD WOMAN, *smiling*: But I'm afraid it's in perfect condition.

SHEN TEH: Yes, a pity. I cannot undertake too much with my shop. The income is small, and there are many expenses.

THE OLD WOMAN: For charity; don't you do so much. When you are starting every bowl of rice counts, eh?

SHEN TEH *tries on the shawl with the hole in it*: Except that I have to; only at present I'm light-headed. Do you think the colour suits me?

THE OLD WOMAN: You had better ask a man that question.

SHEN TEH *calls to the old man*: Does it suit me?

THE OLD MAN: Why don't you ask ...

SHEN TEH, *very politely*: No, I am asking you.

THE OLD MAN, *equally politely*: The shawl suits you. But wear it dull side out.

Shen Teh pays.

THE OLD WOMAN: If you don't like it I will always change it for another. *Draws her aside*: Has he any money?

SHEN TEH, *laughing*: O goodness no.

THE OLD WOMAN: Will you be able to pay your half-year's rent?

SHEN TEH: The rent! It had clean gone out of my mind!

THE OLD WOMAN: I thought it had! And Monday will be the first of the month. I have something to suggest. You know: my husband and I were a little doubtful about the marriage advertisement once we had got to know you. We decided we'd help you out if need be. We've put something by, and we can lend you the 200 silver dollars. If you like you can make over your stock to us as security. But of course we don't need anything in writing.

SHEN TEH: Would you really lend money to such a scatter-brained person?

THE OLD WOMAN: To be honest, we'd think twice about lending it to your cousin, who is definitely not scatter-brained, but we'd gladly lend it to you.

THE OLD MAN *comes up*: All fixed?

SHEN TEH: I wish the gods could have heard your wife just

then, Mr Deng. They are looking for good and happy people. And I'm sure you must be happy, to be helping me out of the troubles that love has brought me.

The two old people smile at one another.

THE OLD MAN: Here is the money.

He hands her an envelope. Shen Teh accepts it and bows. The old people bow too. They go back to their shop.

SHEN TEH, *to Wang, holding up the envelope*: This is six months' rent. Isn't that a miracle? And Wang, what do you think of my new shawl?

WANG: Did you buy it for the man I saw in the park?

Shen Teh nods.

MRS SHIN: You might choose to look at his hand instead of retailing your shady adventures!

SHEN TEH, *alarmed*: What's the matter with your hand?

MRS SHIN: The barber smashed it with his curling tongs in front of our eyes.

SHEN TEH, *horrified at her heedlessness*: And I didn't notice! You must go to the doctor at once, or your hand will go stiff and you'll never be able to work properly again. It's a frightful disaster. Come on, get up! Hurry!

THE UNEMPLOYED MAN: He doesn't want the doctor; he wants the magistrate! The barber's a rich man, and he ought to get compensation.

WANG: Do you think there's a chance?

MRS SHIN: If you really can't use it. Can you?

WANG: I don't think so. It's already very swollen. Would it mean a pension for life?

MRS SHIN: You need a witness, of course.

WANG: But you all saw! You can all of you bear me out.

He looks round. Unemployed man, grandfather, sister-in-law: all are sitting against the wall and eating. No one looks up.

SHEN TEH, *to Mrs Shin*: You yourself saw it, didn't you?

MRS SHIN: I don't want to get mixed up with the police.

SHEN TEH, *to the sister-in-law*: What about you then?

THE SISTER-IN-LAW: Me? I wasn't looking!

MRS SHIN: Of course you were looking. I saw you looking! You're just scared because the barber's got too much pull.

SHEN TEH, *to the grandfather*: I am sure that you will confirm what happened.

THE SISTER-IN-LAW: They wouldn't listen to him. He's gaga.

SHEN TEH, *to the unemployed man*: It may mean a pension for life.

THE UNEMPLOYED MAN: They've taken my name twice for begging. It won't do him much good if I give evidence.

SHEN TEH, *incredulous*: Do you mean to say that not one of you will say what happened? His hand gets broken in full daylight, in front of you all, and not one will open his mouth. *Angrily*:

O you unfortunates!

Your brother is mishandled before you, and you just shut your eyes.

Injured, he screams aloud, and you keep mum.

The bully swaggers round, picks out his victim

And you say: he'll spare us, for we hide our displeasure.

What sort of a town is that, what sort of humans are you?

When an injustice takes place in a town there must be an uproar

And where there is no uproar it is better the town disappears

In flames before the night falls.

Wang, if nobody who saw it will be your witness, then I will be your witness and say that I saw it.

MRS SHIN: It'll be perjury.

WANG: I don't know if I can allow that. But perhaps I have to allow it. *Looking anxiously at his hand*: Do you think it has swollen enough? It looks to me as if it has started to go down?

THE UNEMPLOYED MAN, *calming him*: No, it certainly hasn't gone down.

WANG: Are you sure? Ah yes, I do believe it's swelling a bit

more. Possibly my wrist is broken! I'd better go straight to
the magistrate.

*Holding his hand carefully and still looking at it, he hurries off.
Mrs Shin enters the barber's shop.*

THE UNEMPLOYED MAN: She's gone to the barber's to butter
him up.

THE SISTER-IN-LAW: It's not for us to change the world.

SHEN TEH, *discouraged*: I didn't mean to be rude to you. It's
just that I was shocked. No, I did mean to be rude to you.
Get out of my sight!

*The unemployed man, the sister-in-law and the grandfather go off
eating and grumbling.*

SHEN TEH, *to the audience*:

They cannot respond. Where they are stationed
They stay put, and when turned away
They quickly yield place!
Nothing now moves them. Only
The smell of cooking will make them look up.

An old woman comes hurrying up. It is Sun's mother, Mrs Yang.

MRS YANG, *out of breath*: Are you Miss Shen Teh? My son has
told me everything. I am Sun's mother, Mrs Yang. Think
of it, he has got the chance of a job as a pilot! He got a letter
from Pekin this morning, just now. From one of the superin-
tendents in the postal service.

SHEN TEH: That means he can fly again? Oh, Mrs Yang!

MRS YANG: But it will cost a lot: 500 silver dollars.

SHEN TEH: That's a great deal, but money must not stand in
his way. After all, I've got the shop.

MRS YANG: If you could only do something!

SHEN TEH *embraces her*: If I could help him!

MRS YANG: You would be giving a chance to a very gifted
individual!

SHEN TEH: Why should they stop a man from applying his gifts?
After a pause: Except that I shall not get enough for the shop,

and the 200 silver dollars which I have got in cash are only a loan. Of course you can have those now. I will sell my stock and pay them back out of that.

She gives her the old couple's money.

MRS YANG: O Miss Shen Teh, a friend in need is a friend indeed. And they were all calling him the dead pilot, because they said he has as much chance of flying again as a corpse.

SHEN TEH: We still need 300 silver dollars for the job, though. Mrs Yang, we must think. *Slowly*: I know someone who might perhaps help. Someone who has advised me before. I didn't really want to have to resort to him again; he is too smart and too tough. This will definitely be the last time. But a pilot has got to fly, that is obvious.

Sound of engines in the distance.

MRS YANG: If your friend could only raise the money! Look, there goes the morning mail service to Pekin!

SHEN TEH, *with determination*: Wave to it, Mrs Yang. I'm sure the pilot can see us! *She waves her shawl.* Go on, wave!

MRS YANG, *waving*: Do you know the pilot?

SHEN TEH: No. I know a pilot. For the man without hope shall fly, Mrs Yang. One of us at least shall be able to fly above all this wretchedness; one at least shall rise above us all!

To the audience:

Yang Sun, my loved one, with the clouds for companions!
Daring enormous tempests
Flying through the heavens and bringing
To friends in far countries
The friendly post.

INTERLUDE
in front of the curtain

Shen Teh enters, carrying Shui Ta's mask and costume, and sings the

SONG OF THE DEFENCELESSNESS OF THE GOOD AND THE GODS

SHEN TEH:

In our country
The capable man needs luck. Only
If he has mighty backers
Can he prove his capacity.
The good
Have no means of helping themselves and the gods are powerless.
    So why can't the gods launch a great operation
    With bombers and battleships, tanks and destroyers
    And rescue the good by a ruthless invasion?
    Then maybe the wicked would cease to annoy us.

She puts on Shui Ta's costume and takes a few steps in his way of walking.

The good
Cannot remain good for long in our country
Where cupboards are bare, housewives start to squabble.
Oh, the divine commandments
Are not much use against hunger.
    So why can't the gods share out what they've created
    Come down and distribute the bounties of nature
    And allow us, once hunger and thirst have been sated
    To mix with each other in friendship and pleasure?

She dons Shui Ta's mask and sings on in his voice.

In order to win one's mid-day meal
One needs the toughness which elsewhere builds empires.
Except twelve others be trampled down
The unfortunate cannot be helped.

So why can't the gods make a simple decision
That goodness must conquer in spite of its weakness? –
Then back up the good with an armoured division
Command it to: 'fire!' and not tolerate meekness?

5

The Tobacconist's

Shui Ta sits behind the counter and reads the paper. He takes no notice of Mrs Shin, who is cleaning the place and talking.

MRS SHIN: A small business like this soon goes downhill, believe me, once certain rumours get around locally. This shady affair between the young lady and that fellow Yang Sun from the Yellow Alley, it was high time a proper gentleman like you came and cleared it up. Don't forget that Mr Shu Fu, the hairdresser next door, a gentleman who owns twelve houses and has only one wife, and an old one at that, hinted to me yesterday that he took a rather flattering interest in the young lady. He went so far as to ask about her financial standing. I'd say that showed real partiality.

Getting no answer, she finally leaves with her bucket.

SUN'S VOICE, *from outside*: Is this Miss Shen Teh's shop?
MRS SHIN'S VOICE: Yes. But her cousin's there today.

Shui Ta runs to a mirror, with Shen Teh's light steps, and is just beginning to arrange his hair when he realises his mistake. He turns away with a soft laugh. Enter Yang Sun. Behind him appears the inquisitive Mrs Shin. She goes past him into the back of the shop.

SUN: I am Yang Sun. *Shui Ta bows.* Is Shen Teh in?
SHUI TA: No, she is not in.
SUN: But I expect you're in the picture about me and her? *He begins to take stock of the shop.* A real shop, large as life. I always thought she was putting it on a bit. *He examines the boxes and china pots with satisfaction.* Oh boy, I'm going to be flying again. *He helps himself to a cigar, and Shui Ta gives*

him a light. Do you think we can squeeze another 300 dollars out of the business?

SHUI TA: May I ask: is it your intention to proceed to an immediate sale?

SUN: Why? Have we got the 300 in cash? *Shui Ta shakes his head.* It was good of her to produce the 200 at once. But I've got to have the other 300 or I'm stuck.

SHUI TA: Perhaps she was a bit hasty in offering you the money. It may cost her her business. They say, haste is the wind that blew the house down.

SUN: I need it now or not at all. And the girl's not one to hesitate when it's a question of giving. Between ourselves, she hasn't hesitated much so far.

SHUI TA: Really?

SUN: All to her credit, of course.

SHUI TA: May I ask how the 500 dollars will be used?

SUN: Why not? As you seem to be checking up on me. The airport superintendent in Pekin is a friend of mine from flying school, and he can get me the job if I cough up 500 silver dollars.

SHUI TA: Isn't that an unusually large sum?

SUN: No. He has got to prove negligence against a highly conscientious pilot with a large family. You get me? That's between us, by the way, and there's no need for Shen Teh to know.

SHUI TA: Perhaps not. One point though: won't the superintendent be selling you up the river a month later?

SUN: Not me. No negligence with me. I've been long enough without a job.

SHUI TA *nods*: It is the hungry dog who pulls the cart home quickest. *He studies him for a moment or two*: That's a very big responsibility. You are asking my cousin, Mr Yang Sun, to give up her small property and all her friends in this town, and to place herself entirely in your hands. I take it your intention is to marry Shen Teh?

SUN: I'd be prepared to.

SHUI TA: Then wouldn't it be a pity to let the business go for a few silver dollars? You won't get much for a quick sale. The 200 silver dollars that you've already got would guarantee the rent for six months. Do you not feel at all tempted to carry on the tobacconist's business?

SUN: What, me? Have people see Yang Sun the pilot serving behind a counter? 'Good morning, sir; do you prefer Turkish or Virginia?' That's no career for Yang Suns, not in the twentieth century!

SHUI TA: And is flying a career, may I ask?

SUN takes a letter from his pocket: They're paying me 250 silver dollars a month, sir. Here is the letter; see for yourself. Look at the stamp, postmarked Pekin.

SHUI TA: 250 silver dollars? That is a lot.

SUN: Do you think I'd fly for nothing?

SHUI TA: It sounds like a good job. Mr Yang Sun, my cousin has asked me to help you get this pilot's job which means so much to you. Looking at it from her point of view I see no insuperable objection to her following the bidding of her heart. She is fully entitled to share in the delights of love. I am prepared to realise everything here. Here comes Mrs Mi Tzu, the landlady; I will ask her advice about the sale.

MRS MI TZU enters: Good morning, Mr Shui Ta. I suppose it's about your rent that's due the day after tomorrow?

SHUI TA: Mrs Mi Tzu, circumstances have arisen which make it doubtful whether my cousin will carry on with the business. She is contemplating marriage, and her future husband – he introduces Yang Sun – Mr Yang Sun, is taking her to Pekin where they wish to start a new life. If I can get a good price for my tobacco I shall sell it.

MRS MI TZU: How much do you need?

SUN: 300 in cash.

SHUI TA, quickly: No, no. 500!

MRS MI TZU, to Sun: Perhaps I can help you out. How much did your stock cost?

SHUI TA: My cousin originally paid 1000 silver dollars, and very little of it has been sold.

MRS MI TZU: 1000 silver dollars! She was swindled, of course.

I'll make you an offer: you can have 300 silver dollars for the
whole business, if you move out the day after tomorrow.

SUN: All right. That's it, old boy!

SHUI TA: It's too little!

SUN: It's enough!

SHUI TA: I must have at least 500.

SUN: What for?

SHUI TA: May I just discuss something with my cousin's fiancé?
Aside to Sun: All this stock of tobacco is pledged to two old
people against the 200 silver dollars which you got yesterday.

SUN, *slowly:* Is there anything about it in writing?

SHUI TA: No.

SUN, *to Mrs Mi Tzu after a short pause:* 300 will do us.

MRS MI TZU: But I have to be sure that the business has no
outstanding debts.

SUN: You answer.

SHUI TA: The business has no outstanding debts.

SUN: How soon can we have the 300?

MRS MI TZU: The day after tomorrow, and you had better think
it over. Put the sale off for a month and you will get more.
I can offer you 300, and that's only because I'm glad to help
where it seems to be a case of young love. *Exit.*

SUN, *calling after her:* It's a deal! Lock, stock and barrel for 300,
and our troubles are over. *To Shui Ta:* I suppose we might
get a better offer in the next two days? Then we could even
pay back the 200.

SHUI TA: Not in the time. We shan't get a single dollar over
Mrs Mi Tzu's 300. Have you got the money for both your
tickets, and enough to tide you over?

SUN: Sure.

SHUI TA: How much?

SUN: Anyway, I'll raise it even if I have to steal it!

SHUI TA: Oh, so that's another sum that has to be raised?

SUN: Don't worry, old boy. I'll get to Pekin all right.

SHUI TA: It costs quite a bit for two.

SUN: Two? I'm leaving the girl here. She'd only be a liability
at first.

SHUI TA: I see.

SUN: Why do you look at me as if I was something the cat had brought in? Beggars can't be choosers.

SHUI TA: And what is my cousin to live on?

SUN: Can't you do something for her?

SHUI TA: I will look into it. *Pause.* I should like you to hand me back the 200 silver dollars, Mr Yang Sun, and leave them with me until you are in a position to show me two tickets to Pekin.

SUN: My dear cousin, I should like you to mind your own business.

SHUI TA: Miss Shen Teh...

SUN: You just leave her to me.

SHUI TA: ... may not wish to proceed with the sale of her business when she hears...

SUN: O yes she will.

SHUI TA: And you are not afraid of what I may have to say against it?

SUN: My dear man!

SHUI TA: You seem to forget that she is flesh and blood, and has a mind of her own.

SUN, *amused*: It astounds me what people imagine about their female relations and the effect of sensible argument. Haven't they ever told you about the power of love, the twitching of the flesh? You want to appeal to her reason? She hasn't any reason! All she's had is a life-time of ill-treatment, poor thing! If I put my hand on her shoulder and say 'You're coming with me,' she'll hear bells and not recognise her own mother.

SHUI TA, *laboriously*: Mr Yang Sun!

SUN: Mr ... whatever your name is!

SHUI TA: My cousin is indebted to you because ...

SUN: Let's say because I've got my hand inside her blouse? Stuff that in your pipe and smoke it! *He takes another cigar, then sticks a few in his pocket, and finally puts the box under his arm.* You're not to go to her empty-handed: we're getting married, and that's settled. And she'll bring the 300 with her or else you will: either her or you. *Exit.*

MRS SHIN *sticks her head out of the back room*: How very disagreeable! And the whole Yellow Alley knows that he's got
the girl exactly where he wants her.

SHUI TA, *crying out*: The business has gone! He's not in love.
This means ruin. I am lost! *He begins to rush round like a
captive animal, continually repeating, 'The business has gone!'
– until he suddenly stops and addresses Mrs Shin*: Mrs Shin
you grew up in the gutter and so did I. Are we irresponsible?
No. Do we lack the necessary brutality? No. I am ready to
take you by the scruff of the neck and shake you until you
spit out the farthing you stole from me, and you know it.
Times are frightful, the town is hell, but we scrabble up the
naked walls. Then one of us is overcome by disaster: he is in
love. That is enough, he is lost. A single weakness, and you
can be shovelled away. How can one remain free of every
weakness, above all of the most deadly, of love? It is intolerable! It costs too much! Tell me, has one got to spend one's
whole life on the look-out? What sort of world do we live in?

> Love's caresses merge in strangulation.
> Love's sighs grow into a scream of fear.
> What are the vultures hovering for?
> A girl is keeping an appointment.

MRS SHIN: I think I had better fetch the barber. You must talk
to the barber. He is a man of honour. The barber: that's the
right man for your cousin.

*Getting no answer, she hurries away. Shui Ta continues rushing
around until Mr Shu Fu enters, followed by Mrs Shin, who however is forced to withdraw at a gesture from Mr Shu Fu.*

SHUI TA *turns to him*: My dear sir, rumour has it that you have
shown a certain interest in my cousin. You must allow me to
set aside the laws of propriety, which call for a measure of
reserve, for the young lady is at the moment in great danger.

MR SHU FU: Oh!

SHUI TA: Proprietress of her own business until a few hours ago, my cousin is now little more than a beggar. Mr Shu Fu, this shop is bankrupt.

MR SHU FU: Mr Shui Ta, Miss Shen Teh's attraction lies less in the soundness of her business than in the goodness of her heart. You can tell a lot from the name they give the young lady round here: The Angel of the Slums!

SHUI TA: My dear sir, this goodness has cost my cousin 200 silver dollars in a single day! There are limits.

MR SHU FU: Allow me to put forward a different opinion: is it not time that all limits to this goodness were removed? It is the young lady's nature to do good. What is the sense of her feeding four people, as she so moves me by doing every morning! Why should she not feed four hundred? I hear for instance that she is desperate to find shelter for a few homeless. My buildings across the cattleyard are unoccupied. They are at her disposal. And so on and so forth. Mr Shui Ta, have I the right to hope that such thoughts as these which I have lately been entertaining may find a willing listener in Miss Shen Teh?

SHUI TA: Mr Shu Fu, she will listen with admiration to such lofty thoughts.

Enter Wang with the policeman. Mr Shu Fu turns round and examines the shelves.

WANG: Is Miss Shen Teh here?

SHUI TA: No.

WANG: I am Wang, the water-seller. I suppose you are Mr Shui Ta?

SHUI TA: Quite correct. Good morning, Wang.

WANG: I am a friend of Shen Teh's.

SHUI TA: I know that you are one of her oldest friends.

WANG, *to the policeman*: See? *To Shui Ta*: I have come about my hand.

THE POLICEMAN: He can't use it, there's no denying.

SHUI TA, *quickly*: I see you want a sling for your arm. *He fetches a shawl from the back room and tosses it to Wang.*

WANG: But that's her new shawl.

SHUI TA: She won't need it.

WANG: But she bought it specially to please a particular person

SHUI TA: As things have turned out that is no longer necessary.

WANG *makes a sling out of the shawl*: She is my only witness.

THE POLICEMAN: Your cousin is supposed to have seen Shu Fu
the barber strike the water-carrier with his curling-tongs. Do
you know anything about that?

SHUI TA: I only know that my cousin was not present when this
slight incident took place.

WANG: It's a misunderstanding! When Shen Teh comes she
will clear it all up. Shen Teh will bear me out. Where is she?

SHUI TA, *seriously*: Mr Wang, you call yourself my cousin's
friend. At the moment my cousin has really serious worries.
She has been disgracefully exploited on all sides. From now
on she cannot permit herself the slightest weakness. I am
convinced that you will not ask her to ruin herself utterly by
testifying in your case to anything but the truth.

WANG, *puzzled*: But she told me to go to the magistrate.

SHUI TA: Was the magistrate supposed to cure your hand?

THE POLICEMAN: No. But he was to make the barber pay up.

Mr Shu Fu turns round.

SHUI TA: Mr Wang, one of my principles is never to interfere
in a dispute between my friends.

Shui Ta bows to Mr Shu Fu, who bows back.

WANG, *sadly, as he takes off the sling and puts it back*: I see.

THE POLICEMAN: Which means I can go, eh? You tried your
game on the wrong man, on a proper gentleman that is. You
be a bit more careful with your complaints next time, fellow.
If Mr Shu Fu doesn't choose to waive his legal rights you
can still land in the cells for defamation. Get moving!

Both exeunt.

SHUI TA: I beg you to excuse this episode.

MR SHU FU: It is excused. *Urgently*: And this business about a
'particular person?' *He points to the shawl.* Is it really over?
Finished and done with?

SHUI TA: Completely. She has seen through him. Of course, it will take time for it all to heal.

MR SHU FU: One will be careful, considerate.

SHUI TA: Her wounds are fresh.

MR SHU FU: She will go away to the country.

SHUI TA: For a few weeks. But she will be glad to talk things over first with someone she can trust.

MR SHU FU: Over a little supper, in a small but good restaurant.

SHUI TA: Discreetly. I shall hasten to inform my cousin. She will show her good sense. She is greatly upset about her business, which she regards as a gift from the gods. Please be so good as to wait for a few minutes. *Exit into the back room.*

MRS SHIN *sticks her head in*: Can we congratulate you?

MR SHU FU: You can. Mrs Shin, will you tell Shen Teh's dependents from me before tonight that I am giving them shelter in my buildings across the yard?

She grins and nods.

MR SHU FU, *standing up, to the audience*: What do you think of me, ladies and gentlemen? Could one do more? Could one be more unselfish? More delicate? More far-sighted? A little supper. How crude and vulgar that would normally sound. Yet there will be nothing of that kind, not a thing. No contact, not even an apparently accidental touch when passing the salt. All that will happen will be an exchange of ideas. Two souls will discover one another, across the flowers on the table – white chrysanthemums, by the way. *He notes it down.* No, this will be no exploiting of an unfortunate situation, no profiting from a disappointment. Understanding and assistance will be offered, but almost unspoken. By a glance alone will they be acknowledged, a glance that can also signify rather more.

MRS SHIN: Has it all turned out as you wanted, Mr Shu Fu?

MR SHU FU: Oh, quite as I wanted. You can take it that there will be changes in this neighbourhood. A certain character has been sent packing, and one or two hostile movements against this shop are due to be foiled. Certain persons who have no hesitation in trampling on the good name of the most respectable girl in this town will in future have me to deal with. What do you know about this Yang Sun?

MRS SHIN: He is the idlest, dirtiest . . .

MR SHU FU: He is nothing. He does not exist. He is simply not present, Mrs Shin.

Enter Sun.

SUN: What's this about?

MRS SHIN: Would you like me to call Mr Shui Ta, sir? He won't like strangers wandering round the shop.

MR SHU FU: Miss Shen Teh is having an important discussion with Mr Shui Ta, and they cannot be interrupted.

SUN: She's here, is she? I didn't see her go in! What are they discussing? They can't leave me out!

MR SHU FU *prevents him from going into the back room*: You will have to be patient, sir. I think I know who you are. Kindly take note that Miss Shen Teh and I are about to announce our engagement.

SUN: What?

SHIN: That is a surprise for you, isn't it?

Sun struggles with the barber in an effort to get into the back room; Shen Teh emerges.

MR SHU FU: Forgive us, my dear Shen Teh. Perhaps you will explain.

SUN: What's up, Shen Teh? Have you gone crazy?

SHEN TEH, *breathlessly*: Sun, Mr Shu Fu and my cousin have agreed that I ought to listen to Mr Shu Fu's ideas of how to help the people round here. *Pause.* My cousin is against our relationship.

SUN: And you have agreed?

SHEN TEH: Yes.

Pause.

SUN: Have they told you I'm a bad character?

Shen Teh remains silent.

SUN: Perhaps I am, Shen Teh. And that is why I need you. I am a debased character. No capital, no manners. But I can put up a fight. They're wrecking your life, Shen Teh. *He goes up to her, subdued*: Just look at him! Haven't you got eyes in your head? *Putting his hand on her shoulder*: Poor creature, what are they trying to shove you into now? Into a sensible marriage! If it weren't for me they would simply have put you out of your misery. Tell me yourself: but for me, wouldn't you have gone off with him?

SHEN TEH: Yes.

SUN: A man you don't love!

SHEN TEH: Yes.

SUN: Have you completely forgotten? The rain?

SHEN TEH: No.

SUN: How you hacked me down from the tree, how you brought me a glass of water, how you promised me the money so I could fly again?

SHEN TEH, *trembling*: What do you want?

SUN: Come away with me.

SHEN TEH: Mr Shu Fu, forgive me, I want to go away with Sun.

SUN: We are in love, you know. *He escorts her to the door.* Have you got the key of the shop? *He takes it from her and gives it to Mrs Shin.* Put it on the step when you've finished. Come, Shen Teh.

MR SHU FU: But this is rape! *He shouts into the back room*: Mr Shui Ta!

SUN: Tell him not to make so much row here.

SHEN TEH: Please don't call my cousin, Mr Shu Fu. We are not of one mind, I know. But he is not in the right, I can sense it. *To the audience*:

> I would go with the man whom I love.
> I would not reckon what it costs me.
> I would not consider what is wiser.
> I would not know whether he loves me.
> I would go with the man whom I love.

SUN: Just like that.

Both walk off.

INTERLUDE
in front of the curtain

Shen Teh in her wedding clothes, on her way to the wedding, turns and addresses the audience.

SHEN TEH: I have had a fearful experience. As I stepped out of the door, joyous and full of expectation, I found the carpet-dealer's old wife standing in the street, shakily telling me that her husband was so excited and troubled about the money she lent me that he had fallen ill. She thought it best for me in any case to give her back the money. Of course I promised. She was greatly relieved and, weeping, gave me her good wishes, begging me to excuse her for not completely trusting my cousin, nor, alas, Sun. I had to sit down on the steps when she left, I had so scared myself. In the tumult of my feelings I had thrown myself once more into Yang Sun's arms. I could resist neither his voice nor his caresses. The evil that he had spoken to Shui Ta could not teach Shen Teh a lesson. Sinking into his arms, I still thought; the gods wanted me to be kind to myself too.

> To let none go to waste, not oneself either
> To bring happiness to all, even oneself, that
> Is good.

How could I simply have forgotten the two good old people? Like a small hurricane Sun just swept my shop off in the direction of Pekin, and with it all my friends. But he is not evil, and he loves me. As long as I am near him he will do nothing wicked; what a man tells other men means nothing. He wants to seem big and strong then, and particularly hard-boiled. If I tell him that the old people cannot pay their taxes he will understand. He would rather get a job at the cement works than owe his flying to a wrong action. True, flying is a tremendous passion with him. Shall I be strong enough to call out the goodness in him? At the moment, on the way to my wedding, I am hovering between fear and joy.

She goes off quickly.

6

Private Room in a cheap Suburban Restaurant

A waiter is pouring out wine for the wedding guests. Round Shen Teh stand the grandfather, the sister-in-law, the niece, Mrs Shin and the unemployed man. A priest stands by himself in a corner. Sun is talking to his mother, Mrs Yang, in front. He is wearing a dinner jacket.

SUN: Bad news, mother. She just told me, oh so innocently, that she can't sell the shop for me. Some people are dunning her to pay back those 200 silver dollars she gave you. Though her cousin says there's nothing about it in writing.

MRS YANG: What did you say to her? You can't marry her, of course.

SUN: There's no point in discussing all that with her; she is too pig-headed. I have sent for her cousin.

MRS YANG: But he wants to get her married to the barber.

SUN: I've dealt with that marriage. The barber has been seen off. Her cousin will soon realise the business has gone if I don't produce the two hundred, as the creditors will seize it, but that the job's gone too if I don't get the 300 on top.

MRS YANG: I'll go and look for him outside. Go and talk to your bride now, Sun!

SHEN TEH, *to the audience as she pours out wine*: I was not mistaken in him. Not a line of his face betrayed disappointment. Despite the heavy blow that it must have been to renounce his flying he is perfectly cheerful. I love him very much. *She motions Sun to come to her.* Sun, you have not yet drunk with the bride!

SUN: What shall we drink to?

SHEN TEH: Let it be to the future.

They drink.

SUN: When the bridegroom's dinner jacket is his own!

SHEN TEH: But the bride's dress is still sometimes exposed to the rain.

SUN: To all we want for ourselves!

SHEN TEH: May it come soon!

MRS YANG, *to Mrs Shin as she leaves*: I am delighted with my son. I've always tried to make him realise that he can get any girl he wants. Him, a trained pilot and mechanic. And what does he go and tell me now? I am marrying for love, mother, he says. Money isn't everything. It's a love match! *To the sister-in-law*: Sooner or later these things have to happen, don't they? But it's hard on a mother, very hard. *Calling to the priest*: Don't cut it too short. If you take as long over the ceremony as you did arguing about the fee, that will make it nice and dignified. *To Shen Teh*: We shall have to hold things up a bit, my dear. One of our most valued guests has still to arrive. *To all*: Please excuse us. *Exit.*

THE SISTER-IN-LAW: It's a pleasure to be patient as long as there's something to drink.

They sit down.

THE UNEMPLOYED MAN: We're not missing much.

SUN, *loudly and facetiously in front of the guests*: Before the ceremony starts I ought to give you a little test. There's some point when the wedding's at such short notice. *To the guests*: I have no idea what sort of wife I'm going to get. It's most disturbing. For instance, can you use three tea-leaves to make five cups of tea?

SHEN TEH: No.

SUN: Then I shan't be getting any tea. Can you sleep on a straw mattress the size of that book the priest's reading?

SHEN TEH: Double?

SUN: Single.

SHEN TEH: In that case, no.

SUN: Dreadful, what a wife I'm getting.

All laugh. Behind Shen Teh Mrs Yang appears in the doorway. She shrugs her shoulders to tell Sun that the expected guest is not to be seen.

MRS YANG, *to the priest, who is pointing to his watch*: Don't be in such a hurry. It can't be more than a matter of minutes. There they are, all drinking and smoking, and none of them's in a hurry. *She sits down with her guests.*

SHEN TEH: But oughtn't we to discuss how it's all going to be settled?

MRS YANG: Now, not a word about business today. It so lowers the tone of a party, don't you think?

The bell at the door rings. All look towards the door, but nobody comes in.

SHEN TEH: Who is your mother waiting for, Sun?

SUN: It's to be a surprise for you. By the way, where is your cousin, Shui Ta? I get on well with him. A very sensible fellow! Brainy! Why don't you say something?

SHEN TEH: I don't know. I don't want to think about him.

SUN: Why not?

SHEN TEH: Because I wish you didn't get on with him. If you like me, you can't like him.

SUN: Then I hope the gremlins got him: the engine gremlin, the petrol gremlin and the fog gremlin. Drink, you old obstinate!

He forces her.

THE SISTER-IN-LAW, *to Mrs Shin*: Something fishy here.

MRS SHIN: What else did you expect?

THE PRIEST *comes firmly up to Mrs Yang, with his watch in his hand*: I must go, Mrs Yang. I've got a second wedding, and a funeral first thing in the morning.

MRS YANG: Do you imagine I'm holding things up for pleasure? We hoped that one jug of wine would see us through. Now look how low it's getting. *Loudly, to Shen Teh*: I can't understand, my dear Shen Teh, why your cousin should let us wait for him like this!

SHEN TEH: My cousin?

MRS YANG: But my dear girl, it's him we're waiting for. I am old-fashioned enough to feel that such a close relation of the bride ought to be at the wedding.

SHEN TEH: Oh Sun, is it about the 300 dollars?

SUN, *without looking at her*: You've heard what it's about. She is old-fashioned. I've got to consider her. We'll just wait a quarter of an hour, and if he hasn't come by then it'll mean the three gremlins have got him, and we'll start without!

MRS YANG: I expect you have all heard that my son is getting a position as a mail pilot. I am delighted about it. It's important to have a well-paid job in these days.

THE SISTER-IN-LAW: In Pekin, they say: is that right?

MRS YANG: Yes, in Pekin.

SHEN TEH: Sun, hadn't you better tell your mother that Pekin is off?

SUN: Your cousin can tell her if he feels the same way as you. Between you and me, I don't.

SHEN TEH, *shocked*: Sun!

SUN: God, how I loathe Szechwan! What a town! Do you realise what they all look like when I half shut my eyes? Like horses. They look up nervously: what's that thundering over their heads? What, won't people need them any more? Have they outlived their time? They can bite each other to death in their horse town! All I want is to get out of here!

SHEN TEH: But I promised the old couple I'd pay them back.

SUN: Yes, that's what you told me. And it's a good thing your cousin's coming as you're so silly. Drink your wine and leave business to us! We'll fix it.

SHEN TEH, *horrified*: But my cousin can't come!

SUN: What do you mean?

SHEN TEH: He's not there.

SUN: And how do you picture our future: will you kindly tell me?

SHEN TEH: I thought you still had the 200 silver dollars. We can pay them back tomorrow and keep the tobacco, which is worth much more, and sell it together outside the cement works as we can't pay the rent.

SUN: Forget it! Put it right out of your mind, sister! Me stand in the street and hawk tobacco to the cement workers: me, Yang Sun the pilot? I'd sooner blow the whole 200 in a single night. I'd sooner chuck it in the river! And your cousin knows me. I fixed with him he was to bring the 300 to the wedding.

SHEN TEH: My cousin cannot come.

SUN: And I thought he couldn't possibly stay away.

SHEN TEH: It is impossible for him to be where I am.

SUN: How very mysterious!

SHEN TEH: Sun, you must realise he is no friend of yours. It is I who love you. My cousin Shui Ta loves nobody. He is a friend to me, but not to my friends. He agreed that you should have the old people's money because he was thinking of your pilot's job in Pekin. But he will not bring the 300 silver dollars to the wedding.

SUN: And why not?

SHEN TEH, *looking him in the eyes*: He says you only bought one ticket to Pekin.

SUN: Yes, but that was yesterday, and look what I've got to show him today! *He half pulls two tickets out of his breast pocket*. There's no need for the old woman to see. That's two tickets to Pekin, for me and for you. Do you still think your cousin's against the marriage?

SHEN TEH: No. The job is a good one. And my business has gone.

SUN: It's for your sake I sold the furniture.

SHEN TEH: Don't say any more! Don't show me the tickets! It makes me too afraid that I might simply go off with you. But do you see, Sun, I can't give you the 300 silver dollars, or what is to become of the two old people?

SUN: What's to become of me? *Pause*. You'd better have a drink! Or do you believe in being careful? I can't stick a careful woman. When I drink I start flying again. And you: if you drink there's just the faintest shadow of a possibility you may understand me.

SHEN TEH: Don't think I don't understand you. You want to fly, and I can't be any help.

SUN: 'Here's your plane, beloved, but I'm afraid it's a wing short.'

SHEN TEH: Sun, there's no honourable way for us to get that

job in Pekin. That's why I need you to hand back the 200 silver dollars I gave you. Give them to me now, Sun!

SUN: 'Give them to me now, Sun!' What do you think you are talking about? Are you my wife or aren't you? Because you're ratting on me, don't you realise? Luckily – and luckily for you too – it doesn't depend on you, because it's all been settled.

MRS YANG, *icily*: Sun, are you certain the bride's cousin will be coming? It almost looks as though he had something against this marriage, as he doesn't appear.

SUN: But what are you thinking of, mother! Him and me are like that. I'll open the door wide so that he spots us at once as he comes rushing up to act as best man to his old friend Sun. *He goes to the door and kicks it open. Then he comes back, swaying slightly because he has already drunk too much, and sits down again by Shen Teh.* We'll wait. Your cousin has got more sense than you. Love is an essential part of living, he wisely says. And what's more he knows what it would mean for you: no shop left and no wedding either!

They wait.

MRS YANG: At last!

Footsteps are heard, and all look towards the door. But the footsteps move on.

MRS SHIN: There's going to be a scandal. One can feel it; one can sniff it in the air. The bride is waiting for the ceremony, but the bridegroom is waiting for her honourable cousin.

SUN: The honourable cousin is taking his time.

SHEN TEH, *softly*: Oh, Sun!

SUN: Sitting here with the tickets in my pocket, and an idiot beside me who can't do arithmetic! And I see the day coming when you'll be putting the police on me to get your 200 silver dollars back.

SHEN TEH, *to the audience*: He is evil and he would like me to be evil too. Here am I who love him, and he stays waiting for a cousin. But round me sit the defenceless: the old woman with her sick husband, the poor who wait at the door every morning for rice, and an unknown man from Pekin who is worried about his job. And they all protect me because they all have faith in me.

SUN *stares at the glass jug in which the wine is near the bottom*: The wine-jug is our clock. We are poor people, and once the guests have drunk the wine the clock has run down for ever.

Mrs Yang signs to him to keep silent, and footsteps can be heard once more.

THE WAITER *enters*: Do you wish to order another jug of wine, Mrs Yang?

MRS YANG: No, I think there will be enough. Wine only makes one too hot, don't you think?

MRS SHIN: I imagine it costs a lot too.

MRS YANG: Drinking always makes me perspire.

THE WAITER: Would you mind settling the bill now, madam?

MRS YANG *ignores him*: Ladies and gentlemen, I hope you can be patient a little longer: our relative must be on his way by now. *To the waiter*: Don't interrupt the party.

THE WAITER: My orders are not to let you leave until the bill is settled.

MRS YANG: But I am well known here!

THE WAITER: Exactly!

MRS YANG: The service nowadays is really outrageous! Don't you think so, Sun?

THE PRIEST: I fear that I must leave. *Exit weightily.*

MRS YANG, *desperate*: Please all of you remain seated! The priest will be back in a few minutes.

SUN: Drop it, mother. Ladies and gentlemen, now that the priest has left we cannot detain you any longer.

THE SISTER-IN-LAW: Come on, Grandpa!

THE GRANDFATHER *solemnly empties his glass*: The bride!

THE NIECE, *to Shen Teh*: Don't mind him. He means it friendly-like. He's fond of you.

MRS SHIN: That's what I call a flop!

All the guests leave.

SHEN TEH: Shall I leave too, Sun?

SUN: No, you wait. *He pulls at her wedding finery so that it is askew.* It's your wedding, isn't it? I'm going to wait on, and the old lady will wait on. She is anxious to see her bird in the air again anyhow. It's my opinion that the moon will be nothing but green cheese before she can step outside and see his plane thundering over the house. *To the empty chairs as if the guests were still there:* Ladies and gentlemen, can't you make conversation? Don't you like it here? The wedding has only been somewhat postponed, on account of the non-arrival of influential relations, and because the bride doesn't know what love is. To keep you amused I, the bridegroom, will sing you a song. *He sings:*

THE SONG OF GREEN CHEESE

A day will come, so the poor were informed
As they sat at their mother's knees
When a child of low birth shall inherit the earth
And the moon shall be made of green cheese.
    When the moon is green cheese
    The poor shall inherit the earth.

Then goodness will be a thing to reward
And evil a mortal offence.
'Where there's merit there's money' won't sound quite
        so funny
There will really be no difference.
    When the moon is green cheese
    There won't be this difference.

Then the grass will look down on the blue sky below
And the pebbles will roll up the stream
And man is a king. Without doing a thing
He gorges on honey and cream.
    When the moon is green cheese
    The world flows with honey and cream.

Then I shall become a pilot again
And you'll get a deputy's seat.
You, man on the loose, will find you're some use
And you, ma, can put up your feet.
>When the moon is green cheese
>The weary can put up their feet.

And as we have waited quite long enough
This new world has got to be born
Not at the last minute so there's nothing left in it
But at the first glimmer of dawn
>When the moon is green cheese
>The very first glimmer of dawn.

MRS YANG: He won't come now.

The three of them sit there and two of them look towards the door.

INTERLUDE

Wang's Sleeping Place

Once more the gods appear to the water-seller in a dream. He has fallen asleep over a large book. Music.

WANG: How good that you have come, Illustrious Ones! Permit me a question which disturbs me greatly. In the tumbledown hut belonging to a priest who has left to become an unskilled labourer in the cement works I discovered a book, and in it I found a remarkable passage. I should like to read it to you. It runs: *With his left hand he thumbs through an imaginary book laid over the book in his lap, and lifts this imaginary book up to read from it, leaving the real one lying where it was.* 'In Sung there is a place known as Thorn Hedge. There catalpas, cypresses and mulberries flourish. Now those trees which are nine or ten inches in circumference are chopped down by the people who need stakes for their dog kennels. Those which are three or four feet in circumference are chopped down by rich and respectable families who want planks for their coffins. Those which are seven or eight feet in circumference are chopped down by persons seeking beams for their luxurious villas. And so none reaches its full quota of years, but is brought down prematurely by saw or by axe. That is the price of utility.'

THE THIRDGOD: That would mean that the least useful is the best.

WANG: No, only the most fortunate. The least good is the most fortunate.

THE FIRST GOD: Ah, what things they write!

THE SECOND GOD: Why are you so deeply moved by this comparison, O water-seller?

WANG: On account of Shen Teh, Illustrious Ones! She has failed in her love because she obeyed the commandment to love her neighbours. Perhaps she really is too good for this world, O Illustrious Ones!

THE FIRST GOD: Nonsense. You poor, feeble creature! It seems to me that you are half eaten away by scepticism and lice.

WANG: Certainly, O Illustrious One! I only thought you might perhaps intervene.

THE FIRST GOD: Out of the question. Our friend here – *he points to the third god, who has a black eye* – intervened in a quarrel only yesterday; you see the result.

WANG: But they had to send for her cousin yet again. He is an unusually capable man, I know from experience, but even he could not set things straight. It looks as if the shop were already lost.

THE THIRD GOD, *disturbed*: Do you think perhaps we ought to help?

THE FIRST GOD: My view is that she has got to help herself.

THE SECOND GOD, *strictly*: The worse the difficulties, the better the good man will prove to be. Suffering ennobles!

THE FIRST GOD: We are putting all our hopes in her.

THE THIRD GOD: Our search is not progressing well. Now and again we come across a good start, admirable intentions, a lot of high principles, but it hardly adds up to a good person.

When we do find people who are halfway good, they are not living a decent human existence. *Confidentially*: The nights are getting worse and worse. You can tell where we have been spending them from the straws sticking to our clothes.

WANG: Just one request. Could you not at least . . .

THE GODS: Nothing. We are but observers. We firmly believe that our good person will find her own feet on this sombre earth. Her powers will wax with her burden. Only wait a little, O water-seller, and you will find all's well that ends . . .

The gods' figures have been growing steadily paler, their voices steadily fainter. Now they disappear, and their voices cease.

7
Yard behind Shen Teh's Shop

A few household goods on a cart. Shen Teh and Mrs Shin are taking washing down from the line.

MRS SHIN: I can't think why you don't put up a better fight for your business.

SHEN TEH: How? I can't even pay the rent. I have got to pay the old people their 200 silver dollars back today, and because I've given them to someone else I shall have to sell my stock to Mrs Mi Tzu.

MRS SHIN: All gone, eh? No man, no stock, no home! That comes of trying to set oneself up as a cut above our lot. How do you propose to live now?

SHEN TEH: I don't know. I might earn a bit as a tobacco sorter.

MRS SHIN: What are Mr Shui Ta's trousers doing here? He must have gone off in his shirt.

SHEN TEH: He's got another pair.

MRS SHIN: I thought you said he had gone away for good. What does he want to leave his trousers behind for?

SHEN TEH: Perhaps he's finished with them.

MRS SHIN: Oughtn't you to make a parcel of them?

SHEN TEH: No.

Mr Shu Fu bursts in.

MR SHU FU: Don't tell me. I know it all. You have sacrificed your young love so that two old people who trusted you should not be ruined. It was not for nothing that this malicious and mistrustful district christened you 'The Angel of the Slums'. The gentleman to whom you were engaged proved unable to raise himself to your moral stature; you threw him over. And now you are closing your shop, that little haven of refuge for so many! I cannot stand by and see it. Day after day I have stood at the door of my shop and seen the knot of down-and-outs before your window, and you yourself doling out rice. Must all that vanish for ever? Must goodness be defeated? Ah, if only you will allow me to assist you in your good works! No, don't say a thing! I wish for no assurances. No promises that you will accept my help! But herewith – *he takes out a cheque-book and writes a cheque, which he lays on the cart* – I make you out a blank cheque, which you can fill in for any sum you like; and now I shall go, quietly and modestly, demanding nothing in return, on tiptoe, full of respectful admiration, not a thought for myself.

Exit.

MRS SHIN *examines the cheque*: This'll save you! People like you have some luck! You can always find a mug. Now hurry up. Write in 1,000 silver dollars and I'll run to the bank with it before he comes to his senses.

SHEN TEH: Put the laundry basket on the cart. I can pay for the washing without that cheque.

MRS SHIN: What do you mean? You're not going to take the cheque? That's criminal! Is it just because you feel you would have to marry him? That would be plain crazy. A fellow like that just asks to be led by the nose! That sort really likes it. Are you still wanting to hang on to that pilot of yours, when everyone here and in Yellow Alley knows how badly he's treated you?

SHEN TEH: It all comes from poverty. *To the audience*:

At night I watched him blow out his cheeks in his sleep:
    they were evil

And at dawn I held his coat up to the light, and saw the
    wall through it.
When I saw his sly smile I was afraid, but
When I saw the holes in his shoes I loved him dearly.

MRS SHIN: So you're still sticking up for him? I never heard
anything so idiotic. *Angry:* I shall be relieved when we have
got you out of the district.

SHEN TEH *staggers as she takes down the washing:* I'm feeling a
bit giddy.

MRS SHIN *takes the washing from her:* Do you often feel giddy
when you bend or stretch? Let's only hope it isn't a little
one! *Laughs.* He has fixed you good and proper! If that's it
then the big cheque will turn sour. It wasn't meant for that
sort of situation. *She goes to the rear with a basket.*

*Shen Teh looks after her without moving. Then she examines her
body, feels it, and a great joy appears in her face.*

SHEN TEH, *softly:* Oh joy! A small being is coming to life in my
body. There is nothing to see yet. But he is already there.
The world awaits him in secret. In the cities they have heard
the rumour: someone is coming now with whom we must
reckon. *She presents her small son to the audience:* An airman!
    Salute a new conqueror
    Of unknown mountains, inaccessible countries! One
    Carrying letters from man to man
    Across the wastes where no man yet has trod!
*She begins to walk up and down, leading her small son by the
hand.* Come my son, inspect your world. Here, that is a tree.
Bow politely, greet him. *She performs a bow.* There, now you
know one another. Listen, that is the water-seller coming. A
friend, shake hands with him. Don't be nervous. 'A glass of
cool water for my son, please. It's a hot day.' *She hands him
the glass.* Ah, the policeman! I think we will avoid him. Perhaps we might collect one or two cherries over there, from
rich old Mr Feh Pung's orchard. This is a moment not to be
seen. Come, poor little bastard! You too like cherries! Soft,
soft, my son! *They walk cautiously, looking around them.* No,

round this way, where the bushes will shield us. No, no going straight to the point in this case. *He seems to be dragging away; she resists.* We've got to be sensible. *Suddenly she gives in.* Very well, if you can't do it any other way. . . . *She lifts him up.* Can you reach the cherries? Shove them in your mouth, that's the best place for them. *She eats one herself, which he puts into her mouth.* Tastes fine. O god, the police. This is where we run. *They flee.* Here's the road. Now gently, walk slowly so we don't attract attention. As if nothing whatever had happened. . . . *She sings as she walks along with the child*:

> A plum off my tree
> Bit a man on the knee
> The man had a thirst
> Got his own bite in first.

Wang the water-seller has entered, leading a child by the hand. He watches Shen Teh in astonishment.

SHEN TEH, *as Wang coughs*: Oh, Wang! Good day.

WANG: Shen Teh, I have heard you are in difficulties, that you must even sell your business to pay debts. But here's this child without any home. It was playing about in the slaughter-house. They say it belongs to Lin To the carpenter, who had to give up his workshop a few weeks ago and is now on the drink. His children are wandering around starving. What can be done with them?

SHEN TEH *takes the child from him*: Come on, little man! *To the audience*:

> Here, you! Someone begging for shelter.
> A chip of tomorrow begging you for a today.
> His friend, the conqueror, whom you know
> Can answer for him.

To Wang: He can quite well live in Mr Shu Fu's sheds, where I may be going too. I myself am expecting a child. But do not repeat that, or Yang Sun may hear of it, and we can only hamper him. See if you can find Lin To in the lower town, and tell him to come here.

WANG: Many thanks, Shen Teh. I knew you would find an

answer. *To the child*: See? A good person always knows a way. I'll go off quickly and fetch your father. *He starts to go.*

SHEN TEH: Oh, Wang, I have just remembered. What happened about your hand? I did want to give evidence for you, but my cousin . . .

WANG: Don't bother about my hand. Look, I've already learnt to do without my right hand. I hardly need it at all. *He shows her how he can manage his carrying pole without his right hand*: See how I manage?

SHEN TEH: But you mustn't let it get stiff! Take that cart, sell the lot, and use the money to go to the doctor. I am ashamed of having let you down like that. And what must you think of me for accepting the barber's offer of the sheds!

WANG: The homeless can live there now, and you yourself. After all, that matters more than my hand. I'll go and fetch the carpenter. *Exit.*

SHEN TEH *calls after him*: Promise me you'll let me take you to the doctor!

Mrs Shin has come back and has been making repeated signs.

SHEN TEH: What is it?

MRS SHIN: Are you mad? Giving away the cart with all you've got left? What's his hand to do with you? If the barber gets to know he'll throw you out of the last lodging you're likely to find. You haven't paid me for the washing yet!

SHEN TEH: Why are you so unpleasant?

> To trample on one's fellows
> Is surely exhausting? Veins in your temples
> Stick out with the strenuousness of greed.
> Loosely held forth
> A hand gives and receives with the same suppleness. Yet
> Greedily snatching it has got to strain. Oh
> How tempting it is to be generous. How welcome
> Friendliness can somehow feel. A kindly word
> Escapes like a sigh of contentment.

Mrs Shin goes off angrily.

SHEN TEH, *to the child*: Sit here and wait till your father comes.

The child sits on the ground. Enter the elderly couple who visited Shen Teh on the day of the opening of her shop. Man and wife are dragging big sacks.

THE WOMAN: Are you by yourself, Shen Teh? *When Shen Teh nods she calls in her nephew, who is also carrying a sack.* Where's your cousin?

SHEN TEH: He went away.

THE WOMAN: Is he coming back?

SHEN TEH: No. I'm giving up the shop.

THE WOMAN: So we heard. That's why we've come. These are a few sacks of leaf tobacco which somebody owed us, and we'd be ever so grateful if you could move them to your new home with your own things. We've no place to put them yet, and if we have them in the street people are bound to notice. I don't see how you can refuse to do us this little favour after the bad luck we had in your shop.

SHEN TEH: I will do it for you gladly.

THE MAN: And if anyone happens to ask you whose sacks these are you can say they're yours.

SHEN TEH: Who would want to know?

THE WOMAN, *giving her a sharp look*: The police for one. They've got it in for us, and they're out to ruin us. Where do we put the sacks?

SHEN TEH: I don't know; just at this moment I'd sooner not do anything that might get me into gaol.

THE WOMAN: Isn't that like you? All we've been able to save of our things is a few rotten old sacks of tobacco, and a lot you care if we lose them!

Shen Teh is stubbornly silent.

THE MAN: Don't you see that this stock of tobacco might allow us to start manufacturing in a small way? Then we could work our way up.

SHEN TEH: All right, I'll keep your sacks for you. They can go in the back room for the present.

She goes in with them. The child has been watching her. Now it looks round timidly, goes to the dustbin and starts fishing in it. It begins to eat something that it has found. Shen Teh and the others return.

THE WOMAN: You realise we're completely in your hands?

SHEN TEH: Yes. *She notices the child and stiffens.*

THE MAN: We'll call on you the day after tomorrow in Mr Shu Fu's buildings.

SHEN TEH: Please leave at once; I'm not well. *She pushes them out. Exeunt the three.* He's hungry. *Fishing in the dustbin.*

She lifts up the child and expresses her horror at the fate of poor children in a speech, showing the audience his dirty mouth. She proclaims her determination never to treat her own child in such a heartless way.

> O son, O airman! What sort of a world
> Awaits you? Will you too
> Be left to fish in the garbage? Observe
> The greyness round his mouth! *She exhibits the child.* Is that
> How you treat your fellow-creatures? Have you
> Not the least compassion for the fruit
> Of your bodies? No pity
> For yourselves, you unfortunates? Henceforth I
> Shall fight at least for my own, if I have to be
> Sharp as a tiger. Yes, from the hour
> When I saw this thing I shall cut myself off
> From them all, never resting
> Till I have at least saved my son, if only him.
> What I learnt from my schooling, the gutter
> By violence and trickery now
> Shall serve you, my son: to you
> I would be kind; a tiger, a savage beast
> To all others if need be. And
> It need be.

She goes off to change herself into her cousin.

SHEN TEH, *walking off*: Once more it must be done, for the last time I hope.

She has taken Shui Ta's trousers with her. Mrs Shin returns and stares inquisitively after her. Enter the sister-in-law and the grandfather.

THE SISTER-IN-LAW: Shop shut, all her stuff in the yard! It's the finish!

MRS SHIN: That's what comes of selfishness, irresponsibility and the lusts of the flesh! And where is she heading? Downwards! To Mr Shu Fu's sheds, along with the rest of you!

THE SISTER-IN-LAW: She'll be surprised at what she finds there! We've come to complain! A damp rabbit-warren with half rotten floors! The barber only let us have them because his stock of soap was going bad there. 'I can give you shelter, what do you say to that?' We say, it's a scandal!

Enter the unemployed man.

THE UNEMPLOYED MAN: Is it true Shen Teh's clearing out?

THE SISTER-IN-LAW: Yes. She meant to sneak away so we shouldn't know.

MRS SHIN: She's ashamed because she's broke.

THE UNEMPLOYED MAN, *excited*: She must send for her cousin! All of you, advise her to send for her cousin! He's the only one can do anything.

THE SISTER-IN-LAW: That's right! He's mean enough, but at least he'll save her business, and then she'll be generous.

THE UNEMPLOYED MAN: I wasn't thinking of us, I was thinking of her. But it's a fact: he must be sent for for our sakes too.

Enter Wang with the carpenter. He is leading two children by the hand.

THE CARPENTER: Truly, I can't thank you enough. *To the others*: We're to get a lodging.

MRS SHIN: Where?

THE CARPENTER: In Mr Shu Fu's buildings. And it was little Feng who managed it! Ah, there you are! 'Here's someone begging for shelter', Miss Shen Teh's supposed to have said, and she finds us lodgings there and then. Say thank you to your brother, all of you!

The carpenter and his children make pretence of bowing to the child.

THE CARPENTER: Our thanks, shelter-beggar!

Shui Ta has entered.

SHUI TA: May I ask what you are all doing here?
THE UNEMPLOYED MAN: Mr Shui Ta!
WANG: Good day, Mr Shui Ta. I didn't realise you were back. You know Lin To the carpenter. Miss Shen Teh promised to find him a corner in one of Mr Shu Fu's buildings.
SHUI TA: Mr Shu Fu's buildings are booked.
THE CARPENTER: Does that mean we can't lodge there?
SHUI TA: No. These premises are reserved for another purpose.
THE SISTER-IN-LAW: Have we got to move out too then?
SHUI TA: Unfortunately.
THE SISTER-IN-LAW: But where can we all go?
SHUI TA, *shrugging his shoulders*: Miss Shen Teh, who has left town, gave me to understand that she had no intention of neglecting you. In future however it must all be rather more sensibly arranged. No more free meals without working for it. Instead every man shall have the opportunity to improve his condition honourably by his labour. Miss Shen Teh has decided to find work for you all. Those of you who now choose to follow me into Mr Shu Fu's buildings will not be led into the blue.
THE SISTER-IN-LAW: Do you mean we've all got to start working for Shen Teh?
SHUI TA: Yes. You will shred tobacco. There are three full bales in the back room there. Get them!
THE SISTER-IN-LAW: Don't forget we used to have a shop of our own. We'd rather work for ourselves. We've got our own tobacco.
SHUI TA, *to the unemployed man and the carpenter*: Perhaps you

would like to work for Shen Teh, as you have no tobacco of
your own?

*The carpenter and the unemployed man comply reluctantly, and
exeunt. Mrs Mi Tzu enters.*

MRS MI TZU: Now then, Mr Shui Ta, how about the sale of the
stock? I have your 300 silver dollars here with me.

SHUI TA: Mrs Mi Tzu, I have decided not to sell, but to sign
the lease.

MRS MI TZU: What? Don't you want the money for the pilot
any more?

SHUI TA: No.

MRS MI TZU: And can you find the rent?

SHUI TA *takes the barber's cheque off the cart and fills it in.* I have
here a cheque for 10,000 silver dollars, signed by Mr Shu Fu,
who is taking an interest in my cousin. Look for yourself,
Mrs Mi Tzu! You will get your 200 silver dollars for the next
half-year's rent before six this evening. And now, Mrs Mi
Tzu, you will allow me to go on with my own work. I am
extremely busy today and must ask you to excuse me.

MRS MI TZU: So Mr Shu Fu is in the pilot's shoes now! 10,000
silver dollars! All the same I am astounded that young girls
nowadays should be so frivolous and unstable, Mr Shui Ta.
Exit.

The carpenter and the unemployed man bring in the sacks.

THE CARPENTER: I can't think why I should have to cart your
sacks for you.

SHUI TA: The point is that I can. Your son has a healthy appetite. He wants to eat, Mr Lin To.

THE SISTER-IN-LAW *sees the sacks:* Has my brother-in-law been
here?

MRS SHIN: Yes.

THE SISTER-IN-LAW: I thought so. I know those sacks. That's
our tobacco.

SHUI TA: I advise you not to say that so loudly. That is my
tobacco, as you can see from the fact that it was in my room.

But if you have any doubts about it we can go to the police and clear them up. Do you wish to?

THE SISTER-IN-LAW, *crossly*: No.

SHUI TA: Evidently you haven't got your own stock of tobacco after all. Perhaps under those circumstances you will accept the helping hand which Miss Shen Teh is offering you? Be so good now as to show me the way to Mr Shu Fu's buildings.

Taking the hand of the carpenter's youngest child, Shui Ta walks off, followed by the carpenter, his remaining children, the sister-in-law, the grandfather, the unemployed man. Sister-in-law, carpenter and unemployed man drag out the sacks.

WANG: He is not a wicked man, but Shen Teh is good.

MRS SHIN: I'm not sure. There's a pair of trousers missing from the clothes line, and her cousin is wearing them. That must mean something. I'd like to know what.

Enter the two old people.

THE OLD WOMAN: Is Miss Shen Teh not here?

MRS SHIN, *absently*: Left town.

THE OLD WOMAN: That's strange. She was going to bring us something.

WANG, *looking painfully at his hand*: And she was going to help me. My hand's going stiff. She's sure to be back soon. Her cousin never stays long.

MRS SHIN: He doesn't, does he?

INTERLUDE

Wang's Sleeping Place

Music. In a dream the water-seller informs the gods of his fears. The gods are still engaged on their long pilgrimage. They seem tired. Unresponsive at first, they turn and look back at the water-seller.

WANG: Before you appeared and awoke me, O Illustrious Ones, I was dreaming and saw my dear sister Shen Teh in great distress among the reeds by the river, at the spot where the suicides are found. She was staggering in a strange way and held her head bent as if she were carrying something soft and heavy that was pressing her into the mud. When I called to her she called back that she must carry the whole bundle of precepts across to the other bank, keeping it dry so that the ink should not run. In fact I could see nothing on her shoulder. But I was sharply reminded that you gods had lectured her about the major virtues as a reward for her taking you in when you were stuck for a night's lodging, the more shame to us! I am certain you understand my worries for her.

THE THIRD GOD: What do you suggest?

WANG: A slight reduction of the precepts, Illustrious Ones. A slight alleviation of the bundle of precepts, O gracious ones, in view of the difficulty of the times.

THE THIRD GOD: For instance, Wang, for instance?

WANG: For instance, that only good will should be required instead of love, or . . .

THE THIRD GOD: But that is far harder, you unhappy man!

WANG: Or fairness instead of justice.

THE THIRD GOD: But that means more work!

WANG: Then plain decency instead of honour!

THE THIRD GOD: But that is far more, you man of doubts!

They wander wearily on.

8

Shui Ta's Tobacco Factory

Shui Ta has set up a small tobacco factory in Mr Shu Fu's huts. Horribly constricted, a number of families huddle behind bars. Women and children predominate, among them the sister-in-law, the grandfather, the carpenter and his children. In front of them enter Mrs Yang, followed by her son, Sun.

MRS YANG, *to the audience*: I must describe to you how the wisdom and discipline of our universally respected Mr Shui Ta turned my son Sun from a broken wreck into a useful citizen. Near the cattle-yard, as the whole neighbourhood quickly came to hear, Mr Shui Ta started a small but rapidly prospering tobacco factory. Three months ago I found it advisable to call on him there with my son. He received me after a brief wait.

Shui Ta comes up to Mrs Yang from the factory.

SHUI TA: What can I do for you, Mrs Yang?

MRS YANG: Mr Shui Ta, I should like to put in a word for my son. The police came round this morning, and we heard that you were suing in Miss Shen Teh's name for breach of promise and fraudulent conversion of 200 silver dollars.

SHUI TA: Quite correct, Mrs Yang.

MRS YANG: Mr Shui Ta, in the gods' name can you not temper justice with mercy once more? The money has gone. He ran through it in a couple of days as soon as the idea of the pilot's job fell through. I know he is a bad lot. He had already sold my furniture and was going to set off to Pekin without his poor old mother. *She weeps.* There was a time when Miss Shen Teh thought very highly of him.

SHUI TA: Have you got anything to say to me, Mr Yang Sun?

SUN, *sombrely*: The money's gone.

SHUI TA: Mrs Yang, in view of the weakness which my cousin for some inexplicable reason felt for your broken-down son, I am prepared to give him another chance. She told me she

thought honest work might bring an improvement. I can find
him a place in my factory. The 200 silver dollars will be
deducted in instalments from his wages.

SUN: So it's to be factory or clink?

SHUI TA: It's your own choice.

SUN: And no chance of talking to Shen Teh, I suppose.

SHUI TA: No.

SUN: Show me where I work.

MRS YANG: A thousand thanks, Mr Shui Ta. Your kindness is
overwhelming, and the gods will repay you. *To Sun*: You
have strayed from the narrow path. See if honest work will
make you fit to look your mother in the face again.

*Sun follows Shui Ta into the factory. Mrs Yang returns to the
front of the stage.*

MRS YANG: The first weeks were difficult for Sun. The work
was not what he was used to. He had little chance to show
what he could do. It was only in the third week that a small
incident brought him luck. He and Lin To who used to be
a carpenter were shifting bales of tobacco.

*Sun and the former carpenter Lin To are each shifting two bales of
tobacco.*

THE FORMER CARPENTER *comes to a halt groaning, and lowers
himself on to one of the bales*: I'm about done in. I'm too old
for this sort of work.

SUN *likewise sits down*: Why don't you tell them they can stuff
their bales?

THE FORMER CARPENTER: How would we live then? To get
the barest necessities I must even set the kids to work. A pity
Miss Shen Teh can't see it! She was good.

SUN: I've known worse. If things had been a bit less miserable
we'd have hit it off quite well together. I'd like to know where
she is. We had better get on. He usually comes about now.

They get up.

SUN *sees Shui Ta coming*: Give us one of your sacks, you old
cripple! *Sun adds one of Lin To's bales to his own load.*

THE FORMER CARPENTER: Thanks a lot! Yes, if she were there you'd certainly go up a peg when she saw how helpful you were to an old man. Ah yes!

Enter Shui Ta.

MRS YANG: And a glance is enough for Mr Shui Ta to spot a good worker who will tackle anything. And he takes a hand.

SHUI TA: Hey, you two! What's happening here? Why are you only carrying one sack?

THE FORMER CARPENTER: I feel a bit run down today, Mr Shui Ta, and Yang Sun was so kind . . .

SHUI TA: You go back and pick up three bales, my friend. If Yang Sun can do it, so can you. Yang Sun puts his heart in it, and you don't.

MRS YANG, *while the former carpenter fetches two more bales*: Not a word to Sun, of course, but Mr Shui Ta had noticed. And next Saturday, at the pay desk . . .

A table is set up and Shui Ta comes with a small bag of money. Standing next the overseer – the former unemployed man – he pays out the wages. Sun steps up to the table.

THE OVERSEER: Yang Sun – 6 silver dollars.

SUN: Sorry, but it can't be more than five. Not more than 5 silver dollars. *He takes the list which the overseer is holding.* Look, here you are, you've got me down for six full days, but I was off one day, as I had to go to cóurt. *Ingratiatingly*: I wouldn't like to be paid money I hadn't earned, however lousy the pay is.

THE OVERSEER: 5 silver dollars, then! *To Shui Ta*: Very unusual that, Mr Shui Ta!

SHUI TA: How do you come to have six days down here when it was only five?

THE OVERSEER: Quite correct, Mr Shui Ta, I must have made a mistake. *To Sun, coldly*: It won't occur again.

SHUI TA *calls Sun aside*: I have noticed lately that you have plenty of strength and don't grudge it to the firm. Now I see that you are to be trusted too. Does it often happen that the overseer makes mistakes to the firm's loss?

SUN: He's friends with some of the workers, and they count him as one of them.

SHUI TA: I see. One good turn deserves another. Would you like a bonus?

SUN: No. But perhaps I might point out that I have also got a brain. I have had a fair education, you know. The overseer has the right ideas about the men, but being uneducated he can't see what's good for the firm. Give me a week's trial, Mr Shui Ta, and I think I can prove to you that my brains are worth more to the firm than the mere strength of my muscles.

MRS YANG: They were bold words, but that evening I told my Sun: 'You are a flying man. Show that you can get to the top where you are now! Fly, my eagle!' And indeed it is remarkable what brains and education will achieve! How can a man hope to better himself without them? Absolute miracles were performed by my son in the factory directed by Mr Shui Ta!

Sun stands behind the workers, his legs apart. They are passing a basket of raw tobacco above their heads.

SUN: Here you, that's not proper work! The basket has got to be kept moving! *To a child*: Sit on the ground, can't you? It takes up less room! And you might as well get on with a bit of pressing: yes, it's you I'm talking to! You idle loafers, what do you think you're paid for? Come on with that basket! O hell and damnation! Put grandpa over there and let him shred with the kids! There's been enough dodging here! Now take your time from me! *He claps time with his hands and the basket moves faster.*

MRS YANG: And no enmities, no slanderous allegations by the uneducated – for he was not spared that – could hold my son back from the fulfilment of his duty.

One of the workers begins singing the song of the eighth elephant. The others join in the chorus.

WORKERS' CHORUS:

SONG OF THE EIGHTH ELEPHANT

I

Seven elephants worked for Major Chung
And an eighth one followed the others.
Seven were wild and the eighth was tame
And the eighth had to spy on his brothers.
> Keep moving!
> Major Chung owns a wood
> See it's cleared before tonight.
> That's orders. Understood?

2

Seven elephants were clearing the wood
The eighth bore the Major in person
Number eight merely checked that the work was correct
And spared himself any exertion.
> Dig harder!
> Major Chung owns a wood
> See it's cleared before tonight.
> That's orders. Understood?

3

Seven elephants got tired of their work
Of shoving and digging and felling.
The Major was annoyed with the seven he employed
But rewarded the eighth one for telling.
> What's up now?
> Major Chung owns a wood
> See it's cleared before tonight.
> That's orders. Understood?

4

Seven elephants, not a tusk in their heads
The eighth's were in excellent order.
So eight used his wits, slashed the seven to bits
And the Major had never laughed harder.

> Dig away!
> Major Chung owns a wood
> See it's cleared before tonight
> That's orders. Understood?

Shui Ta has lounged forward, smoking a cigar. Yang Sun has laughingly joined in the chorus of the third verse and quickened the tempo in the fourth verse by clapping his hands.

MRS YANG: We really owe everything to Mr Shui Ta. With wisdom and discipline, but with hardly a word of interference, he has brought out all the good that lay in Sun! He made no fantastic promises like his much overrated cousin, but forced him to do good honest work. Today Sun is a different person from what he was three months ago. I think you will admit it! 'The noble soul is like a bell, strike it and it rings, strike it not and it rings not', as our forebears used to say.

9

Shen Teh's Shop

The shop has been turned into an office, with easy chairs and fine carpets. It is raining. Shui Ta, now become fat, is showing out the old couple of carpet-dealers. Mrs Shin watches with amusement. It is plain that she is wearing new clothes.

SHUI TA: I regret that I cannot say when she will be back.

THE OLD WOMAN: We had a letter today enclosing the 200 silver dollars we once lent her. It didn't say who from. But it can only be Shen Teh who sent it. We'd like to write to her: what's her address?

SHUI TA: I'm afraid I don't know that either.

THE OLD MAN: We'd better go.

THE OLD WOMAN: Sooner or later she is bound to come back.

Shui Ta bows. The two old people go off uncertain and upset.

MRS SHIN: It was too late when they got their money back. Now they've lost their shop because they couldn't pay their taxes.

SHUI TA: Why didn't they come to me?

MRS SHIN: People don't like coming to you. I expect they started by waiting for Shen Teh to come back as they'd got nothing in writing. Then the old man got ill at the critical moment, and his wife had to nurse him night and day.

SHUI TA *has to sit down because he feels sick*: I feel giddy again.

MRS SHIN *fusses around him*: You're six months gone! You mustn't let yourself get worked up. Lucky for you you've got me. Everyone can do with a helping hand. Yes, when your time comes I shall be at your side. *She laughs.*

SHUI TA, *feebly*: Can I count on that, Mrs Shin ?

MRS SHIN: You bet! It'll cost money of course. Undo your collar, and you'll feel better.

SHUI TA, *pitifully*: It's all for the baby's sake, Mrs Shin.

MRS SHIN: All for the baby's sake.

SHUI TA: I'm getting fat so quickly, though. People are bound to notice.

MRS SHIN: They think it's because you're doing so well.

SHUI TA: And what will happen to him?

MRS SHIN: You're always asking that. He will be looked after. The best that money can buy.

SHUI TA: Yes. *Anxiously*: And he must never see Shui Ta.

MRS SHIN: Never. Only Shen Teh.

SHUI TA: But all the gossip round here! The water-seller and his rumours! They're watching the shop!

MRS SHIN: As long as the barber doesn't hear there's no harm done. Come on dear, have a drop of water.

Enter Sun in a smart suit carrying a business man's brief-case. He is amazed to see Shui Ta in Mrs Shin's arms.

SUN: Am I disturbing you?

SHUI TA *gets up with difficulty and goes unsteadily to the door*: Till tomorrow, then, Mrs Shin!

Mrs Shin puts on her gloves and goes off smiling.

SUN: Gloves! How, why, what for? Is she milking you? *On Shui Ta not replying*: Don't tell me even you have your softer moments. Curious. *He takes a document from his briefcase.* Anyway, you haven't been on form lately, not on your old förm. Moody. Hesitant. Are you ill? It's doing no good to the business. Here's another notice from the police. They want to shut the factory. They say they can't possibly allow more than twice the legal number of people to a room. It's about time you took some action, Mr Shui Ta!

Shui Ta looks at him distractedly for a moment. Then he goes into the back room and returns with a box. He takes out a new bowler and throws it on the table.

SHUI TA: The firm wishes its representatives to dress according to their position.
SUN: Did you get that for me?
SHUI TA, *indifferently*: See if it fits.

Sun looks astounded, then puts it on. Shui Ta tries adjusting it at the right angle.

SUN: At your service, sir. But don't try and dodge the question. You must see the barber today and talk about the new scheme.
SHUI TA: The barber makes impossible conditions.
SUN: I wish you'd tell me what conditions.
SHUI TA, *evasively*: The sheds are quite good enough.
SUN: Good enough for the riffraff who work there, but not good enough for the tobacco. The damp's getting in it. Before we have another meeting I'll see Mrs Mi Tzu again about her premises. If we can get them we can chuck out this rag, tag and bobtail. They're not good enough. I'll tickle Mrs Mi Tzu's fat knees over a cup of tea, and we'll get the place for half the money.
SHUI TA, *sharply*: That is out of the question. For the sake of the firm's reputation I wish you always to be coolly business-like, and to be reserved in personal matters.
SUN: What are you so irritable for? Is it the unpleasant local gossip?

SHUI TA: I am not concerned with gossip.

SUN: Then it must be the weather again. Rain always makes you so touchy and melancholic. I'd like to know why.

WANG'S VOICE, *from without*:

> I sell water. Who would taste it?
> – Who would want to in this weather?
> All my labour has been wasted
> Fetching these few pints together.
> I stand shouting Buy my Water!
> And nobody thinks it
> Worth stopping and buying
> Or greedily drinks it.

SUN: There's that bloody water-seller. Now he'll be nagging us again.

WANG'S VOICE, *from without*: Isn't there a good person left in this town? Not even on the square where the good Shen Teh used to live? Where is the woman who once bought a mug of water from me in the rain, months ago, in the joy of her heart? Where is she now? Has nobody seen her? Has none of you heard from her? This is the house which she entered one evening and never left!

SUN: Hadn't I better shut his mouth for good? What's it got to do with him, where she is? Incidentally, I believe the only reason why you don't say is so that I shouldn't know.

WANG *enters*: Mr Shui Ta, I ask you once more: when is Shen Teh coming back? It's now six months since she went off on her travels. *On Shui Ta remaining silent*: Since then a lot has happened which could never have taken place if she'd been here. *On Shui Ta still remaining silent*: Mr Shui Ta, the rumour round here is that something must have happened to Shen Teh. Her friends are very worried. Would you please be so good as to let us know her address?

SHUI TA: I fear I have no time at the moment, Mr Wang. Come again next week.

WANG, *worked up*: People have also begun to notice that the rice she used to give the needy is being put out at the door again.

SHUI TA: What do they conclude from that?

WANG: That Shen Teh hasn't gone away at all.

SHUI TA: But? *On Wang's remaining silent*: In that case I will give you my answer. It is final. If you consider yourself a friend of Shen Teh's, Mr Wang, then you will refrain from enquiring as to her whereabouts. That is my advice.

WANG: Marvellous advice! Mr Shui Ta, Shen Teh told me before she disappeared that she was pregnant!

SUN: What?

SHUI TA, *quickly*: A lie!

WANG, *most seriously, to Shui Ta*: Mr Shui Ta, please don't think Shen Teh's friends will ever give up the search for her. A good person is not easily forgotten. There are not many. *Exit.*

Shui Ta stares after him. Then he goes quickly into the back room.

SUN, *to the audience*: Shen Teh pregnant! That makes me livid! I've been done! She must have told her cousin, and of course that swine hurried her off at once. 'Pack your bags and clear out, before the child's father gets wind of it!' It's utterly against nature. Inhuman, in fact. I've got a son. A Yang is about to appear on the scene! And what happens? The girl vanishes, and I'm left here to work like a slave. *He is losing his temper.* They buy me off with a hat! *He tramples on it.* Crooks! Thieves, kidnappers! And the girl has nobody to look after her! *Sobbing is heard from the back room. He stops still.* Wasn't that someone crying? Who's there? It's stopped. What's that crying in the back room? I bet that half-baked swine Shui Ta doesn't cry. So who's crying? And what's the meaning of the rice being put outside the door every morning? Is the girl there after all? Is he simply hiding her? Who else could be crying in there? That would be a fine kettle of fish! I've absolutely got to find her if she's pregnant!

Shui Ta returns from the back room. He goes to the door and peers out into the rain.

SUN: Well, where is she?

SHUI TA *raises his hand and listens*: Just a moment! Nine o'clock. But one can't hear today. The rain is too heavy.

SUN, *ironically*: What do you hope to hear?

SHUI TA: The mail plane.

SUN: Don't be funny.

SHUI TA: I thought they told me you were interested in flying? Have you dropped that?

SUN: I have no complaints about my present job, if that's what you mean. I'd sooner not do night work, you know. The mail service means flying at night. I've begun to get a sort of soft spot for the firm. After all, it is my former fiancée's firm, even if she is away. She did go away, didn't she?

SHUI TA: Why do you ask?

SUN: Maybe because her affairs don't leave me entirely cold.

SHUI TA: My cousin might like to hear that.

SUN: Anyway I'm concerned enough to be unable to shut my eyes if I find, for instance, that she is being deprived of her freedom.

SHUI TA: By whom?

SUN: By you!

Pause.

SHUI TA: What would you do in such an eventuality?

SUN: I might start by wanting to reconsider my position in the firm.

SHUI TA: Indeed. And supposing the firm – that is to say I – found a suitable position for you, would it be able to count on your giving up all further enquiries about your former fiancée?

SUN: Possibly.

SHUI TA: And how do you picture your new position in the firm?

SUN: Full control. For instance, I picture chucking you out.

SHUI TA: And suppose the firm chucked you out instead?

SUN: Then I should probably return, but not on my own.

SHUI TA: But?

SUN: With the police.

SHUI TA: With the police. Let us suppose the police found no one here.

SUN: Then I presume they would look in that room! Mr Shui

Ta, my longing for the lady of my heart cannot be suppressed.
I feel I shall have to take steps if I am to enfold her in my
arms once more. *Quietly*: She's pregnant, and needs a man
beside her. I must talk it over with the water-seller. *He leaves.*

*Shui Ta looks after him without moving. Then he goes quickly into
the back room once more. He fetches all kinds of everyday articles
of Shen Teh's: underwear, dresses, toilet things. He looks lengthily
at the shawl which Shen Teh bought from the old carpet-dealers.
Then he packs it all into a bundle and hides it under the table, as he
hears sounds. Enter Mrs Mi Tzu and Mr Shu Fu. They greet
Shui Ta and dispose of their umbrellas and galoshes.*

MRS MI TZU: Autumn's on the way, Mr Shui Ta.

MR SHU FU: A melancholy time of year!

MRS MI TZU: And where is that charming manager of yours?
A shocking lady-killer! But of course you don't know that
side of him. Still, he knows how to reconcile his charm with
his business obligations, so you only profit from it.

SHUI TA *bows*: Will you please sit down?

They sit and start smoking.

SHUI TA: My friends, an unpredictable eventuality, which may
have certain consequences, compels me to speed up the
negotiations which I have recently initiated as to the future
of my business. Mr Shu Fu, my factory is in difficulties.

MR SHU FU: It always is.

SHUI TA: But now the police are frankly threatening to shut it
down if I cannot show that I am negotiating for a new
arrangement. Mr Shu Fu, what is at stake is nothing less
than the sole remaining property of my cousin, in whom you
have always shown such interest.

MR SHU FU: Mr Shui Ta, it is deeply repugnant to me to discuss
your ever-expanding projects. I suggest a small supper with
your cousin, you indicate financial difficulties. I offer your
cousin buildings for the homeless, you use them to set up a
factory. I hand her a cheque, you cash it. Your cousin
vanishes, you ask for 100,000 silver dollars and tell me my
buildings are not big enough. Sir, where is your cousin?

SHUI TA: Mr Shu Fu, please be calm. I can now inform you that she will very shortly be back.

MR SHU FU: 'Shortly.' When? You have been saying 'shortly' for weeks.

SHUI TA: I have not asked you to sign anything further. I have simply asked whether you would be more closely associated with my project supposing my cousin came back.

MR SHU FU: I have told you a thousand times that I am not prepared to go on discussing with you, but will discuss anything with your cousin. However, you seem to want to put obstacles in the way of such a discussion.

SHUI TA: Not now.

MR SHU FU: Can we fix a date?

SHUI TA, *uncertainly*: In three months.

MR SHU FU, *irritably*: Then you can have my signature in three months too.

SHUI TA: But it must all be prepared.

MR SHU FU: You can prepare everything yourself, Shui Ta, if you are sure this time that your cousin really is coming.

SHUI TA: Mrs Mi Tzu, are you for your part ready to certify to the police that I can have your workshops?

MRS MI TZU: Certainly, if you will let me take over your manager. I told you weeks ago that that was my condition. *To Mr Shu Fu*: The young man is so conscientious, and I must have someone to run things.

SHUI TA: Please understand that I cannot let Mr Yang Sun go at this moment: there are all these problems, and my health has been so uncertain lately. I was always prepared to let you have him but . . .

MRS MI TZU: Ha! But!

Pause

SHUI TA: Very well, he shall report at your office tomorrow.

MR SHU FU: I am glad you could arrive at this decision, Mr Shui Ta. If Miss Shen Teh really comes back it will be most undesirable that this young man should be here. We all know that in his time he has had a most pernicious influence on her.

SHUI TA, *bowing*: No doubt. Forgive my undue hesitation in these questions relating to my cousin Shen Teh and Mr Yang Sun: it was quite unworthy of a business man. These two were once very close to each other.

MRS MI TZU: We forgive you.

SHUI TA, *looking towards the door*: My friends, it is time for us to come to a decision. At this spot, in what used to be the drab little shop where the poor of the district bought the good Shen Teh's tobacco, we, her friends, herewith resolve to establish twelve fine new branches, which from now on shall retail Shen Teh's good tobacco. I am told that people have begun calling me the Tobacco King of Szechwan. But the fact is that I have conducted this enterprise solely and exclusively in my cousin's interest. It will belong to her, and to her children, and to her children's children.

From without come sounds of a crowd of people. Enter Wang, Sun and the policeman.

THE POLICEMAN: Mr Shui Ta, I am extremely sorry, but in view of the disturbed state of the district I have to follow up certain information received from your own firm, according to which you are alleged to be keeping your cousin Miss Shen Teh under illegal restraint.

SHUI TA: That is not true.

THE POLICEMAN: Mr Yang Sun here states that he heard crying from the room behind your office, and that it can only have proceeded from a female person.

MRS MI TZU: That is absurd. Mr Shu Fu and I, two respected citizens of this town whose word the police can hardly doubt, will witness that there has been no crying here. We have been smoking our cigars perfectly quietly.

THE POLICEMAN: I'm afraid I have an order to search the aforementioned room.

Shui Ta opens the door. The policeman bows and crosses the threshold. He looks in, then turns round and smiles.

THE POLICEMAN: Perfectly true, there's no one there.

SUN, *who has accompanied him*: But someone was crying! *His eye falls on the table under which Shui Ta shoved the bundle. He pounces on it.* That wasn't there before!

He opens it and reveals Shen Teh's clothes, etc.

WANG: Those are Shen Teh's things! *He runs to the door and calls out*: They've found her clothes!

THE POLICEMAN, *taking charge of things*: You state that your cousin is away. A bundle containing her property is found concealed beneath your desk. Where can the young lady be contacted, Mr Shui Ta?

SHUI TA: I don't know her address.

THE POLICEMAN: That is a great pity.

SHOUTS FROM THE CROWD: Shen Teh's things have been found! The Tobacco King did the girl in and got rid of her!

THE POLICEMAN: Mr Shui Ta, I must ask you to come to the station with me.

SHUI TA, *bowing to Mrs Mi Tzu and to Mr Shu Fu*: Please forgive this disturbance, my dear colleagues. But we still have magistrates in Szechwan. I am sure it will all be cleared up quickly.

He precedes the policeman out.

WANG: There has been a most frightful crime!

SUN, *overcome*: But I did hear somebody crying!

INTERLUDE

Wang's Sleeping-Place

Music. For the last time the gods appear to the water-seller in a dream. They are greatly changed. It is impossible to mistake the symptoms of prolonged travel, utter exhaustion and unhappy experiences of every kind. One of them has had his hat knocked off his head, one has lost a leg in a fox-trap, and all three are going barefoot.

WANG: At last you have appeared! Fearful things are happening in Shen Teh's shop, Illustrious Ones! Shen Teh has again been away, this time for months! Her cousin has been grabbing everything! Today they arrested him. He is supposed to have murdered her in order to get hold of her shop. But I cannot believe that, for I had a dream in which she appeared to me and said that her cousin was keeping her a prisoner. Oh, Illustrious Ones, you must come back at once and find her.

THE FIRST GOD: That is terrible. Our whole search has been in vain. We found few good people, and those we found were not living a decent human existence. We had already decided to settle on Shen Teh.

THE SECOND GOD: If only she is still good!

WANG: That she surely is, but she has vanished!

THE FIRST GOD: Then all is lost!

THE SECOND GOD: You forget yourself.

THE FIRST GOD: What's wrong with forgetting oneself? We shall have to give up if she cannot be found! What a world we have found here: nothing but poverty, debasement and dilapidation! Even the landscape crumbles away before our eyes. Beautiful trees are lopped off by cables, and over the mountains we see great clouds of smoke and hear the thunder of guns, and nowhere a good person who survives it!

THE THIRD GOD: Alas, water-seller, our commandments seem to be fatal! I fear that all the moral principles that we have evolved will have to be cancelled. People have enough to do to save their bare lives. Good precepts bring them to the edge

of the precipice; good deeds drag them over. *To the other
gods*: The world is unfit to live in, you have got to admit it!
THE FIRST GOD, *emphatically*: No, mankind is worthless!
THE THIRD GOD: Because the world is too chilling!
THE SECOND GOD: Because men are too feeble!
THE FIRST GOD: Remember your dignity, my friends! Brothers,
we cannot afford to despair. We did discover one who was
good and has not become evil, and she has only disappeared.
Let us hasten to find her. One is enough. Did we not say that
all could still be redeemed if just one can be found who
stands up to this world, just one?

They swiftly disappear.

10

Courtroom

*In groups: Mr Shu Fu and Mrs Mi Tzu. Sun and his mother.
Wang, the carpenter, the grandfather, the young prostitute, the two
old people. Mrs Shin. The policeman. The sister-in-law.*

THE OLD WOMAN: He is too powerful.
WANG: He means to open twelve new branches.
THE CARPENTER: How can the magistrate give a fair verdict
when the defendant's friends, Shu Fu the barber and Mrs Mi
Tzu the property owner, are his friends too?
THE SISTER-IN-LAW: Last night old Shin was seen carrying a
fat goose into the judge's kitchen on Mr Shui Ta's orders.
The grease was oozing through the basket.
THE OLD WOMAN, *to Wang*: Our poor Shen Teh will never be
found again.
WANG: Yes, it will take the gods to get at the truth.
THE POLICEMAN: Silence! The court is assembling.

*The three gods appear in magistrates' robes. As they pass along the
front of the stage to go to their places they can be heard whispering.*

THE THIRD GOD: There will be trouble. The certificates were
most incompetently forged.

THE SECOND GOD: And people will be curious about the magistrate's sudden indisposition.

THE FIRST GOD: It is natural enough after eating half a goose.

MRS SHIN: We've got new magistrates!

WANG: And very good ones!

*The third god, last of the three, hears him, turns and smiles at him.
The gods take their seats. The first god taps on the table with a
hammer. The policeman brings in Shui Ta, who is received with
catcalls but maintains an air of arrogance as he enters.*

THE POLICEMAN: This may be a shock to you. Fu Yi Cheng is
not on the bench. But the new magistrates look pretty soft too.

Shui Ta catches sight of the gods and faints.

THE YOUNG PROSTITUTE: What's happened? The Tobacco
King has fainted.

THE SISTER-IN-LAW: As soon as he saw the new magistrates!

WANG: He seems to know them! That's beyond me.

THE FIRST GOD: Are you Shui Ta, tobacco merchant?

SHUI TA, *very faintly*: Yes.

THE FIRST GOD: You are charged with having made away with
your cousin Miss Shen Teh, in order to gain control of her
business. Do you plead guilty?

SHUI TA: No.

THE FIRST GOD, *thumbing through the papers*: The court will
begin with the local constable's evidence as to the characters
of the accused and his cousin.

THE POLICEMAN *steps forward*: Miss Shen Teh was a girl who
made herself pleasant to everyone – live and let live, as they
say. Mr Shui Ta, on the other hand, is a man of principle.
The young lady's warm-hearted nature sometimes drove him
to strict measures. But unlike the girl he was always on the
side of the law, your worships. There were some people whom
his cousin had trusted and taken in, and he was able to show
them up as a gang of thieves, and another time he barely

managed to save Shen Teh from straight perjury. Mr Shui Ta is known to me as a respectable citizen who respects the law.

THE FIRST GOD: Are there other witnesses in court who wish to testify that the accused is incapable of a crime of the sort attributed to him?

Mr Shu Fu and Mrs Mi Tzu step forward.

THE POLICEMAN *whispers to the gods*: Mr Shu Fu, one of our more prominent citizens!

MR SHU FU: The town looks up to Mr Shui Ta as an able business man. He is vice-chairman of the chamber of commerce and has been proposed as a justice of the peace.

WANG, *interrupting*: By you! You two are hand in glove with him.

THE POLICEMAN, *whispering*: An undesirable character!

MRS MI TZU: In my capacity as Chairman of the Charitable Welfare Association I should like to point out to the court that Mr Shui Ta is not only turning over the best possible rooms in his tobacco works – all light and healthy – to a considerable number of the homeless, but also makes regular subscriptions to our Disabled Persons' Institution.

THE POLICEMAN, *whispering*: Mrs Mi Tzu, a close friend of our magistrate Fu Yi Cheng!

THE FIRST GOD: Yes, yes, but now we must also hear whether anyone has a less favourable report to make on the accused.

There step forward: Wang, the carpenter, the old couple, the unemployed man, the sister-in-law, the young prostitute.

THE POLICEMAN: The scum of the district.

THE FIRST GOD: Tell us, what do you know of Shui Ta's general conduct?

CRIES, *confusedly*: He ruined us! He bled me white! Led us into bad ways! Exploited the helpless! Lied! Swindled! Murdered!

THE FIRST GOD: Accused, what have you to say for yourself?

SHUI TA: All I did was to save my cousin's bare means of existence, your worships. I only came when she was in danger of losing her small business. Three times I had to come. I never meant to stay. Circumstances were such that last time I was forced to remain. All the time I have had nothing but trouble. They loved my cousin, and I had to do the dirty work. That is why they hate me.

THE SISTER-IN-LAW: You bet we do. Look at our boy, your worships. *To Shui Ta*: Not to mention the sacks.

SHUI TA: Why not? Why not?

THE SISTER-IN-LAW, *to the gods*: Shen Teh put us up, and he had us arrested.

SHUI TA: You were stealing cakes!

THE SISTER-IN-LAW: Now he's pretending he cared about the baker and his cakes! He wanted the shop for himself!

SHUI TA: The shop wasn't a dosshouse, you selfish brutes!

THE SISTER-IN-LAW: But we had nowhere to go!

SHUI TA: There were too many of you!

WANG: And these two! *He points to the old couple.* Are they also too selfish?

THE OLD WOMAN: We put our savings into Shen Teh's business Why did you do us out of our own?

SHUI TA: Because my cousin was helping an airman to get back into the air again. I was supposed to find the money!

WANG: She may have wanted that, but you had your eye on that good job in Pekin. The shop wasn't good enough for you.

SHUI TA: The rent was too high!

MRS SHIN: I can confirm that.

SHUI TA: And my cousin had no idea of business.

MRS SHIN: That too! Besides, she was in love with the airman.

SHUI TA: Hadn't she the right to love?

WANG: Of course she had! So why did you try to make her marry a man she didn't love: the barber there?

SHUI TA: The man she loved was a crook.

WANG: Him?

He indicates Sun.

SUN *leaps up*: Was it because he was a crook you took him into your office?

SHUI TA: To help you! To help you improve!

THE SISTER-IN-LAW: To turn him into a slave-driver!

WANG: And when you had finished improving him, didn't you sell him to her? *He indicates Mrs Mi Tzu.* She was crowing all over the place about it!

SHUI TA: Because she wouldn't let me have her workshops unless he tickled her knees!

MRS MI TZU: Lies! Don't ever mention my workshops again! I'll have nothing more to do with you. Murderer!

She rushes off in a dudgeon.

SUN, *firmly*: Your worships, I must put in a word for him!

THE SISTER-IN-LAW: You've got to; he's your boss.

THE UNEMPLOYED MAN: He's the worst slave-driver there ever was. They completely broke him.

SUN: Your worships, whatever the accused made of me he is not a murderer. A few minutes before his arrest I heard Shen Teh's voice from the room behind the shop!

THE FIRST GOD, *intrigued*: She was alive, was she? Describe exactly what you heard.

SUN, *triumphantly*: Crying, your worships, crying!

THE THIRD GOD: You could recognise it?

SUN: Absolutely certain. Don't I know her voice?

MR SHU FU: Yes, you've made her cry often enough!

SUN: But I've also made her happy. And then he wanted – *pointing to Shui Ta* – to sell her to you.

SHUI TA, *to Sun*: Because you didn't love her!

WANG: No: for the money!

SHUI TA: But what was the money needed for, your worships? *To Sun*: You would have liked her to give up all her friends, but the barber offered his buildings and his money so that she could help the poor. I had to promise her to the barber even to allow her to do good.

WANG: Why didn't you allow her to do good when the big cheque was filled in? Why did you shove Shen Teh's friends in your stinking sweat-shops, your tobacco factory, you tobacco king?

SHUI TA: It was for the child's sake!

THE CARPENTER: And what about my children? What did you do to them?

Shui Ta remains silent.

WANG: That has made you think! The gods gave Shen Teh her shop to be a little source of goodness. And she always tried to do good, and you always came and brought it to nothing.

SHUI TA, *beside himself*: Because they'd have stifled the source, you fool.

MRS SHIN: That's quite true, your worships!

WANG: What's the good of a source that can't be drawn on?

SHUI TA: Good deeds are the road to ruin!

WANG, *wildly*: And evil deeds are the road to the good life, I suppose? What have you done with the good Shen Teh, you evil man? How many good people are there left, Illustrious Ones? She was certainly good! When that barber broke my hand she wanted to give evidence for me. And now I'm giving evidence for her. She was good, I swear it.

He raises his hand to swear.

THE THIRD GOD: What is wrong with your hand, water-seller? It seems stiff.

WANG *points to Shui Ta*: He's to blame, no one else! She was going to give me the money for the doctor, then he came along. You were her mortal enemy!

SHUI TA: I was her only friend!

ALL: Where is she?

SHUI TA: Gone away.

WANG: Where to?

SHUI TA: I shan't tell!

ALL: What made her go?

SHUI TA, *screaming*: You were tearing her to bits!

There is a sudden silence.

SHUI TA *has collapsed on to his chair*: I can't go on. If the court can be cleared so that only the magistrates are present I will make a confession.

ALL: Confession! We've won!

THE FIRST GOD *taps on the table with his hammer*: Clear the court.

The policeman clears the court.

MRS SHIN, *as she goes out, laughing*: They've got a surprise coming!

SHUI TA: Have they gone? All of them? I cannot hold out any longer. Illustrious Ones, I have recognised you!

THE SECOND GOD: What have you done with our good person of Szechwan?

SHUI TA: Let me confess the frightful truth. I am your good person!

He takes off his mask and rips away his costume. Shen Teh stands there.

THE SECOND GOD: Shen Teh!

SHEN TEH:

Yes, it is me. Shui Ta and Shen Teh, I am both of them.
Your original order
To be good while yet surviving
Split me like lightning into two people. I
Cannot tell what occurred: goodness to others
And to myself could not both be achieved.
To serve both self and others I found too hard.
Oh, your world is arduous! Such need, such desperation!
The hand which is held out to the starving
Is quickly wrenched off! He who gives help to the lost
Is lost for his own part! For who could
Hold himself back from anger when the hungry are dying?
Where could I find so much that was needed, if not
In myself? But that was my downfall! The load of command-
ments
Forced me into the sludge. Yet if I broke the rules
I strode proudly around, and could eat myself full!
Something is wrong with this world of yours. Why
Is wickedness so rewarded, and why is so much suffering

Reserved for the good? Oh, I felt such
Temptation to treat myself kindly! I felt too
A secret awareness inside me, for my foster-mother
Washed me with slops from the gutter! So I acquired
A sharp eye. And yet pity
Brought me such pain that I at once felt wolfish anger
At the sight of misery. Then
I could feel how I gradually altered and
My lips grew tight and hard. Bitter as ashes
The kind word felt in my mouth. And yet
I should gladly have been an Angel to the slums. For giving
Was still my delight. A smiling face
And I walked in the clouds.
Condemn me: each of my crimes
Was committed to help out my neighbour
To love my beloved or
To save my young son from going without.
O gods, for your vast projects
I, poor human, was too small.

THE FIRST GOD, *with every indication of horror*: Speak no further,
you unhappy creature! What are we to think, who so rejoice
to have found you again?

SHEN TEH: But do you not understand that I am the wicked
person whose many crimes you have heard described?

THE FIRST GOD: The good person, of whom no one speaks anything but good!

SHEN TEH: No, the wicked person as well!

THE FIRST GOD: A misunderstanding! A few unfortunate incidents. One or two hard-hearted neighbours! A little too much
zeal!

THE SECOND GOD: But how is she to go on living?

THE FIRST GOD: She can manage! She is strong, healthy and
well-built, and can endure much.

THE SECOND GOD: But didn't you hear what she said?

THE FIRST GOD, *emphatically*: Muddled, completely muddled!
Hard to accept, extremely hard to accept! Are we to admit
that our commandments are fatal? Are we to sacrifice them?

Grimly: Never! Is the world to be altered? How? By whom? No, everything is as it should be.

He taps rapidly on the table with his hammer. And now – at a sign from him – music is heard. A rosy glow is seen.

> Now we return to heaven. This little world
> Still fascinates us. All its joys and hurts
> Encouraged us or caused us pain. And still
> We'll gladly think, away beyond the planets
> Of you, Shen Teh, the good person we sought
> Who makes our spirit manifest down here
> And through this bitter darkness bears the tiny lamp.
> Farewell, good luck!

At a sign from him the ceiling opens. A pink cloud descends. On it the three gods mount slowly upwards.

SHEN TEH: Oh no, Illustrious Ones! Do not go away! Don't leave me! How am I to face the two good old people who lost their shop, or the water-seller with his stiff hand? And how can I protect myself against the barber, whom I don't love, and how against Sun, whom I do? And my body has been blessed; soon my little son will be there and wanting to eat. I cannot remain here!

She looks frantically towards the door through which her tormentors will come.

THE FIRST GOD: You can manage. Only be good, and all will be well!

Enter the witnesses. They are amazed to see the magistrates floating on their pink cloud.

WANG: Show your respect! The gods have appeared among us! Three of the mightiest gods have come to Szechwan in search of a good person. They thought they had found one, but . . .

THE FIRST GOD: No but! Here she is!

ALL: Shen Teh!

THE FIRST GOD: She was not dead, she lay but hidden. She will remain among you, a good person!

SHEN TEH: But I must have my cousin!

THE FIRST GOD: Not too often!

SHEN TEH: Once a week anyway!

THE FIRST GOD: Once a month: that will be enough!

SHEN TEH: Oh, do not go away, Illustrious Ones! I haven't told you all! I need you terribly!

THE GODS *sing*:

TRIO OF THE VANISHING GODS ON THEIR CLOUD

> All too long on earth we lingered.
> Swiftly droops the lovely day:
> Shrewdly studied, closely fingered
> Precious treasures melt away.
> Now the golden flood is dying
> While your shadows onward press
> Time that we too started flying
> Homeward to our nothingness.

SHEN TEH: Help!

THE GODS:

> Now let us go: the search at last is o'er
> We have to hurry on!
> Then give three cheers, and one cheer more
> For the good person of Szechwan!

As Shen Teh stretches desperately towards them they disappear upwards, waving and smiling.

EPILOGUE

A player appears before the curtain and addresses the audience apologetically in an epilogue:

THE PLAYER:

Ladies and gentlemen, don't feel let down:
We know this ending makes some people frown.
We had in mind a sort of golden myth
Then found the finish had been tampered with.
Indeed it is a curious way of coping:
To close the play, leaving the issue open.
Especially since we live by your enjoyment.
Frustrated audiences mean unemployment.
Whatever optimists may have pretended
Our play will fail if you can't recommend it.
Was it stage fright made us forget the rest?
Such things occur. But what would you suggest?
What is your answer? Nothing's been arranged.
Should men be better? Should the world be changed?
Or just the gods? Or ought there to be none?
We for our part feel well and truly done.
There's only one solution that we know:
That you should now consider as you go
What sort of measures you would recommend
To help good people to a happy end.
Ladies and gentlemen, in you we trust:
There must be happy endings, must, must, must!

recht's Plays, Poetry and Prose

nnotated and edited in hardback and paperback

y John Willett and Ralph Manheim

The following plays are also available (in paperback) in unannotated editions:
The Caucasian Chalk Circle; The Days of the Commune; The Life of Galileo;
The Measures Taken and other Lehrstücke; The Messingkauf Dialogues; The Mother
*in preparation

Methuen World Classics

Aeschylus (two volumes)
Jean Anouilh
John Arden
Arden & D'Arcy
Aristophanes (two volumes)
Peter Barnes
Brendan Behan
Aphra Behn
Edward Bond (four volumes)
Bertolt Brecht (three volumes)
Howard Brenton (two volumes)
Büchner
Bulgakov
Calderón
Anton Chekhov
Caryl Churchill (two volumes)
Noël Coward (five volumes)
Sarah Daniels
Eduardo De Filippo
David Edgar (three volumes)
Euripides (three volumes)
Dario Fo
Michael Frayn (two volumes)
Max Frisch
Gorky
Harley Granville Barker
Henrik Ibsen (six volumes)
Lorca (three volumes)
Marivaux
Mustapha Matura
David Mercer
Arthur Miller (three volumes)
Anthony Minghella
Molière
Tom Murphy (two volumes)
Peter Nichols (two volumes)
Clifford Odets
Joe Orton
Louise Page
A. W. Pinero
Luigi Pirandello
Stephen Poliakoff
Terence Rattigan (two volumes)
Ntozake Shange
Sophocles (two volumes)
Wole Soyinka
David Storey
August Strindberg (three volumes)
J. M. Synge
Ramón del Valle-Inclán
Frank Wedekind
Oscar Wilde